CLOSED DOORS, OPEN MINDS

Also by Meir Persoff

The Running Stag: The Stamps and Postal History of Israel
1973

Immanuel Jakobovits: a Prophet in Israel
(Foreword by Elie Wiesel; Prologue by Jonathan Sacks)
2002

Faith Against Reason: Religious Reform and the British Chief Rabbinate, 1840–1990
(Introduction by Todd M. Endelman)
2008

Another Way, Another Time: Religious Inclusivism and the Sacks Chief Rabbinate
(Foreword by Geoffrey Alderman)
2010

Hats in the Ring: Choosing Britain's Chief Rabbis from Adler to Sacks
(Foreword by Stefan C. Reif)
2013

CLOSED DOORS, OPEN MINDS

British Jewry's Secret Disputations

MEIR PERSOFF

ACADEMIC STUDIES PRESS
Boston 2018

First published in 2018 by Academic Studies Press

28 Montfern Avenue
Brighton, MA 02135
United States of America

press@academicstudiespress.com
www.academicstudiespress.com

Copyright © 2018 Meir Persoff
Meir Persoff has asserted his right under the Copyright, Designs and
Patents Act 1988 to be identified as the author of this work.

ISBN 9781618117557 (cloth)
ISBN 9781618117564 (paper)
ISBN 9781618117571 (ebook)

Library of Congress Cataloging-in-Publication Data: a catalog record has been applied for.

Book design by Kryon Publishing Services (P) Ltd.
www.kryonpublishing.com
Typeset in Joanna MT 11/13

Front cover photo: Chief Rabbi Immanuel Jakobovits in earnest discussion with Rabbi Hugo Gryn, senior minister of the West London (Reform) Synagogue and a key figure in the 'peace process.'

All rights reserved. No part of this publication may be reproduced, stored in or introduced into a retrieval system, or transmitted, in any form or by any means, electronic, mechanical, photocopying, recording, or otherwise without the prior written permission of the publisher of this book.

For five generations of
Family Persoff
with fondest love

Closed Doors: The Chief Rabbi's residence in Hamilton Terrace, North-West London, where many of the religious disputations took place in utmost secrecy

'How good and pleasant it is
to dwell together as brothers in unity.'

Psalms 133:1

Contents

Foreword, by Aubrey Newman	xi
Preface	xv
Chapter One: 1945–1960: Strife and Sanctity	1
Chapter Two: 1960–1970: Gestures and Concessions	12
Chapter Three: 1970–1980: Disputes and Divisions	44
Chapter Four: 1980–1990: Dissent and Disunity	97
Chapter Five: 1990–2000: Kinship and Courtesy	176
Notes	202
Bibliography	222
Index	233

Open Minds: Immanuel Jakobovits and his four main disputants (clockwise from top left), John Rayner (Liberal), Dow Marmur (Reform), Tony Bayfield (Reform), Sidney Brichto (Liberal)

Foreword

In his latest work on the British Chief Rabbinate, Meir Persoff explores uncharted territory in the tenures of Immanuel Jakobovits and Jonathan Sacks and, through exclusive access to personal and other archives, reveals consistent attempts to find common ground within the various strands of Anglo-Jewry. Allied to his forty-year career on the *Jewish Chronicle*, he presents a rare insight into controversial aspects of their work, demonstrating the dilemmas facing them over a range of issues, and leading to the view (posited elsewhere) that the institution of the Chief Rabbinate may have outlasted its usefulness and should cease to exist.

This case, supported by others in the field – and beyond – is not new. As long ago as 1911, in the run-up to the election of Joseph Herman Hertz, it was enunciated by a group of foreign-born, strictly Orthodox rabbis, who argued that the Office of the Chief Rabbi was no longer required, or should never have been established. If examined in purely historical terms, a strong case could well be argued that the position had developed in a society that was changing so dramatically that it was indeed time to seek an alternative.

It is almost universally accepted today that changes within British Jewry over the past two generations have dug deep. One feature of early Anglo-Jewry was the central role played by laymen, above all by the so-called Cousinhood, who between them ran virtually every communal institution until the end of the Second World War. When the last of their number, Ewen Montagu, was succeeded as president of the United Synagogue by Sir Isaac Wolfson, the Glasgow-born son of a Russian immigrant, a forceful signal went forth that Anglo-Jewry had changed.

At one time, debates between the Chief Rabbi and his contemporaries involved almost exclusively the lay leaders of the community, adamant in their belief that it was they, and not their ecclesiastical head, who could – and should – decide which limited areas of authority came under his jurisdiction. The post-war era has produced no lay leaders of comparable strength, and one of the notable features of this book is their relative absence from the disputations taking place.

This is not to say that the lay leaders are unaware of the issues. One of the arguments adduced during the discussions over Lord Jakobovits' successor was the extent to which the successful candidate could bridge the gulf so apparent in the Jewish world. What seemed to be overlooked was that a bridge is there to be walked over.

A forceful development within the community is the growing cohesiveness of the Progressive group, uniting the rabbinates and lay leaders of Reform and Liberal persuasion. The creation of a Reform Beth Din in Britain emerged, to some extent, as a result of opposition to the widespread disunity among American Reform congregations, and testified to a desire to sink their differences, paralleled by the appearance of figures who could be regarded as spokespersons for the group as a whole. Simultaneously, there has been a considerable strengthening of the ultra-Orthodox groups, which have never accepted the pre-eminence of a Chief Rabbi, and were part of the gulf that had to be bridged.

The extent to which there remains a recognisable 'mainstream' within Anglo-Jewry has also been thrown into doubt. The growth of 'alternative' religious groupings of various hues, the issues of female participation in synagogue services and the management of communal institutions, have all gone far towards undermining one of the foundation-stones of the Chief Rabbinate — its financial base.

Early desires to establish the institution on a sound footing coincided with attempts to establish the institution itself. With every vacancy, congregations contributing towards its upkeep were instructed to participate in the election process, and the conflict between the United Synagogue and the Federation of Synagogues revolved as much around this issue as around anything else. But, continually, it was left to the United Synagogue to fund the Chief Rabbinate and the London Beth Din, and in today's climate the parent organisation has found its own financial basis increasingly unsound.

Its membership, moreover, is steadily shrinking. Fewer families now feel the imperative to 'join' a synagogue; in fact, the very religiosity of the community has continued to change. What might in the Brodie era have been described as a cylinder stretching from the ultra-Orthodox to the ultra-non-Orthodox now increasingly resembles a dumbbell, with the two extremes developing at the expense of the middle. With numbers falling, the danger increases that the middle ground will largely disappear, leaving the community irredeemably split. And a growing tendency towards intermarriage poses a further menace.

None of this is new to informed opinion. Early in the Jakobovits era, the Chief Rabbi sought to forge links with involved academics, hoping to benefit from their broader insights. The establishment of unofficial, and highly confidential, meetings with non-Orthodox leaders – strikingly revealed in this volume – formed another aspect of that endeavour, though it largely failed to achieve its goal. In an earlier work, Dr Persoff explored possible reasons for this failure; indeed, the incumbents are faced with a near-impossible task. Some did not mix in the strictly Orthodox yeshivah world and were thereby unlikely to gain its acknowledgement or support.

When Jonathan Sacks was chosen, he delayed his induction for a year so as to study in Jerusalem with the *gedolim*. His appointment was greeted with enthusiasm by many in the community because of his undisputed reputation as a scholar and publicist, perhaps without recognising that not all of his talent was focused on the Jewish community. In effect, the Chief Rabbi was expected to be all things to all men, even though this would have involved squaring the circle.

Is it therefore accurate, and inevitable, that the Office of the Chief Rabbi has reached the end of its journey? Should the community accept that there is no longer any need of it, and no possibility of finding an ideal incumbent? Paradoxically, it might well be suggested that current divisions within the broad sweep of Anglo-Jewry make the position of the Chief Rabbinate more necessary than ever.

When there was a Lord Rothschild to represent the entire community, and to whom the Government would invariably address important issues; when publication of a major news story could be delayed so as to allow the *Jewish Chronicle* virtual exclusivity, no one thought of consulting the Chief Rabbi. But the disappearance of such lay leadership has thrown into higher prominence the Chief Rabbinical role.

The growing precariousness of Jews within modern society means more than ever that those who recognise their own Jewishness require a leader who can be acknowledged as such. Issues arise – involving shechitah and milah, for example – which are fundamental to many who would not describe themselves as 'fundamentalist'. These are matters on which a Chief Rabbi must give guidance, both to the Jewish community and to the outside world – as did Hertz when he led the fight against the adoption by the League of Nations of a universalist calendar.

Within today's broader Anglo-Jewry, there are enormous differences. But, as Hertz remarked in another context, while we recognise religious differences, more troubling still is religious indifference. It was the Reform rabbi Harold Reinhardt who pushed his congregations towards a degree of unity, having experienced the apparent chaos which had befallen his fellow Jews in the United States.

In these circumstances, it appears that the one Office which might help to instil unity within British Jewry – the Chief Rabbinate – should not be allowed to wither and die. The jury of history is out, and we must await its verdict.

AUBREY NEWMAN
Emeritus Professor of History,
University of Leicester

Preface

In March 1993, a brief report in the London *Jewish Chronicle* drew the public's attention to a communal body that had been kept under wraps for almost a decade. A closed-door 'liaison committee' of prominent Orthodox and Progressive Jews, it disclosed, 'has decided to shed an eight-year-old veil of secrecy in a bid to encourage "respect and tolerance" across doctrinal divides.

> A co-founder of the group – Rabbi Maurice Unterman, emeritus minister of the Marble Arch (United) Synagogue – said that wider communication was essential. 'Human beings who don't speak will always quarrel,' he declared. 'There is too much collective position-taking in Anglo-Jewry and not enough respect, sympathy and communication among individuals.'
>
> The committee, which also includes prominent members of the Masorti, Reform and Liberal movements, was set up with the aim of 'agreeing to disagree amicably' on differences of doctrine, while trying to work for compromise solutions to other problems. 'We are present in individual, not organisational, capacities,' said Jonathan Lew, the United Synagogue's chief executive. 'What has made the arrangement work is the honesty and trust that exist among all of us.'
>
> The main focus of the group – which began in 1985 as an informal response to a series of perceived attacks by a Progressive rabbi on the then Chief Rabbi, Sir Immanuel Jakobovits – has been to take the 'personal sting' out of relations between the various religious groups, one member said. 'We've had successes, partial successes, and failures,' said Rabbi Tony Bayfield, the chief executive-designate of the Reform movement. 'But the attempt has always been to address the real issues without posturing.'[1]

What the report did not reveal – indeed, did not know – was that the 'eight-year-old veil of secrecy' was a good deal older. Closed-door meetings at the Chief Rabbi's residence in Hamilton Terrace, North-West London,[2] had been taking place almost from the beginning of the Jakobovits Chief Rabbinate, and were to continue, clandestinely, for several years after this revelation was announced.

* * *

As readers of my earlier studies will be aware, intra-communal strife has been a hallmark of Anglo-Jewish life almost from the start of the modern era. Following the rise of Reform in the early 1840s, it dominated relations between the factions for more than fifty years, until a modus vivendi (of sorts) was reached towards the end of the century.

Confrontation re-emerged, however, with the founding of the Liberal movement in the early 1900s, exacerbated by growing warfare between the Chief Rabbinate and London Beth Din, on the one hand, and the Progressives – and, much later, the Masorti (Conservatives) – on the other. The arrival of Immanuel Jakobovits as Chief Rabbi in the mid-1960s, after the upheaval of the so-called 'Jacobs Affairs',[3] saw the first solid attempts to calm troubled waters.

In preparing for his role, the future Chief Rabbi had set certain boundaries:

> I believe I can assume that all parties to the recent conflict are by now thoroughly tired of the costly strife, disenchanted with the sterile results achieved, saddened by the bitterness and disunity which have disrupted the once-solid structure of the community, and anxious to find an honourable solution.
>
> For my part, I am prepared to go a very long way in my quest for a lasting reconciliation, based on friendliness and mutual trust, as well as on respect for our sacred traditions. Of course, I realise there will have to be some give-and-take on a few matters of substance, but primarily I think the situation calls for a new outlook and attitude on all sides, the creation of an atmosphere of goodwill, and an amicable 'agreement to disagree' within some well-defined limits.[4]

When, after a short time – despite assurances from all sides of peace and accord – Jakobovits found that the atmosphere was as toxic as ever, he took steps to harmonise relations, first through public means and then, when these failed, by going underground. More precisely, he opened the doors of his home to a select few of the combatants, and then closed them firmly once the parties were inside.

For some twenty years from the late 1960s, and thereafter following a break, representatives of the various orientations held confidential meetings in attempts to bridge their communal and halachic differences. So secret were these contacts that no word reached the outside world until well after they were broken off, and hitherto the details of their often fiery disputations – both verbally and in writing – have never been revealed. This volume opens the doors for the first time on that combative world.

* * *

Within the past year, a report published in London by the Institute of Jewish Policy Research (JPR), in conjunction with the Board of Deputies, noted that the number of households affiliated to synagogues in Britain had fallen by 20% over the previous quarter-century.[5]

Centrist Orthodox synagogues, including those under the Chief Rabbinate, were the biggest losers, shedding more than one-third of their members during that period. While they were the most dominant synagogal group in 1990, representing 70% of shul members (including Sephardim), that number had fallen to 56% by 2016. Non-Orthodox membership, meanwhile, had risen from 26% to 31%.

The report also noted that data from the JPR's community survey of 2013 indicated that 'a significantly higher number and proportion of mainstream Orthodox-affiliated Jews have moved towards more non-Orthodox or Progressive movements than the other way round'.

According to Jonathan Boyd, JPR's executive director and co-author of the report, 'because the more Progressive wing is largely stable, representing just under one-third of the total, the trends point to a future in which stricter forms of Orthodoxy will hold an increasingly prominent position, not only in synagogue membership, but in how Judaism is practised and how Judaism is seen and understood by others'.

Commenting on this trend, Rabbi Danny Rich, chief executive of Liberal Judaism, said that 'mainstream Jewry – and mainstream Orthodoxy in particular – has failed to respond by offering an attractive alternative to the false certainties of fundamentalism. I believe we need to be more open, more inclusive and more flexible.'

In a brief analysis, written for the *Jewish Chronicle*, Boyd commented: 'Belonging to a synagogue matters. More than anything else, it is where we encounter Jewish community and find our place within it. News of continuing decline should wake us up, and prompt us to get involved to make our synagogues more vibrant, dynamic and purposeful for everyone.'⁶

The survey's findings have a clear bearing on the contents of this volume – and on another report published in 1992, when the United Synagogue released *A Time for Change*, the results of an extensive review conducted under the chairmanship of Stanley (now Lord) Kalms.⁷

The review was set up 'against a background of crisis and opportunity – crisis in the form of declining membership, and opportunity represented by growing interest and participation in Jewish life, as well as the challenge of a new Chief Rabbi. Many possibilities were considered, including the notion that this once-vital lynchpin in Anglo-Jewry was no longer relevant or needed....

'Along with financial malaise, other symptoms were manifest. These included a loss of morale at every tier within the organisation, confused and conflicting approaches to the United Synagogue's objectives, lack of role definition at both a lay and professional level, and, above all, a deep dissatisfaction with the centre.'⁸

Many of these problems were corrected over the years, but at least one remained: the possibility of members leaving the United Synagogue. 'For the non-Orthodox respondents', the Kalms review noted, 'the Masorti and Reform communities were real options. For the reasonably Orthodox, Masorti was a powerful magnet.

'For respondents who consider themselves traditional, many are annoyed by the perceived new-found extremism of the United Synagogue and its unwillingness to develop halachah in the ways that they believe it has been developed over the centuries. For this group, Masorti synagogues are a real attraction, especially those that still retain separate seating for men and women.'⁹

In a section on 'quantitative research' (by questionnaires), the review found that 'about a quarter of those who had considered leaving had done so because of geographical considerations, and the majority of these would move to another United or Orthodox synagogue. If such cases are removed from the analysis, the majority of potential (dissatisfied) leavers would move to the Left – that is, to Reform (35%), Masorti (17%) or Liberal (3%) synagogues, or to no synagogue at all (4%). The remaining 41% would move to another Orthodox synagogue.

'Allowing for the proportion of respondents who have probably never heard of the Masorti movement, the percentage selecting this type of synagogue is surprisingly high. Combined with the Progressive sector, it would seem that the main threat to United Synagogue membership comes from the Left. The dramatic growth in the Right-wing sector appears to be fuelled mainly by the natural growth of Chasidic communities, and by the attraction of previously unaffiliated Jews, rather than by any sizeable defection from the central Orthodox community.'[10]

Nearly twenty years on, the JPR report noted that, 'while the Orthodox middle has suffered a squeeze, there has been a 139% increase in membership of strictly Orthodox congregations since 1990, and their overall synagogue market had risen from 4% to 13%. The Progressive wing is largely stable and, apart from the strictly Orthodox, the only stream to grow is Masorti, which has more than doubled its membership since 1990 and is no longer the smallest grouping, having overtaken the Sephardim.'

In light of these statistics, the narrative related in the coming chapters assumes contemporary significance. With numbers shrinking in the wider Jewish community, let alone in the congregational establishment, its leaders need to learn the lessons of past disputes and, with open doors and open minds, find new paths to an Anglo-Jewry at peace with itself. One fact appears certain: in terms of size, structure and sympathies, centrist Orthodoxy is on the wane, and another review may be necessary if it is to revive in the coming decades.

* * *

Over some forty years, as a member of the *Jewish Chronicle* editorial staff, I established close contacts – and friendships – across the communal divide. Many were the meetings I had with rabbis, organisational leaders, community workers, academics, fellow journalists, counsellors and politicians, and a host of other professionals and pundits, all as eager to impart as I was to receive.

In the context of my research, they included Chief Rabbi Professor Jonathan Sacks and, earlier, the late Chief Rabbi Dr Immanuel (Lord) Jakobovits, Haham Dr Solomon Gaon, and Rabbi Dr Louis Jacobs, of blessed memory; and from each and all, my storehouse of communal knowledge and interest steadily grew. To me, and to countless others throughout the world, Lord Sacks remains a source of profound inspiration. Week after week, and year after year, he does what he does best – producing teachings and volumes of the highest calibre, enriching the field of Jewish scholarship, and enlightening generations of young and old with words and thoughts that leave one spellbound.

To the late Rabbi Dr Sidney Brichto, I owe much for the mound of material he shared with me, and for the hours we passed discussing the

Jewish world around us. Far above all, I am deeply indebted to the late Lady (Amélie) Jakobovits, who, almost to the day of her passing, encouraged me to continue working in my chosen subject – the relationship between the British Chief Rabbinate and the non-Orthodox movements, in which field her beloved husband was so closely involved.

I extend warm thanks to Nicola Avery, Principal Archivist (Culture, Heritage and Libraries) at London Metropolitan Archives (LMA), and to Mary Cockerill, Archivist at the Hartley Library of the University of Southampton (USL, Archives and Special Collections) for their invaluable assistance in the preparation of this study; and to Rabbi Dr Tony Bayfield and David Jacobs, of Reform Judaism, for their constant advice and support over many years. My early research owes much to Erla Zimmels, librarian of the London School of Jewish Studies (formerly Jews' College), whose help and expertise have proved of inestimable value.

I am also grateful to Professor Aubrey Newman, of the University of Leicester, for so kindly contributing the foreword to this book. He has written extensively in the field of Anglo-Jewish history, most notably provincial Jewry since the eighteenth century, and is the author of the highly acclaimed *The United Synagogue, 1870–1970*. In the late 'eighties, he sat on the seven-man committee responsible for selecting Jonathan Sacks as Chief Rabbi. Now Emeritus Professor of History at Leicester University, he was instrumental in the establishment of its Stanley Burton Centre for Holocaust and Genocide Studies, and continues his work on modern Anglo- Jewry.

MEIR PERSOFF
Jerusalem
December 2017, Tevet 5778

CHAPTER ONE

1945–1960

Strife and Sanctity

British Jewry emerged from the Second World War in a fraught and fragile state. Within months of Victory in Europe (VE) Day – 8 May, 1945 – Chief Rabbi Joseph Herman Hertz[1] died, leaving behind a fractured community beset by internecine strife and religious differences, primarily in the fields of marriage, divorce and conversion.

The rise and spread of Reform Judaism throughout much of the nineteenth century, and its Liberal counterpart in the ensuing decades, had led to escalating friction between the Orthodox and Progressive factions, aggravated by Hertz's diminishing authority as failing health, clashes within the United Synagogue hierarchy, and the growing dominance of the London Beth Din, sapped his strength.

As early as 1856, during the Chief Rabbinate of Nathan Marcus Adler, and after considerable disputation between the opposing synagogal bodies, an 'Act to amend the Provisions of the Marriage and Registration Acts' had received royal assent, authorising the Registrar General 'to furnish marriage register books and forms to each certified secretary of the [Reform] West London Synagogue of British Jews,' and of 'some other Synagogue... being in connexion with the West London Synagogue and having been established for not less than one year.... Every marriage solemnised under any of the said recited Acts or of this Act shall be good and cognisable in like manner as marriages before the passing of the first-recited Act according to the rites of the Church of England.'[2]

Eight decades later, the Liberals – until then compelled by statute to have a civil registrar at each of their weddings – similarly sought a marriage secretary of their own. In June 1934, they approached Neville Laski,[3] president of the Board of Deputies, who in turn (as again required by law) asked Hertz for a ruling that the Liberal congregation was 'a synagogue of persons professing the Jewish religion'. This the Chief Rabbi initially declined to do, until six months later when, after a fiery exchange with United Synagogue vice-president Sir Robert Waley Cohen,[4] he issued the following statement:

> Although I strongly disapprove of the religious practices and principles of the Liberal Synagogue, I am not justified in declaring that its members have left the ranks of Jewry, and do not profess Judaism. If that had been the case, they could not have been given representation on the Board of Deputies.
>
> Moreover, if the recognition requisite for the appointment of a marriage secretary is now denied them, they will, as Berkeley Street [West London Reform] have done years ago, seek relief by Act of Parliament. Such a course would in all probability bring with it a discussion in Parliament of minor religious differences. I feel that such a discussion would be especially undesirable at the present moment.
>
> In the circumstances, I am prepared to agree to the formality of certifying that the body in question is an organisation for purposes of worship and kindred activities on the part of Liberal Jews, and therefore constitutes for the purposes of the Act of Parliament a synagogue of persons professing the Jewish religion.
>
> However, it must be clearly understood that, by this formal act of certification, the Chief Rabbinate can take no responsibility for the legality or otherwise in Jewish law of any ritual act performed by the ministers of that Congregation.[5]

The appointment a year later of Yechezkel Alter Abramsky as senior dayan of the London Beth Din[6] foreshadowed a diametrically different approach to non-Orthodox marriages, heightened by the growing incidence of intermarriage during the Second World War. In this connection, the number of applications for conversions to the West London Synagogue had risen annually from around thirty before the war to more than 100 by its close.[7]

Gone were the days when the Beth Din felt comfortable in passing on to the West London Synagogue would-be converts who wished to marry nominally observant Jews. 'The fact that the gentleman concerned is not a strictly Orthodox Jew,' wrote Dayan Mark Gollop to the Rev Vivian Simmons in 1930, regarding one such case, 'would seem to point to her [the prospective convert] being more at home with you than with us. It would be almost absurd to train an applicant for strictly Orthodox Judaism when the man she proposes to marry does not observe the religion she is presumed to undertake. I see no reason why you should not deal with the case if he wishes to place it in your hands.'[8] Observant applicants to Berkeley Street were on occasion similarly referred to the London Beth Din.

The establishment of the Reform Beth Din in 1948, and its internal recognition soon after as 'The Court of the Assembly of Ministers,' marked a new and increasingly hostile chapter in Orthodox–Progressive relations. Initially, the dayanim ignored its existence, but their growing opposition in the early 1960s sparked the flames of a conflict that spilled over into the next Chief Rabbinate, and well beyond. Liberal Jews, meanwhile, after their partial success twenty-five years earlier, welcomed the 1959 Marriage (Secretaries of Synagogues) Act, which – as Hertz had predicted – accorded to them similar rights as the Reform in nominating marriage secretaries direct to the Registrar General without needing to employ the Board of Deputies.

Two years earlier, addressing a Conference of European Rabbis, in Amsterdam, Ireland's 37-year-old Chief Rabbi Immanuel Jakobovits had told his colleagues that 'the Reform movement, it seems to me, is not our chief problem. It is merely a symptom, not the cause, of the general malaise. Reform has not drawn its ranks from the Orthodox camp, but from those already lost to us....

> I believe we have to decide whether to write off the Reform movement and its followers as a dead loss, and try to insulate it completely from the adherents of Orthodoxy, or go all out to retrieve what can be salvaged even at the cost of some formal compromise with them. In the havoc wrought by these dissenters, we must distinguish between irreparable damage, which will leave sores festering on the body of our people for generations to come, and purely temporary infractions of the sanctities of Jewish life, causing wounds which can be healed by individual acts of repentance....
>
> It might be worthwhile to explore the possibility of offering the Reformers, as an earnest of our anxiety for the preservation of Jewish unity, some kind of truce based on their acceptance of our exclusive jurisdiction in all matters affecting marriage and conversion, even if this meant closing our eyes to their forms of

synagogue services and religious education for the time being. Their agreement to this suggestion would, to my mind, constitute an invaluable gain and possibly pave the way to their eventual return to our fold.

On the other hand, if they rejected the offer, we would at least win a substantial moral victory. Their refusal would publicly reveal more clearly than ever before who are the real disruptive influences in Jewish life today. The true causes for disunity and strife would be exposed for all to see.[9]

Disturbed by reports of, and reactions to, the conference as subsequently published in the *Jewish Chronicle*, Jakobovits reconstructed his remarks. 'It appears,' he wrote the following week, 'that the spokesmen of "Progressive" Judaism now seek to become the apostles of Jewish "unity" in much the same way as the Communists have appropriated the plea for "peace" as their watchword. The logic, let alone the justice, of the Reformers' argument is really hard to see for any fair-minded person.

'First they break away from the historic traditions of our people, assault the unity of our Torah and the integrity of our law by choosing what they like and rejecting what they do not understand; sow bitterness and strife by their secession from our established communities and their propagation of unlawfulness; and then they have the audacity to pontificate to the loyal element on the dangers of disunity!...

'If [they] are really as concerned to heal the breach which they have created as they profess to be, let them demonstrate their anxiety for unity by deeds, not words. Let them cease to solemnise marriages which contravene Biblical and rabbinic law, let them stop disrupting the unity of our people by issuing "admissions" to Judaism which no law-abiding Jew can conscientiously recognise, let them join with us in our hard battle for the unconditional submission of all Jews to the Divine Law. Let them show at least some respect and understanding for those who, in the face of constant provocation and denigration, genuinely labour day and night to "salvage our Jewish heritage."'[10]

In 1962, a Beth Din publication, *Jewish Marriage and Divorce*, written by Dayan Morris Swift with a foreword by then Chief Rabbi Israel Brodie,[11] contained a lengthy denunciation of Reform and Liberal developments. 'Anglo-Jewry,' declared Swift, 'must be guarded against the danger of their practices, particularly in cases of marriage, divorce and conversions. Their rulings are not recognised by any authentic rabbinic body in the world.

In Jewish law, the *get* [divorce] they issue is no *get*, and the conversions they perform have no validity....

'As a result of their widespread interference with our marriage laws, the term "intermarriage," which hitherto applied to marriages "out" of the Jewish fold, now applies equally to many marriages within the Jewish fold. Many of the marriages performed by them have no validity in Jewish law and have made a tragic impact on hundreds of Jewish families in this country; they have caused untold pain and suffering to the issue of these marriages which can never be repaired.'

In response to Swift's booklet, the Reform Assembly of Ministers issued a statement defending 'the sacred character' of its marriages and upholding the validity of its court; lay members of the movement threatened an action for libel against the London Beth Din; and the Chief Rabbi held a covert meeting with Werner Van der Zyl, the Assembly's chairman and senior minister at Berkeley Street.[12]

The libel threat was later dropped, but not before Brodie was said to have given an assurance that copies of the booklet, having been exhausted, would not be reissued. In his meeting with Van der Zyl, held without the knowledge of the United Synagogue officers, the Chief Rabbi raised issues of marriage, divorce and conversion; hinted that if *tevilah* [ritual ablution] were introduced, recognition of Reform proselytes might be granted; and confirmed that, 'as far as he was concerned, marriages in Reform synagogues between halachically acceptable Jews were valid.'[13]

Some three years later, the Liberals' Rabbi Sidney Brichto,[14] who was to assume a major role in the controversy over the coming years, had occasion to refer to 'rumours which can only cause greater dissension in our already regrettably divided community. It is being suggested in certain circles that the marriage ceremony of Liberal and Progressive synagogues is not recognised as religiously valid by Orthodox Jewish authorities.

> The Orthodox may refuse to accept as valid those few marriages in which they consider one or both parties to be ineligible – for example, a divorcee without an Orthodox *get*; a case involving *chalitzah*; an *agunah* ['chained wife'],[15] etc. However, where marriages are performed in Liberal and Progressive synagogues between two Jews whose eligibility for Jewish marriage is unquestionable, even according to their own rulings, I challenge any responsible spokesman of Orthodox Judaism to state publicly and categorically that such marriages are invalid. As they cannot question the

validity of these marriages, I would call upon all Orthodox rabbis to refrain from causing personal distress and communal friction, either by encouraging these false and malicious rumours or by allowing them to go unchecked.[16]

Addressing a public gathering some days later, Swift rose to the challenge and asserted that Reform and Liberal marriages could be considered valid, but 'no more so than those performed in a register office. They are merely contractual agreements between men and women and lack any sanctity.'[17]

In response, the ministers' bodies of the Union of Liberal and Progressive Synagogues and the Reform Synagogues of Great Britain declared: 'We reaffirm – and this has never before been officially challenged – that, where the eligibility of the partners to marry each other is unquestionable, even from the point of view of Orthodoxy, such marriages are unimpeachable on the basis of rabbinic law, for they satisfy all its essential requirements....

'Unless the present Orthodox leaders are persuaded to refrain from abusing their ecclesiastical authority – whose basis should be Torah, of which it is said that all its paths are peace – through the sowing of dissension and the infliction of grief in the household of Israel, Anglo-Jewry will find itself the victim of self-imposed religious persecution and oppression, which must lead to the decline and disintegration of Jewish communal life.'[18]

* * *

The last years of Brodie's Chief Rabbinate were dominated by issues far removed from the marriage arena. In 1959, he approved the appointment of Rabbi Dr Louis Jacobs, then minister of London's New West End Synagogue, as moral tutor and lecturer in pastoral theology at Jews' College, Anglo-Jewry's foremost Orthodox seminary (of which Brodie was president). The honorary officers had indicated to Jacobs that, 'subject to the Chief Rabbi's approval of his candidature, they intended to recommend to the council his appointment as principal when the post became vacant.'[19]

In the event, some thirty months later, Brodie withheld his approval 'on various grounds' (as Jacobs described it),[20] 'the one recurring most often being that views I have expressed in writing render me unsuitable for the position. These views are contained in my books *We Have Reason to Believe* and *Jewish Values*. I remain firmly convinced that the approach to traditional Judaism I have sketched in these books is one that must commend itself to all who are aware of modern thought and scholarship. I have tried to show that intense loyalty to Jewish tradition and observance need not be synonymous with reaction and fundamentalism. Furthermore, I would claim that no reputable scholar in the world has an approach that is basically different from mine.'

Giving their own version of events, the dayanim of the London Beth Din subsequently asserted: 'Dr Jacobs follows the critical hypotheses of predecessors and of scholars who ignore Orthodox tenets and traditional canons. His rejection of the doctrine of verbal inspiration, his acceptance of textual criticism of the Torah, and his compromising attitude to higher criticism which denies the divine origin and unity of the Torah, Torah min hashamayim – the truth of which is expressed in the familiar words which we repeat when the Scroll is held up after the Reading of the Law: "And this is the Law which Moses set before the children of Israel, according to the commandment of the Lord by the hand of Moses" – do not fit in with any Orthodox school of thought.'[21]

The ramifications of the episode were lengthy and far-reaching, particularly when allied to a second so-called 'Jacobs Affair' in 1964. Unexpectedly, the pulpit of the New West End Synagogue fell vacant with the departure to New York of Jacobs' successor, Chaim Pearl,[22] and the congregation's honorary officers – keen to secure their former minister – approached the Chief Rabbi for his required approval.

Unsurprisingly, Brodie declined to issue his certificate,[23] whereupon the officers, going over his head, invited Jacobs to preach; this he did, arising from the minister's seat and dressed in canonicals. As a result, the United Synagogue's leaders – headed by their president, Sir Isaac Wolfson – called an extraordinary meeting to discharge the rebels and instal their own men.

Jacobs and his supporters responded by establishing an alternative congregation, the New London Synagogue, thus laying the foundation of what, in due course, was to become the Masorti (Conservative) movement – and of which Brodie himself had predicted some five years earlier when, addressing a rabbinical conference in Westcliff-on-Sea, he gave what he described as 'an emphatic warning' directed at the United Synagogue of America:

'This body,' he declared, 'which represents the Conservative elements in the United States and Canada, is now making an attempt to spread its wings and to have a world organisation. As far as Jewish communities in

Europe are concerned which rally under the flag of the Torah, there can be no association with this movement. We shall discourage and resist these efforts by the Conservatives of America to infiltrate into Europe, even if they may speak to us in terms of traditional Judaism.'[24]

* * *

Early in 1964, at the height of the New West End controversy – behind the scenes, and well before serious interest emerged in the Chief Rabbinical succession – came backing for Brodie from Immanuel Jakobovits, then rabbi of Fifth Avenue Synagogue, New York. Acknowledging a message from Jakobovits, the Chief Rabbi wrote:

> Thank you very much for your letter of 16 April. I found its contents most heartening, particularly at this time.
>
> I have been considerably encouraged by the support which my stand has received from religious leaders at home and abroad. When I was in Israel, I had a word with the Chief Rabbis, who assured me that they were with me in the decision that I had made.
>
> I did not know that, during my absence [on a cruise to Australia, recovering from ill-health], you had been approached by the Beth Din to obtain a statement from Rabbi [Joseph] Soloveitchik[25] in support of my ruling. While normally I would not like to involve Rabbis of other communities in an issue which is domestic, the publicity which has been given to the whole matter, in the general press and on radio outside the United Kingdom, does make it necessary for spiritual leaders of the stature of Rabbi Soloveitchik to make a pronouncement. I entirely agree with you that support would be more effective, as far as America is concerned, if it came from individuals like Rabbis Soloveitchik and [Leo] Jung,[26] and one or two others, rather than from official Orthodox bodies.
>
> I have this day written a letter to Rabbi Soloveitchik in which I suggest that he, together with Rabbi Jung and others, might be prepared to make a supporting statement which could be used effectively. Up to the present, I have maintained silence and have not communicated in any way to the press, and have resisted the importunate demands of the journalists. Now, however, it has become essential for me to break that silence.

For this purpose, I have decided to call a meeting of all Rabbis and Preachers in the United Kingdom for next Tuesday, before whom I will make a statement[27] on the situation against the background of the religious problems which challenge the integrity and survival of the Anglo-Jewish community. The statement will, of course, be printed and distributed, and will go to the press.

I have taken a long time before reaching a decision to make a statement because I did not wish to be associated with the grievous sin of *chillul Hashem* committed by those who – directly or indirectly – were responsible for the matter to be publicised and written about in the national, and now world, press, and also on radio. I feel that I cannot desist any longer.

I have been considerably helped by the attitude of the Honorary Officers of the United Synagogue, who have loyally maintained the authority and dignity of my Office.

With all good wishes, and thanking you sincerely for your ready undertaking to help.[28]

The following week, in response to Brodie's letter, Jakobovits told the Chief Rabbi that he had met Soloveitchik that day for a lengthy discussion. 'Subject to whatever practical suggestions you may have made to him, he is now quite prepared to come out with a statement. In strictest confidence, he further told me that he may be able to prevail on Professor Saul Lieberman – of all people[29] – to join him in such a statement, following discussions on the issue the two of them had yesterday. Evidently, support may still come from some quite unexpected quarters.

'A further suggestion on which I sounded Rabbi S. was for him to visit England, and it appears that he might be quite receptive to an invitation from you. For tactical purposes, such an invitation might be for the purpose of consultations, though his presence could then be taken advantage of for some public appearances which, I imagine, would be highly effective.

'Since [Israel's Ashkenazi] Chief Rabbi [Issar Yehudah] Unterman is due here at the beginning of June, he too might be prevailed upon to include England in his itinerary. By concerting the visits of the two chief Orthodox spokesmen in the world, the rebellion might be crushed by sheer weight of intellect and mass solidarity. Such a unique demonstration of superior knowledge and universally recognised authority could well provide embattled Orthodoxy in England with the requisite *chizuk* [strengthening] to ensure its triumph and consolidation.'

Jakobovits added that Rabbis Jung and Emanuel Rackman[30] were prepared to make or endorse any statement that might be required, and that a meeting with them and Soloveitchik had been proposed for the following week, 'on our hearing from you in the meantime, so that a concerted plan of action can be devised.'[31]

A fortnight later, Jakobovits sent Soloveitchik the draft of a letter subsequently forwarded to Brodie. In an aside to his New York colleague, he added: 'As you will note, I prefer a somewhat pragmatic approach to a purely ideological one. I also thought it advisable to introduce our arguments by a statement explaining our concern and involvement in the crisis.... I do hope that our efforts may prove of some use to you in providing Rabbi Brodie with the support he so anxiously awaits.'

Addressing their letter to Brodie, the American rabbis wrote:

> The present religious dissension in the ranks of your community has caused us the deepest distress. Quite apart from our obvious concern with Jewish interests everywhere, the fortunes of Judaism in America too are bound to be gravely affected by the destruction of the religious unity of Anglo-Jewry, hitherto the most solid bulwark of Orthodox Judaism in the Diaspora.
>
> Moreover, the highly unsavoury reports on internal Jewish strife, as fed in such profusion (and distortion) to the public press in America as elsewhere, have reached the proportions of a major *chillul Hashem*, with the prospects of adverse effects beyond calculation. For all these reasons, we cannot be indifferent to the outcome of the present crisis and its ramified repercussions.
>
> Together with traditional and fair-minded Jews throughout the world, we acclaim your courageous stand, in the face of intolerable pressures to coerce your conscience, as recently exemplified by your historic statement to your British colleagues. In support of the cause which united us with you, we wish to assert
>
> 1. The belief in *Torah min hashamayim* – that is, the Divine origin of the entire Torah, and its identity with the Law Moses received at Sinai, as adumbrated in the Thirteen Principles of Faith listed by Maimonides – has never been challenged or compromised in our history until the rise of Reform Judaism

in the last century. Nor is this principle today disputed by any leading Orthodox rabbi, scholar, scientist or thinker anywhere. No one, therefore, who denies or qualifies this axiom of Judaism can legitimately claim to be Orthodox, however observant he may be in practice.

2. We resent the widely publicised insinuation that only Jews who have abandoned this belief are 'thinking' and 'modern'. The incontestable truth is that just the uncompromising supporters of this principle are today the spiritually and communally most creative element in Jewry. These are the Jews who have built the worldwide network of Jewish day-schools and yeshivot, thus giving new dimensions and meaning to Jewish education; who have galvanised religious observance and community life to a degree of intensity never known before in the Western world; who have pioneered the burgeoning movements of religious scientists and college students, thus recreating a Jewish religious intelligentsia; who apply the principles of Jewish law to contemporary problems in voluminous responsa to vindicate the relevance of Judaism to our times; and who are in the forefront of every endeavour in the spheres of biblical research, religious scholarship, and literary and publishing enterprises.

3. To subject religious teachings to the fickle claims of Bible Criticism (a Christian nineteenth-century product now largely discarded) and to plead for an adulterated Orthodoxy in the name of 'tolerance' is to put back the clock of history. The battle of the Haskalah movement (inspired by Bible Criticism) against Jewish tradition has been fought and lost long ago, and the religious *laisser-faire* rampant thirty years ago or more has been rendered obsolete by the resurgence of an enlightened, militant Orthodoxy in Anglo-Jewry, as anywhere else in the Jewish world. Those who want to restore the former conditions of liberalism within organisations labelled as 'Orthodox' are, and will remain, out of step with the dynamic forces governing Orthodox Jewish life today all over the world.

The letter concluded: 'We fervently hope that, even at this late hour, it will be possible to reach a settlement compatible with the teachings representing the very definition of Judaism. To achieve such understanding, we gladly offer any assistance we may be called upon to render in healing the present tragic breach in the ranks of our people.'[32]

CHAPTER TWO

1960–1970

Gestures and Concessions

Within weeks of his New West End statement to the rabbis and ministers, Brodie's retirement was foreshadowed by Wolfson. In June 1964, he announced that the Chief Rabbi would step down on his seventieth birthday the following spring, and the United Synagogue council took its first steps in 'the complex process of choosing a successor' by convening a conference of bodies contributing to the Chief Rabbinate's maintenance.[1]

Brodie's last public engagement was a sermon preached at the Western Synagogue in May 1965,[2] and days later he and his wife, Fanny, moved into a flat in London's Portland Place, gifted them through a fund set up by Wolfson.[3] During the interregnum, the dayanim of the London Beth Din were appointed to act as the Chief Rabbinate-in-Commission.[4]

Among early names mentioned as a possible successor was that of Yaacov Herzog,[5] director-general of Israel's Foreign Ministry and younger son of the country's late Ashkenazi Chief Rabbi, Isaac Halevi Herzog. Jakobovits was known to be Wolfson's preference, but when the New York rabbi initially declined the post,[6] the reluctant Herzog was offered – and accepted – it.[7] He withdrew, however, four months later, due to 'a serious deterioration of his health'.[8]

Both before and during the Chief Rabbinical interregnum, with emotions running high among the non-Orthodox movements, several calls went out for the abolition of the Office. 'The rabbis of Anglo-Jewry who are under the jurisdiction and supervision of a Chief Rabbi,' declared Reform's Ignaz Maybaum, 'are no longer free. Why should young men choose the rabbinical profession under such undignified conditions?... The jurisdiction of the Chief Rabbi is also responsible for the present sterility of Anglo-Jewish public life. The best brains and the finest characters turn with disgust from public life. The Office of the Chief Rabbi must disappear from the scene or be changed into an honorary position, with a new occupant, say, every third year.'[9]

'We must make it abundantly clear,' wrote the Liberals' Sidney Brichto, 'that we do not believe in a Chief Rabbinate, that we do not believe in a hierarchy of religious leaders, that we do not accept a form of Judaism in which there is an inseparable gulf between the religious and lay leaders in belief and practice. Anglo-Jewry must hear that we believe in a form of Judaism in which all may participate with full honesty. We believe in the equality of all rabbis, and we reject the idea of a Chief Rabbinate as the sole source of religious authority.'[10]

Chaim Pearl, who had left the New West End congregation to become rabbi of the Conservative Synagogue of Riverdale, New York, wrote of his newly established counterpart in Britain: 'The New London can present a focal point of organised and articulate opposition to the Chief Rabbinate. Its present religious leadership is against the institution of the Chief Rabbinate in principle, and argues against the extremist position which the London Beth Din has adopted in recent years.... The Jew [whom it represents] doesn't want Reform, yet he cannot accept the fundamentalist legalism of the present-day leaders of the Establishment. He must find another way, and the New London – and what it represents – may be his answer.'[11]

* * *

Against this background of strife and disharmony, the Board of Deputies stepped in to mediate. In January 1966, an attempt 'to prevent an irrevocable split in Anglo-Jewry, threatened by the controversy over the religious validity of Reform and Liberal marriages,' was launched by its president, Solomon Teff, with the aim 'not to resolve the religious issues involved, but to preserve communal cohesion.'

Revealing 'this unprecedented initiative' to the Board's members, following a meeting of its executive committee, Teff said that he had been asked to consider the implications and repercussions of the controversy, sparked off by statements from dayanim in London and Manchester that marriages performed in Reform and Liberal synagogues were not valid in Jewish law.

He added that, while the committee 'considered the Board, as the representative body of all Jews in this country holding different religious views, an unsuitable forum for the discussion of the religious issues involved', it was 'very seriously concerned with pronouncements and incidents that may adversely affect the cohesion and unity of the community. The committee agreed that I, as president of the Board, make certain approaches and engage in appropriate consultations with a view to the maintenance of harmony in the community, which must be our main concern.'[12]

Six months later, a meeting of religious leaders – Dayan Myer Lew, representing the Chief Rabbinate-in-Commission; the Haham, Rabbi Solomon Gaon, the Sephardi community; Van der Zyl, the Reform Synagogues of Great Britain; and Brichto and Jakob Kokotek, the Union of Liberal and Progressive Synagogues – took place under Teff's chairmanship. A statement noted that the meeting, of a preliminary nature, was held 'in a spirit of goodwill and discussed possibilities of co-operation between the different religious trends in matters of common Jewish interest, with a view to preserving the integrity of the community.'[13]

Addressing a gathering in Brighton the same week at the laying of the foundation-stone for the Brighton and Hove New Synagogue (Reform), Teff declared in his capacity as chairman of the local Jewish communal council: 'None of the millions of Jews exterminated at wartime concentration camps was ever asked whether he was Orthodox, Reform or Liberal. To the non-Jew, a Jew was a Jew, whatever his religious outlook.'

Judge Alan King-Hamilton, president of the West London Synagogue, asserted: 'It is lamentable, at a time when different sections of Christianity are drawing together, and Jews and Christians becoming more closely associated, that the gulf between the United Synagogue and Progressives is becoming wider.' The fault, he added, was 'not with the Progressives'.

The synagogue's minister, Erwin Rosenblum, remarked that the various sections of the Brighton community worked together in many ways, thanks largely to Teff. 'The gulf is being narrowed, and representatives of the Orthodox and Liberal synagogues of the town are present here.' He was supported by Van der Zyl who, in an appeal for unity, declared: 'Let us differ where, in all sincerity, we have to differ. But let us join and strengthen our efforts to the glory of Judaism.'[14]

King-Hamilton's appearance coincided with a series of meetings in London held under his name and chairmanship, aimed at enhancing non-Orthodox representation in the communal and national arenas, and at strengthening areas of co-operation with the Orthodox establishment. However, after a drawn-out succession of unproductive approaches, Malcolm Slowe, the Liberals' chairman, wrote to Brichto: 'The King-Hamilton Committee first met over a year ago and, although it has been quite an interesting talking-shop, it has achieved absolutely nothing. Unless it can take some useful action, I shall feel bound to advise the Union representatives to withdraw from it. I should be reluctant to take this step, but some action is required of the Union or we will soon find ourselves in an embarrassing position.'[15]

The King-Hamilton group later re-emerged as the Joint Standing Committee on Anglo-Jewish Relations, having made several approaches – ultimately unfruitful – to Teff, Gaon, Jacobs and Van der Zyl, and to Harris Swift, of the (independent Orthodox) Western Synagogue, with a view to establishing a so-called British Council of Synagogues or National Rabbinical Council.[16]

Regarding Teff's lukewarm reaction to the proposal, Slowe told Brichto: 'I am not surprised that Mr Teff would regard the establishment of a Synagogue Council as a rival to the Deputies, but so long as the Deputies feel compelled to refer all matters appertaining to religious questions to the Beth Din, it is perhaps necessary that they should have a rival which will recognise other religious authorities. Indeed, the establishment of a rival might well lead to a union of the two bodies in the same way as the historical foundation of the Deputies.'[17] While the 'rival' did not surface at the time, a challenge to the Beth Din's supremacy was eventually successful.

Teff's committee, meanwhile, occasionally convened, and at one stage the Haham met with Brichto, who subsequently wrote: 'It was a great pleasure to have the opportunity of meeting with you, and I hope that we shall do so many times again, and that all our discussions will lead to a deeper relationship between you and me.... The Federation [of Synagogues] should be approached to come to the next meeting, at which it should also be decided to extend an invitation to the trend of the Jewish community which Rabbi Jacobs represents.'[18]

Gaon responded: 'Mr Teff is at present away on holiday, but I shall be seeing him as soon as possible after his return, probably towards the beginning of September. I shall, of course, contact you in order to inform you what transpires at our meeting. I entirely agree with the suggestions put forward in your letter, and trust that we may see their fulfilment.'[19]

Partially fulfilling that assurance, Teff later told deputies that talks on communal unity among the various religious groups in Anglo-Jewry, initiated by the Board, 'are to be continued, with the blessing of the Chief Rabbi-elect of the United Hebrew Congregations, and probably also with the participation of representatives of the Federation of Synagogues.' He added that he regarded the initiative for the talks as 'one of the really important things we have done here'.

During the discussion that followed, deputies criticised the Federation's absence from the first round of talks, held some weeks earlier under Teff's chairmanship and attended by representatives of the Spanish and Portuguese, Reform and Liberal Synagogues, as well as of the Chief Rabbinate-in-Commission. With a view to 'exploring possibilities of co-operation between them, in the interest of preserving the integrity of Anglo-Jewry,' they were adjourned to await the appointment of the new Chief Rabbi.[20]

* * *

Teff's reference to 'the Chief Rabbi-elect of the United Hebrew Congregations' came after Wolfson's lengthy drive, following Herzog's withdrawal, aimed at persuading Jakobovits to reconsider. The United Synagogue president was finally successful when, in August 1966, he received a positive response.

'With deepest humility,' wrote Jakobovits from New York,[21] 'I can now inform you of my willingness to accept the historic challenge of the Chief Rabbinate of Great Britain and the Commonwealth, if your Council decide to offer me this supreme honour, together with the awesome responsibilities vested in this Office, subject to the official ratification of the attached terms and conditions[22] previously agreed upon between us.' These were formally approved weeks later, when the Chief Rabbinate Conference voted, 'without dissent or discussion,' to welcome the appointment.[23]

In his 'terms and conditions,' following meetings with a cross-section of communal leaders[24] while on a visit to London the previous month, Jakobovits had included a passage headed 'Resolving the Religious Crisis.' Aimed in part at 'the Left-wing', he declared of that body:

> It would be premature at this stage to spell out in detail the proposals for a formula I have in mind. Meanwhile, the following basic terms of an understanding should not be beyond reach or reason:
>
> The 'Left wing' must agree
> a. to respect the Chief Rabbinate as an institution which is and will remain Orthodox, reflecting the religious loyalties, if not necessarily the views, of the overwhelming majority of religious Jews;

b. to leave the determination and interpretation of Jewish law to duly qualified experts, and to oppose any incitement against their rulings by pressure groups, newspapers or especially individuals who themselves neither acknowledge nor practise the dictates of the halachah;
c. to refrain from subversion, abuse and denigration directed at any established communal institution or its leaders; and
d. to make the maximum positive contribution to the enrichment and unity of Jewish life.[25]

The Liberal Union's response was soon forthcoming: 'After the recent years of turbulence,' wrote the leader-writer of *Pointer*, its quarterly journal, 'it is understandable that some sections of Anglo-Jewry should hail Dr Jakobovits' appointment with relief, seeing in him a cure for all troubles and the healing of all divisions. Such optimism may be unrealistic if it is not freely acknowledged that there are different, and legitimate, interpretations of Judaism. The unity of Anglo-Jewry is now conditional upon the recognition that, while the Chief Rabbi represents a large section of the Orthodox community, there are other religious groups within Anglo-Jewry which have the right to representation on appropriate bodies and occasions, and whose views are entitled to be heard with respect.'[26]

Invited to reply, Jakobovits wrote: 'Your leader rightly emphasises my expressed anxiety to "build bridges of understanding across factional differences", and you may have discovered already that I intend to leave no stone unturned in these efforts at communal reconstruction following Anglo-Jewry's recent agony of bitter and sterile conflict. I know that trust, respect and understanding cannot be cultivated unilaterally; if I do not demonstrate these to others, I cannot expect them in return. Nor can Jews in Britain acknowledge me as their spokesman unless I, in turn, acknowledge them as such....

'First and foremost, we can forswear intolerance and personal acrimony in our relations. I can oppose "heresy-hunts" looking for a deviant in every cupboard, and you can oppose "heresy-hunts"' in reverse, whereby every little incident of Orthodox zeal is inflated into a cause célèbre or a public scandal. We can generate goodwill and banish despondency, by confounding the prophets of doom who hold out, and preach, nothing but strife and disintegration for the community. We can jointly fight all attempts to sow subversion and secession, breeding further disunity within Anglo-Jewry.'[27]

In the same issue of *Pointer*, Brichto hit back. 'Only on the basis of mutual respect,' he retorted, 'will it be possible for us to build together along the lines you suggest. It would certainly not be possible for us to accept you as our spokesman to the non-Jewish community were you unable, after expressing your own view on a matter upon which we were divided, to inform the questioner that there was a non-Orthodox Jewish view which you would respect. It would, I think, even be difficult for us to acknowledge you as the representative of the Jewish community, were you not prepared, in that capacity, to attend certain Progressive Jewish services.

'I assure you that it is not our intention to "force the pace" in our attempt to achieve co-operation and understanding. But you will realise that we owe it to ourselves to assert our principles and to defend them when defence is necessary. It will be your responsibility as leader of the Orthodox community to restrain its zeal, when misplaced. While we shall not "look for issues", we cannot allow abuse or slander to go unanswered, for silence in such instances may be taken for acquiescence.'[28]

In a private response to Brichto following his *Pointer* rebuttal, a typewritten copy of which the Liberal spokesman had mailed to Jakobovits, the Chief Rabbi-designate wrote:

Many thanks for your thoughtful letter, which I have read with much care and interest. It raises several points and issues which are, I think, best left to personal discussions. I certainly look forward to opportunities for such discussions once I am settled in London. Meanwhile, I would just like to comment on a few basic items.

You reject my argument that the same God cannot be satisfied with conflicting observances by Jews, by suggesting that He could not care whether we pray three or five times a day. This was hardly my point. I contrasted the obligation to pray three times daily with not praying at all, and, more importantly, the difference between accepting and rejecting such fundamental practices as our laws of divorce and conversion. It is scarcely conceivable that the same religion could allow some Jews to be remarried without a *get* and brand others doing so as guilty of the capital crime of adultery. Similar considerations apply to our far-reaching divergencies on the validity of the laws of Sabbath, kashrut, conversion, etc.

You state: 'There is no reason why you should not worship in our synagogues.' That may be so according to your religious convictions, but it is definitely not so according to the rules of halachic Judaism guiding me. If, in fact, Progressive Jews cannot worship in Orthodox synagogues without violating their religious dictates, I would not expect them to do so, any more than I want you to expect me to break faith with the authentic halachah as I find it.

You state: 'While I may not disapprove of your religious practices, I cannot endorse them all. Nor do I ask you to endorse all our religious practices.' You here identify 'disapprove' with 'not endorse'. There's the rub! The crucial difference is that, while my convictions compel me to 'disapprove' of some of your practices as a grave and sometimes capital violation of Jewish Law, the very philosophy of Progressive Judaism at worst refuses to 'endorse' – but never brands as grossly offensive – Orthodox practices sanctioned by halachic standards.

Above all, I find in your letter, in contrast to mine submitted to Pointer, a purely unilateral demand for concessions, without any indication of substantial modifications on your part to narrow the gap between us. After all, you must realise that the proposals I have made represent a most revolutionary departure from Orthodox attitudes in the past, proposals which have already encountered much bitter opposition from among some of my friends.

I cannot hope gradually to win widespread support for this new outlook unless a similar earnestness in the search for goodwill and understanding is manifested on your side, without a dogmatic take-it-or-leave-it attitude. What we want to initiate are historic developments leading to a gradual relaxation of tensions produced by such challenges as 'you must attend my religious services'.

Altogether, I feel that the understanding we seek will be more readily forthcoming through private discussions and unobstrusive gestures rather than through public debates and widely advertised 'concessions'. Thus, I would like to feel that, in time, we can exchange speakers on each other's platforms without arousing public comment, inevitably leading to acrimonious arguments each time we do so.

In short, what is needed is a sincere, quiet quest for a fresh climate of 'live and let live', and not a noisy clamour for panaceas or causes célèbres. To achieve this détente, and to open up such a new era of communal reconstruction, I am committed, and I hope you will enthusiastically share this commitment with me.[29]

* * *

Earlier that month, in response to Jakobovits' letter in *Pointer*, John Rayner wrote confidentially to Malcolm Slowe excusing himself from a forthcoming meeting of the King-Hamilton Committee. 'Indeed,' he added, 'I have written to Judge King-Hamilton to say that I should prefer not to serve on his Committee any more. I have never been completely clear or happy about the raison d'être of the Committee, and I have repeatedly found myself out of accord with the tenor of the approach to the Chief Rabbinate problem of most of the members....

'I feel that I should have greater freedom to act in my own name if I were not a member of the Committee. The ULPS has been very anxious for some time to establish the principle that no special status within the Union attaches to the Senior Minister of the Liberal Jewish Synagogue, so that the invitation extended to me to serve on the King-Hamilton Committee was something of a concession to the slightly different situation in the RSGB to which I should perhaps not have lent myself.

> Nevertheless, let me briefly comment on Dr Jakobovits' letter, in case it is wished that my views should be reported. (1) A great deal of the letter strikes me as sincere and reasonable. (2) However, he evidently thinks that reciprocity in the matter of attendance at religious services, or joint participation in religious services, would imply mutual endorsement and is therefore impossible. In this I believe him to be mistaken; but I am prepared to respect his view.
>
> (3) He indicates that he regards Progressive Judaism as Orthodox Judaism minus X, and of this mistaken view he must be disabused. (4) Most serious of all, the letter makes it obvious that he still regards himself as appointed to the religious leadership of Anglo-Jewry as a whole. This is evident especially where he says that *he* intends to leave no stone unturned in these efforts at *communal* reconstruction, and where he expresses the hope that Jews in Britain will acknowledge him as their spokesman.

It is also evident from the way he signs himself as 'Chief Rabbi-Elect' sans phrase. This strongly confirms my view that the efforts of the King-Hamilton Committee have completely failed to achieve what I have considered all along to be their most important purpose: to make it clear to all and sundry that Dr Jakobovits will be the Chief Rabbi of the United Hebrew Congregations and of nobody else.

In my view, our policy should be as follows: On the one hand, we should co-operate with Dr Jakobovits in every possible way, as far as our religious principles permit (which is evidently somewhat farther than his religious principles would permit him to co-operate with us). And within these limits, we should accord to him all the respect, tact, restraint and patience which he can legitimately expect.

On the other hand, we must make it clear to him that he has no jurisdiction, authority or spokesman-status whatever vis-à-vis those sections of Anglo-Jewry, including ours, which had no share in electing him; and that if he steps one inch outside these limits, he must expect from us polite but resolute opposition.

Concluding his letter, Rayner added: 'Naturally, I hope that the King-Hamilton Committee may still see fit to adopt this approach. Meanwhile, I must reserve the right to act in this spirit in my own name and as Senior Minister of the LJS.'[30]

* * *

During the period following his appointment, Jakobovits sought to reach out to the variegated strands of British Jewry. At one stage, obliquely – though not exclusively – addressing the 'Left-wing', he wrote in a lengthy letter to the *Jewish Chronicle*: 'I will stretch out my hand in friendship to all who care to give me theirs, whether they share my beliefs or not; I will respect them even if I have to oppose their views. I have every faith in the yearning of most British Jews for turning a new leaf to inaugurate a fruitful era of reconciliation and religious reawakening. I hope you will sustain this faith by helping me to restore the solidarity of our people with its origin and its destiny as the proud bearers of our timeless heritage.'[31]

Several leaders representing Anglo-Jewry's non-Orthodox movements were quick to respond. 'We assume,' they wrote, 'that this gesture is intended to include Reform and Liberal Jews, and we gladly extend our hands in return. Indeed, in our case, it will be but a renewal of handshaking, for when Rabbi Jakobovits came to London at the end of July, he was the recipient of warm good wishes sent to him by leading personalities in Progressive Jewry, coupled with the earnest wish for a happy co-operation in communal matters.

'We think it is a very good augury for the future that the new Chief Rabbi of the United Synagogue not only appreciates that there are independent movements within Anglo-Jewry which exercise religious autonomy, but also respects them and is prepared to work with them. We trust, indeed we regard it as essential, that this attitude should extend to a recognition of the fact that, as fellow-Jews, we are entitled to express our own independent views and be represented on appropriate communal and national occasions. For, as Rabbi Jakobovits said in his letter, albeit in another context, we ought to be partners, not rivals or antagonists.'[32]

Days after his installation at the St John's Wood Synagogue, London, in April 1967,[33] Jakobovits hinted strongly at 'the proposals for a [peace] formula I have in mind.' Interviewed by Rabbi Dow Marmur in the Reform journal, Living Judaism,[34] the Chief Rabbi was asked: 'You have spoken of bridges. What exactly do you have in mind?' He replied: 'First of all, we must establish personal contacts. That is the most important bridge. The next thing is to promote such joint efforts as do not involve controversy or religious divisions.

'And then there is an even more important factor: If every time a little concession is made here or there, a little breach in the rigid walls that have separated us until now, there is going to be a public issue over it, we shall not be able to afford to take such steps. For, through such publicity, I am bound to arouse opposition and indignation in my own quarters. However, it we can learn to work quietly and discreetly, we could not only build bridges, but walk on them too. We need a commonsense approach to things. I don't have to tell you that there are enough hot-heads on all sides who are only waiting for a chance to pounce on us. I want to keep them at bay.'

Pressed on the effectiveness of the Teff Committee, Jakobovits told Marmur: 'I certainly think it has possibilities ... but again let me stress that its work must be done discreetly, on a personal level. I am not sure whether it will be necessary to retain it under the aegis of the Board of Deputies; I hope that eventually we will be able to carry on under our own steam. For my part, I will certainly encourage it, provided we can keep it discreet.'

Asked further on his desire to 'build bridges and introduce concessions,' he replied: 'When I speak of concessions, I have in mind steps that would break down the ostracism, the abuse and the impregnable wall of separation. One day, we may understand each other better, and so come closer together. For this purpose, I am eager to encourage and promote the mood of reconciliation.'

* * *

In his memorandum to Wolfson the previous summer, Jakobovits had included an appeal to the 'Right-wing,'[35] who, he declared, 'must agree (a) to look upon the Chief Rabbinate as serving to unite all segments of the community; (b) to accept that dissent from tradition and authority is an inescapable fact of modern life, to be most effectively met by friendly persuasion and intelligent argument, not by denunciation and ostracism; (c) to concentrate its energies on enhancing its own position and public respect, not on attacking others; and (d) to work together with others in all areas that have no bearing on halachic considerations.' These demands were unfavourably received by those to the Right.

Once in office, the Chief Rabbi lost little time in furthering his aims, and followed up his *Living Judaism* interview with a closed-door meeting attended by leaders from across the religious divide, though somewhat fewer than expected. Among participants in the meeting was Brichto, who wrote to Jakobovits within days, apologising for his early departure. He then continued:

> I am very concerned about reports regarding the meeting, and the fact that there were so many absentees. I applaud your efforts to bring the religious leaders of the community closer together, but I fear that unless the matter is very carefully handled, your efforts will be thwarted.
>
> If during this period, when Jewry has felt the threat of annihilation in Israel and has seen a miraculous salvation [a reference to the Six-Day War of the previous month], the rabbis of Anglo-Jewry are not inspired to work together, there is little hope that they ever will.
>
> Because of the murmurings I have heard, I feel it is urgent that we meet as soon as possible – perhaps together with the Haham – so that we can ensure the success of your efforts to bring the community together. I realise that you are facing

opposition within the Orthodox camp, and I would not like you to be faced with opposition from our quarter.

I will do everything possible, together with my colleagues, to see that this does not take place. However, if this is to be avoided, there must be closer consultation.[36]

In a letter to Jakobovits several weeks later, delivered prior to a meeting with him that day, Brichto's colleague John Rayner – as rabbi of the Liberal Jewish Synagogue, St John's Wood – spelled out similar concerns. 'It is unfortunately obvious,' he wrote, 'that your efforts to establish communication, consultation and co-operation between the rabbis of all sections of Anglo-Jewry have run into difficulties, owing to opposition from the "Right-wing". Nevertheless, I hope you will not abandon these efforts. Perhaps the objectors can yet be persuaded to become more co-operative; perhaps they will have to be ignored for the good of the rest of the community.

'In any case, it seems to me that the next step is to hold an absolutely private – indeed, secret – discussion between yourself, the Haham, Dr Kirzner [Rav Rashi of the Federation of Synagogues], and certain other individuals. These other individuals should be invited personally and not as representatives of their organisations, and they should be chosen on the basis of their Jewish learning, their knowledge of Anglo-Jewry, their influential status as religious thinkers and leaders, and the trust which can be placed in them to be open-minded and co-operative, and to treat the matter in the strictest confidence.... The object would be to try to formulate an overall strategy which we would pledge ourselves to implement, however gradual the implementation would have to be.'[37]

Typical of the opposition Jakobovits faced from his colleagues to the Right was a plea he received in January 1968 from Rabbi Mordechai Dov (Ber) Rogosnitzky, the Rav and Av Beth Din of Cardiff:

Arising out of the recent controversy regarding Progressive marriages, I feel I must write out in words fully what previously I have only said on many occasions.

Up to now, under the leadership of Rabbi Brodie, the Beth Din and the mass of Orthodox Rabbonim, a policy has been developed whereby Reform and Liberal groups are virtually regarded as outside the fold, deeming it impossible to regard them as within Jewry. Whereas it is true that since each group in Germany knew its place, and lay people knew the difference, it was possible to talk to Reform – even to have 'friendship' with them. In this country, Reform is belligerent and militant, and any recognition or contact will be regarded by the laity as acceptance on an equal basis, inside and outside the community....

It would seem that you regard your appointment as Chief Rabbi to include suzerainty over the Reform, and therefore you feel the need to build bridges so that they will feel you belong to them, while you hope to take charge of the problems of marriage and proselytisation. I feel that you underestimate the intelligence of the Reform people, for since in practice probably 90 per cent of the so-called Orthodox laity are non-observant, and do not appreciate ideology or the meaning of differences, it is only marriage which keeps them within the fold of Orthodoxy. This fact is as much known to the Reform as to the Orthodox, so that it is surely naive to believe that the Reform will give way to what constitutes their greatest source of increasing their numbers.

I know it is your feeling that it should be possible to fraternise with the Reform and regard them as '*yidden*' and hope that proximity will help to 'convert' them back to Judaism. This blinds itself to the harm this will do to the youth who, seeing such contact, will misinterpret and consider the equal status in religion of the two groups. I know what regard you have for the need to educate our children and youth, but unfortunately we are still very much at the stage when very superficial appearances count a great deal. We will thus be giving the appearance of encouraging our youth to go to Reform, since it would seem that you recognise the groups and that, in any event, they are 'good people'....

I concur fully with your oft-repeated remarks of the necessity for communal support for educational establishments, for the provision of essential educational needs, and for the provision of talmidim for training and service as rabbis, teachers and communal leaders to man our spiritual defences. When these ideals have been brought to fruition, and when we have an adequately educated Jewish laity, we will be able to reappraise the situation, perhaps on the lines you suggest. Until then, it is my earnest appeal that you withdraw from your present policy of rapprochement with the Reform, Liberal or so-called Progressive movements....

I feel strongly that any closer association by you with these 'Progressive movements' will only serve to alienate further Right-wing Orthodoxy. Basically, I know that you expect little from the

Reform; why then do you need to do harm to yourself by diminishing the confidence of your most ardent supporters? I must end by emphasising that modern days and modern English Jewry require strong fences before proper bridges can be built.[38]

Jakobovits' response was unequivocal. 'While I certainly appreciate this invitation to exchange views on some of the most important challenges facing me with colleagues as close to me as you are,' he began, 'I fear that the value of such correspondence may be compromised by the fact that, as I have heard, you send copies of it to others. Quite obviously, I cannot enter into these delicate discussions with complete frankness if the confidence of our exchanges cannot be assured.

'I, of course, entirely agree with your major conclusion that it would be futile to befriend the Left-wing at the cost of alienating the Right-wing, which, after all, represents by far the most vital and creative force in our community. What I do not agree with are your premises, particularly your interpretation of my motivation.

'I have no intention whatever of regarding my "appointment as Chief Rabbi to include suzerainty over the Reform". None of my overtures to the Left are in any way designed to claim or assert such suzerainty. Nor, frankly, am I at this stage primarily concerned with reclaiming Reform people to the Orthodox fold.

'What I am desperately concerned with is to prevent further large-scale defections to Reform from the great mass of our non-committed Orthodox members. It is my firm conviction – unless you or anyone else can persuade me otherwise – that what alienates nominally Orthodox people from us, and has caused them to swell the ranks of Reform, is precisely our public debate with them, and the bitterness engendered by it.

'Reform thrives on attack and denigration; this not only publicises them and their heresies, but wins them the sympathy of the underdog, while gaining for our Rabbinate the denunciation of guilt for "intolerance" and disunity. These factors, and not any "fraternisation", have so alarmingly strengthened the Reform camp in recent times.

'Moreover, this obsessive preoccupation with Reform has gravely stifled our own efforts to intensify Orthodox Jewish life, particularly in the sphere of education. I need hardly convince you that a monopoly of marriage authorisations will scarcely secure the Torah-loyalties of the next generation; only proper *chinuch* [education] can do this.

'Hence my immediate objective is to eliminate the acrimonious attacks and counter-attacks with the Reform from public attention – in other words, to silence that front, so that we can go to work on the constructive challenges before us. In order to achieve this, I must from time to time make some gestures of goodwill and understanding. This could be done in most cases in complete privacy and confidence if our own Right-wing would not always publicise these encounters by their intemperate and ill-advised public attacks on me.

'I would add that I would accept their criticism and opinions with far greater assurance if they would not always be limited to purely negative factors. I have yet to have a single approach from these quarters urging me to positive action and offering me their help in constructive enterprises in the manner in which they issue a constant stream of prohibitions, bans and threats....

'If we want to rescue Orthodoxy from disintegration, we had better begin to revitalise our own image rather than rely on disgracing that of our opponents. It is for the very reason that I agree with you that times have changed – and that we cannot go by earlier precedents – that I am advocating so consistently a drastic change of tactics if we are not to suffer further catastrophic losses.'[39]

* * *

Two years after Brichto's challenge regarding the religious validity of Liberal and Progressive marriages[40] – and within range of Jakobovits' retort to Rogosnitzky on the 'monopoly of marriage authorisations' – the matter was officially clarified in a letter to Brichto from Rabbi Maurice Rose, the Chief Rabbinate's secretary. Rabbi Jakobovits, he wrote, had asked him to confirm Brichto's declaration 'that no responsible Orthodox authority would ever deny that where a marriage took place in a Liberal synagogue which could just as well have taken place in an Orthodox synagogue, the children of such a marriage could become members of, and indeed be married in, an Orthodox synagogue'.

The ruling was read to a meeting of Liberal executive members by their president, Lord Cohen of Walmer, who stated that 'it refuted certain views expressed prior to Dr Jakobovits' appointment which misrepresented the true situation'.

The letter, Cohen added, additionally expressed the Chief Rabbi's view that 'the crucial issue between the communities was not that of marriages which could take place in an Orthodox synagogue, but those marriages which contravene traditional Jewish law, but are permitted by us – for example, cases of *chalitzah, agunah*, etc.'

On these subjects, Rose had written, 'the Chief Rabbi feels that the proviso "where a marriage … could just as well have taken place in an Orthodox synagogue" should receive more emphasis than it did, since quite obviously the crucial point of issue, leading often to such tragic results, concerns the very marriages performed at Liberal synagogues which contravene traditional Jewish law'.

Cohen conveyed Brichto's assurance, and that of David Goldstein, chairman of the Liberals' rabbinic conference, that 'the rabbis of our Union will co-operate fully in any attempt to alleviate the hardships caused by the differences between the two movements.

'In this connection, I am told that they look forward to the reconvening of the Teff Committee of religious representatives, and to further discussion with the authorities of the Orthodox community. I am sure that our Union will not spare any effort in working for the greater unity of our community which will result from the mutual respect and goodwill among all its religious sections.'[41]

Jakobovits' statement was followed in due course by further discussions on aspects of conversion and divorce. In July 1969, Rose wrote to Brichto: 'After careful consultation with the Haham, the Chief Rabbi has drawn up the enclosed statement which he thinks would sum up the tentative understanding reached with you following your recent discussions with the Chief Rabbi. Until such time as full agreement is reached, he suggests that this matter be kept confidential.'[42]

The attached text stated:

> In order to remove a major obstacle to communal harmony, and indeed a growing threat to the unity of the Jewish people created by the rising marriage barriers between the Orthodox and non-Orthodox sections of the community, the Union of Liberal and Progressive Synagogues agrees
>
> 1. not to entertain or undertake any action in respect of the divorce of any members of an Orthodox congregation, nor to effect the conversion of any person contemplating marriage with a member of an Orthodox congregation, nor to effect the remarriage of any person who belongs or belonged to an Orthodox congregation, without ensuring that no impediment exists in Jewish law.
> 2. not to deal with a divorce, remarriage or conversion of any person whose application is currently being dealt with by an

Orthodox Rabbinical authority or has previously been rejected by such an authority.[43]

Dismissing Rose's description of their meeting as 'giving a false impression of what took place during my discussion with you on 8 May', Brichto contended that 'there was no "tentative understanding", and there was no question at this juncture of drawing up a statement....

'I listened sympathetically to your point of view and, because we were rushed as a result of my car accident, I asked you to send me some proposals for my private consideration. These proposals would be the basis for a future discussion, the results of which – if acceptable to both you and me – I would be prepared to put before my Rabbinic Conference.

> I must confess that I was disturbed by the contents of Rabbi Rose's covering letter, suggesting that we have reached the point of considering the implementation of the enclosed proposals, which he refers to as a statement. I am afraid that we have not come that far.
>
> I want to be absolutely clear on this matter. While I understood your point of view, this understanding should not be interpreted as a tentative understanding in the way Rabbi Rose uses these words in his letter to me. I do hope that his letter is only badly phrased and does not imply an interpretation of our discussion which I could not accept.
>
> Believe me, I wish to do everything to heal as many breaches as possible between our two sections, but I will not be rushed or pushed into a position before a true understanding has been reached.
>
> As to the proposals themselves, I could not think of putting them before our Rabbinic Conference in their present form. They are too vague in general when they must be absolutely specific. I can see the justice in certain points, but not in others.
>
> I am prepared to meet with you and the Haham to discuss your suggestions, but I do not want it to be thought that I am undertaking any commitment on behalf of the Union of Liberal and Progressive Synagogues before we come to a real understanding, and before our Rabbinic Conference accepts the understanding reached between us.
>
> If we proceed on any other basis, it could lead to ill-will developing between us, as you might feel that I had not kept my undertaking. I would not like this to happen, and I am disturbed by Rabbi

Rose's letter because I feel that its contents could lead to such a misunderstanding developing between us.

I am sending a copy of Rabbi Rose's letter, and of my letter to you, to Solomon, as you have consulted with him and as I hope he will be at our next meeting.[44]

Thus, Jakobovits was later to declare of Brichto, 'he was a party to these intensive discussions, and to the rejection of the proposals made. Alas, we had to drop the effort, made quietly and with perfect goodwill on all sides, because no agreement could be reached.'[45] Once again, the issue faded, although in future encounters the parties felt encouraged to explore further.[46]

* * *

Despite muted expressions of goodwill on both sides, the closing months of the decade bode badly for the Orthodox–Progressive relationship, highlighted by a long and detailed exchange between Jakobovits and Rayner within a year of the Chief Rabbi's installation. Quoting Joshua ben Levi's talmudic statement, 'Jerusalem rebuilt is a city which makes all Israel friends',[47] Rayner declared in a sermon on 'Anglo-Jewish Unity': 'A year ago [during the Six-Day War], some of us permitted ourselves to hope that that day was drawing near.... But the new mood did not last long, and today it seems to have almost evaporated.

> Two or three weeks ago, there was a golden opportunity to demonstrate that the new spirit of unity had come to stay, for there could have been a united service in celebration of the twentieth anniversary of the establishment of the State of Israel. But a suggestion to that effect on behalf of Progressive Jewry was turned down by the Chief Rabbi of the United Hebrew Congregations. Consequently, two services were held: one at the West London Synagogue, and the other a stone's throw away at the Marble Arch Synagogue.
>
> It is true, of course, that there never has been a united Anglo-Jewish service on Israel Independence Day. Consequently, Dr Jakobovits, as he has pointed out, did not disallow anything that his predecessor had allowed. But that is hardly the point. The point is that the new spirit of communal unity engendered by last year's crisis created a fresh opportunity, and that that opportunity was, in this particular instance, thrown away.

Nevertheless it would have been no worse than a regrettable incident if Dr Jakobovits had not felt obliged to justify his decision and, in so doing, to make remarks which threaten to undermine other attempts at co-operation. Whereas Dr Goldberg, speaking at the West London Synagogue, went out of his way to avoid any recrimination, and contented himself with saying that the holding of a separate service was 'through no fault of the Progressives', Dr Jakobovits prefaced his sermon with a 'statement of clarification' in which he said: 'My sharing the pulpit, reserved for the authentic proclamation of Jewish religious teachings, with those who fundamentally reject traditional Judaism as I understand it, would be an act of betrayal and of gross hypocrisy.'

The implication is clear. It is not merely that Dr Jakobovits felt that if he had taken part in a joint service, his Orthodoxy would have been compromised. That would have been merely, in my view, a mistaken judgment.... What cannot be accepted is the implication that Progressive Judaism lacks 'authenticity' and that it 'rejects fundamentally' the Judaism of the past.

Even so, the matter might have been forgotten if Dr Jakobovits had not, a few days later, come out with a still more intolerant and inflammatory remark. At a meeting of Orthodox ministers in Manchester, he is reported to have said that 'it was inconceivable that the Orthodox could give authenticity to men in the Reform movement who undermined Judaism and who did not profess the same religion, ethics or morality'. It is difficult to know how to deal with such a statement, for it is so patently absurd that any tolerably informed person would reject it instantly; and therefore it is impossible to refute it without appearing to treat it with a seriousness which it does not merit.

After detailing the differences between Orthodox and Progressive Judaism, Rayner continued: 'What is disturbing is [Jakobovits'] underlying attitude: his refusal to concede that there can be legitimate differences of opinion; his insistence that any view which differs from his own is not only mistaken but "inauthentic"; his exaggeration of the differences to such an extent that he does not see the common ground; and his insensitivity which permits him to accuse of "undermining" Judaism those who are, like himself, devoting their whole lives to its preservation and rejuvenation.'[48]

Rayner thereupon sent the Chief Rabbi a copy of the sermon – which Jakobovits annotated and returned – triggering a dialogue that was to become increasingly contentious with every reciprocal message. 'I have made it abundantly clear to you and your colleagues all along,' Jakobovits began, 'that I could not share the conduct of religious services with those who did not share my basic religious convictions. You knew perfectly well that I could not surrender this attitude without violating my innermost conscience, and that this reservation was an integral part of our broad understanding.

'I must therefore take pained exception to your devious efforts now to lambast me for my alleged "throwing away" of an opportunity for communal unity (an opportunity, incidentally, created not – as you claim – by last year's crisis, but by my response to it in convening joint ministerial conferences for the first time in Anglo-Jewish history). It is this intolerance for my religious convictions, as well as the grossly unfair presentation of the case, against which I protest, and which increasingly undermines my faith in an honourable understanding.'

Spelling out 'countless gestures and concessions' he had made across the communal arena, 'officially under the Board of Deputies, and privately in each other's homes ... all in the face of often vehement Orthodox opposition', Jakobovits declared: 'All I now receive in return is abuse from the Left for not making further concessions, and abuse from the Right for having made these concessions.

'As I told Dr Van der Zyl in a frank personal discussion last week, this lamentable lack of any substantive response to my overtures may now compel me to subject my policies of reconciliation to an agonising reappraisal. Your widely heralded decisions, at this stage in our efforts to achieve greater communal unity – first to appoint your own independent religious spokesman as a provocative new token of disunity, and then to hold your own Independence Day service for the first time in twenty years, together with your complete failure to acknowledge or match my gestures of goodwill – represent grave setbacks to the prospects of success.

'I fear that only some dramatic step on your part to narrow our differences can now save the situation from reverting to the breach in Orthodox–Progressive relations as it existed before my arrival on the local scene.'[49]

Rayner replied – over three closely-typed foolscap sheets – with a 21-point rebuttal of Jakobovits' comments, 'which give me an opportunity to try to clear up a number of misunderstandings':

> As you know, I have consistently respected, and urged others to respect, your right to say: 'My conscience does not permit me

to conduct religious services jointly with non-Orthodox Jews.' I have said so privately and publicly, and I said it again in the sermon under discussion – and if my language there sounded condescending, that was not intended. Consequently, I cannot see on what ground you accuse me of 'intolerance' for your religious convictions.

While I respect your conscience in this matter, as in other matters, it is natural to wonder what is the reason behind it, especially since other Orthodox rabbis have taken, and do take, a different view. I can only guess that, in your opinion, a jointly conducted service would be taken to imply that you approved of the religious point of view of the non-Orthodox participants. If that is your reason, then I believe it to be mistaken. In my opinion, no such false inference would be drawn by the great majority of people....

However justified your refusal may have been from your own point of view, you must surely see that it left us no other option but to hold our own service. To do so was not to disrupt any unity, for in this matter, as I have pointed out, there *never* was any unity. We wished to have it this year *for the first time*; you did not....

You ask what concessions we should have made if you had agreed to a united service. I cannot, of course, answer that question authoritatively, since the matter was not put to the test. But to the best of my belief, we should have been satisfied if we had been a co-sponsor, and if one of our rabbis had played a minor part in the service, such as reading a psalm or two. Beyond that, I believe, we should willingly have agreed to the service taking place in an Orthodox synagogue, with segregation of the sexes and covering of the head, and according to a liturgy unexceptionable from an Orthodox point of view, and with you as the preacher. Of course we should also have wanted a part of the service to be spoken in English, but a small proportion would have sufficed, and I dare say that was done in any case at the Marble Arch Synagogue.

Turning to other issues, Rayner described as 'a serious misrepresentation of the truth' the Chief Rabbi's assertion that Progressive Jews 'fundamentally reject traditional Judaism as you understand it, implying that there is *no* agreement worth mentioning on *any* fundamentals, and that we do not "profess the same religion, ethics or morality," implying that Progressive Judaism is not only not identical with Orthodox Judaism, but not even broadly similar and derived from the same traditional heritage. But even if these allegations were true, to express them in such language was bound, as you must have known, to cause the greatest resentment on our part and to have the precise opposite effect of your declared intention of "forswearing the hostility of the past".

> The truth of the matter is surely very simple. We agree about many things, and we disagree about many things. Where we differ, you think we are mistaken, and we think you are mistaken. There is *no* need to say more than that (together with our reasons); and if we want to work harmoniously together, we *must* not say more than that.
>
> I did not say that the differences were slight, but only that they were slight *compared with the common ground*. Even that, I appreciate, may not be true from your point of view. But then I was not speaking from your point of view, but from my own. And to say that, from our point of view, the differences are slight compared with the common ground, how can that possibly be construed as 'hardly courteous or respectful'?
>
> In any case, however we may variously assess the extent of the common ground, it is obviously considerable. And what is more, it is the basis of any co-operation between us. We want to co-operate precisely because we do share a common heritage and, derived from that common heritage, common convictions, practices and ideals.
>
> If so, then the acknowledgement of that common ground is the fundamental prerequisite of any co-operation between us. Consequently, it seems to me, we must make it a basic rule of conduct in our public relations never to allude to our differences without *at the same time* setting them against the background of what we share in common.

Rayner then turned to the Chief Rabbi's 'charge that we have failed to reciprocate your goodwill gestures. First, I do acknowledge that you have made such gestures. I have done so privately and publicly, and there was also such an acknowledgement in the recent statement on behalf of the Council of Reform and Liberal Rabbis to the press. But I do not agree at all that they have not been reciprocated. Let me itemise:

1. You say that it was you who promoted communal unity at the time of the last year's crisis. So you did, but so did we. You initiated the joint ministerial conferences. We initiated other co-operative projects – for example, the Jewish youth groups co-ordinating committee.
2. You invited us to the joint ministerial conferences. We accepted your invitation, even though we were not consulted about the agenda and did not sit at the 'top table'. Would *you* have accepted if *we* had convened a conference of all Anglo-Jewish ministers?
3. You invited us to your home. We accepted your invitation, and we reciprocated it.
4. You talk to us at the Teff Committee (which, so far as I know, was not initiated by you). We talk to you.
5. You were good enough to accept our invitation to lecture at the Leo Baeck College. We are more than willing to lecture at Jews' College.
6. As you know, we have been more than co-operative over the Chaplaincy Commission.

What more do you want from us? So far as I am aware, we have neither demanded nor received any gestures from you which we have not reciprocated, and more than reciprocated. We are willing to co-operate with you in *any* sphere; the only limitations have been imposed by you, not by us.

We have treated you with the respect due to the spiritual head of Anglo-Jewry's largest synagogal body, as well as on account of your learning, eloquence and other personal qualities. We have not denied that you teach Judaism; you have denied that we teach Judaism. We have not accused you of undermining Judaism; you have accused us of doing so.

Then you speak of 'concessions' and of 'narrowing the differences'. But you have not made any concessions, and we do not expect you to make any concessions. Neither should you expect any concessions from us. Of course, as we have repeatedly said, we are willing to discuss particular points of difference with a view to exploring whether, here and there, there might be some modification of policy, without any sacrifice of principle, which would narrow the differences.

But don't you understand that the whole enterprise of co-operation depends on a mutual acceptance of differences? That is what it is all about! Don't you understand the difference between unity and uniformity? We do not desire uniformity. It does not exist, and it will not exist, at any rate in the foreseeable future. If there were uniformity, there would be no problem about unity. It is precisely because there is diversity that we are faced with the challenge of creating unity in spite of it....

We are not suppliants. We are not asking for any favours. We believe that the various synagogal bodies of Anglo-Jewry should co-operate with one another – not for our sake, nor for your sake, but for the sake of the good of the community as a whole. They should co-operate as independent, autonomous bodies, on a basis of equality, with mutual courtesy and goodwill.

'We have made it abundantly clear by word and deed,' Rayner concluded, 'that we are willing to co-operate, and Anglo-Jewry knows this. The only "agonising reappraisal" required of you is to decide whether *you* are willing to co-operate on that basis. Are you prepared to acknowledge that we are an integral part of Anglo-Jewry and that we have the same rights in communal affairs as the other major synagogal bodies? It is really as simple as that. If the answer is "yes", we can co-operate. If "no", then we can't. In either case, we shall of course insist on our rights, and you would not expect us to do otherwise.'[50]

'While I much appreciate the thoughtfulness of your detailed letter,' replied Jakobovits days later, 'I wonder whether our correspondence is not really an exercise in futility. I have the uncomfortable feeling that we not only profess different brands of Judaism, but that we also live in different worlds, in which identical words and phrases have entirely dissimilar meanings, or in which the laws of logic so vary as to make the same premises lead to completely different conclusions.

Without entering into all your arguments, in which you appear to force so many open doors while feigning to see open so many locked doors, let me just give you a couple of examples to illustrate my perplexity in finding a common wavelength in our disputation.

I am in substantial agreement with your premises as stated. But they would fundamentally be just as true if they substituted 'Christianity', 'Christians', and 'Christian Ethics' for 'Progressive Judaism', 'Progressive Jews', and 'Jewish Ethics'. (For surely the common ground between Judaism and Christianity, as understood in your sense, is also greater than the differences between them.) Nevertheless, with the premises thus amended, even you will agree that some of your paragraphs no longer follow.

In particular, I must disagree with your statement on common ground and co-operation. We can and should co-operate not because of any convictions we have in common (which are at present slight and irrelevant to our co-operation), but because we are brothers, belonging to the same people and sharing the same responsibilities before our Creator.

A similar diversity of meaning and logic separates us elsewhere. When I speak of gestures and concessions, I mean tangible steps towards unity taken solely in order to accommodate the other side, even if they impose upon me the need for modifications of views and policies I would not otherwise be prepared to affirm. Thus, all my gestures referred to decisions – some of them quite drastic and unprecedented – which have involved me in a good deal of personal heart-searching and violent attack from my friends.

The gestures you referred to in all your illustrations are invariably responses to opportunities for which you clamoured all along and which involved you in neither personal qualms nor vehement opposition from your own side. Or do you seriously suggest that your readiness to lecture at Jews' College is a reciprocal gesture for my lecturing at the Leo Baeck College, etc, etc? No, the only gestures that would make the efforts at unity and reconciliation bilateral and meaningful are (1) to stop your denigration of Orthodoxy and my leadership, now increasingly frequent in the Jewish press; and (2) to initiate some significant steps towards eliminating the havoc created by your marriages and conversions in disregard of Jewish law.

After all, even you will admit that the disunity of two separate Yom Ha'atzmaut [Independence Day] services pales against the prospect of disunity sundering our people into two sects who will eventually be unable to marry with one another. So far, 'our common destiny' – which you claim as your title-deed to unity – is in fact the vindication of my challenge to you to prevent disunity by narrowing your distance from traditional Judaism.

Unless such or similar gestures will be forthcoming before long by way of true reciprocity, I am afraid we will have to regard more than this correspondence as closed. Of course, this has really been clear to you from the very beginning of our contacts, however successfully this crux of the whole issue may have been sidetracked from time to time.[51]

'I am indeed sorry,' wrote Rayner three weeks later, after returning from a visit to Israel, 'that mutual comprehension is proving so difficult to achieve, even as I am intrigued to know which words and phrases carry different meanings for us, and which laws of logic vary in our respective universes of discourse.

'Personally, I feel that mutual comprehension *ought* to be attainable. But if you think otherwise, or if you feel that this correspondence is taking up too much of your valuable time, do please feel free to close it at any stage. I shall not be offended, and I shall remain appreciative that you pursued it as far as you did. Meanwhile, however, let me respond to the issues which you singled out in your last letter.

> To say, as you do, that the common ground between Orthodox Judaism and Progressive Judaism is not appreciably more extensive than the common ground between Judaism and Christianity seems to me utterly fantastic. So much so that I can only assume that your knowledge of Progressive Judaism is virtually non-existent.
>
> If so, it is indeed futile for the present to pursue this extremely important aspect of the matter. However, even if our mutual co-operation were to be based merely on the fact of our belonging to the same people, I should still find myself unable to accept what you say about reciprocity.
>
> Of course I agree that mutual denigration must cease. I am, however, not aware that we, on the Progressive side, have denigrated Orthodoxy, as distinct from expressing our disagreement with it on specific issues. Neither am I aware that we have denigrated your leadership over those sections of British and Commonwealth Jewry which elected you: we have merely, from time to time, endeavoured to correct the erroneous assumption that your leadership extends beyond those limits.
>
> Indeed, I think I can say that we have been scrupulous in observing the correct proprieties. If, however, it should ever happen that a public spokesman of Progressive Judaism expresses himself in language offensive to Orthodox Judaism, do please bring the matter to our attention so that we can deal with it, just

as we drew your attention to the extremely offensive effect upon us of your Manchester speech.

But when you ask us to modify our marriage laws, you are asking something which does not come under the heading of reciprocity. For you have not done anything comparable on your side, nor have you indicated any willingness to consider anything comparable.

I appreciate, of course, that it is not *possible* for you to modify the halachah. But are there not some areas in which the halachah is flexible to the extent that the tradition records divergent views, giving the modern halachist some latitude as to whether he will follow the stricter or the more lenient view? Does this not apply, for example, to the conversion of minors?

For our part, we remain willing to consider any proposals which, while not infringing any principles important to us, would diminish the divergence between our policies and those of Orthodoxy. But I must repeat what I said previously – that, however desirable such a narrowing of the gap may be, our mutual co-operation should be entirely independent of how much or how little success we may ultimately achieve in that regard. What we desire is co-operation between divergent entities *even while their divergence persists*. That, as I understand it, is the meaning of unity as distinct from uniformity.

At any rate, the record is clear. Hitherto, you have co-operated with us in ways which did not involve any infringement of your principles, although they caused you to be criticised by your 'Right wing'. Similarly, we have co-operated with you in ways which involved no infringement of our principles. (The fact that our 'Left wing' is less intolerant than your 'Right wing' made it easier for us, but is completely irrelevant to the question of reciprocity.) There has been, therefore, complete reciprocity. Indeed, as you know, we are willing to have co-operation in areas where it is not at present acceptable to you, such as joint services.

It is therefore entirely up to you whether this co-operation is to be continued and extended, or not. We are willing – even while Orthodoxy does not give up one iota of its Orthodoxy. The question is whether you are willing to co-operate with Progressive Jewry even while it remains as it is. If not, the responsibility for discontinuing the co-operation will be yours and yours alone, and any attempt on your part to blame it on us will be attributed by the overwhelming majority of British Jews to a private logic of yours which they neither share nor understand.⁵²

A fortnight later, having also returned from Israel, Jakobovits told Rayner: 'I am afraid your letter has not convinced me that our correspondence is bringing us any closer to mutual understanding, or even to tuning in on a similar wavelength. If I nevertheless again reply, it is only so that you should not think that I have broken off our exchange for lack of time, as you suggested I might have, only too true as this reason would be. Let me then refer to just three points raised in your letter.

> It is quite absurd to suggest, as you did, that I had stated that 'the common ground between Orthodox Judaism and Progressive Judaism is not appreciably more extensive than the common ground between Judaism and Christianity'. I had said or implied nothing of the kind.
> What I did state was that the areas of agreement between Orthodox and Progressive Judaism *as defined by you* – such as 'many fundamental things', ethics and teachings 'derived from the same traditional heritage' – could just as well be applied to similarities between Judaism and Christianity and yet not lead to your conclusions. If you will now reread the relevant paragraphs in your letter of 24 June in this light, I am sure you will understand the justice and logic of my argument without branding it as 'utterly fantastic'.
> Your devious casuistry on reciprocity leaves me as baffled as I was at the beginning of our correspondence. Nothing you have now stated has in any way persuaded me that any of the alleged counter-gestures listed by you can even remotely be regarded as reciprocal gestures. You surely are not serious in suggesting that, by my lecturing at your college *and* inviting you to lecture at ours, I would not, in fact, extend two gestures to you, instead of having one reciprocated.
> Your uncompromising reference to your 'marriage laws' (sic) makes particularly painful and disappointing reading. After all, this was the very basis upon which we so hopefully entered into our discussions over a year ago.
> You and your colleagues made it clear again and again at that time that you would gladly give the most serious consideration to some far-reaching return to tradition in this sphere in exchange

for the agreement by the Orthodox community to acknowledge the Progressive congregations as an integral part of the wider community. At that time, you and we understood perfectly well that any détente in our communal relations would have to be built on some such reciprocity and mutual concessions.

I am particularly disturbed by the tone of your final paragraph, telling me – in the rather crude language we are accustomed to hear from the spokesmen of power politics – that you would hold me responsible for any break in our relations if I did not agree to submit to your thinking and your diktat. I rather prefer the more simple logic of attributing such responsibility to the party which brought about the rift in the first place.[53]

Rayner opened his response by referring to the paragraph in his 24 June letter listing 'certain books that, if inspected, would prove that the content of Progressive Judaism is to a very large extent identical with the content of Orthodox Judaism.[54] In the light of that, your counter-comment in your letter of 28 June could, I think, justly be interpreted in the way I did.

'I am, however, glad to have your assurance that you do *not* think that "the common ground between Orthodox Judaism and Progressive Judaism is not appreciably more extensive than between Orthodox Judaism and Christianity". There is therefore no need to pursue this matter any further.'

Turning to the issue of reciprocity, Rayner wrote: 'We are obviously talking at cross-purposes. I understand this term to refer to co-operation. So far as that is concerned, it is surely clear beyond the slightest doubt that we have been, and are, willing to co-operate with the United Synagogue in *all* areas in which it is willing to co-operate with us, and even in some areas in which it is *not* at present willing to co-operate with us.

> Your understanding of reciprocity is obviously quite a different one. You wish us to change our policies and, in return, you would be willing to acknowledge that our congregations are 'an integral part' of the Anglo-Jewish community. How such a proposal can be called reciprocity is beyond my understanding, since *we* acknowledge that the United Synagogue is an integral part of Anglo-Jewry without demanding any changes of policy on its part.
>
> However, terminology apart, I must assure you that it was never my understanding – and I feel sure that it was never the understanding of anyone else on our side – that we agreed to co-operate, or

even to establish a peaceful relationship, *on the condition* that Progressive Judaism would amend its policies. This does not mean that we are not willing to *consider* changes, particularly in the matter of marriage law, which might diminish certain differences without offending our principles.

This is a point which I reiterated in my letter of 17 July, when I said that 'we remain willing to consider any proposals which, while not infringing any principles important to us, would diminish the divergence between our policies and Orthodoxy.' Consequently, I am totally at a loss to understand what you mean by my 'uncompromising reference' on this subject.

Let me therefore make one last attempt to state the position as I see it. The question, it seems to me, is whether the Orthodox and Progressive sections of Anglo-Jewry, even while each remains as it is now, are willing to co-operate with one another in those areas where their respective consciences do not prevent such co-operation, and to respect reciprocally their differences while these remain. The exploration of possible changes of policy on the part of one side or the other is indeed desirable, but is a separate issue, not dependent on the former.

In my view, the foregoing paragraph describes the sort of relationship which we should try to establish, and the simple question to which I should still like to have a clear answer from you is whether you do or do not share that view. In other words, do you or do you not believe in mutual co-operation irrespective of any changes of policy on our part? If not, you are really saying to us: 'I am willing to co-operate with you provided that you cease to be what you are at present.' If so, this is obviously not a basis on which we *could* co-operate and, what is more, this fact will be appreciated by the overwhelming majority of the community.

In that case, therefore, any discontinuation of such co-operation as exists between us at present will clearly be, and will be clearly seen to be, your responsibility. I am sorry if this way of putting the matter is unpalatable to you, but it seems to me to be the undeniable truth.[55]

On the point of 'leaving on my holidays,' the Chief Rabbi replied briefly: 'All I can here comment is, in response to your last two paragraphs, to suggest that the wide divergence now separating us is based on your entirely mistaken assumption that the co-operation you seek requires no greater change of policy on our part than I seek from you.

'A year ago, you and your friends understood this very well; now that some radical changes of policy have in fact taken place on our side, you no longer understand this point. How unrealistic our discussion has now become is surely demonstrated by your revealing remark that reciprocity to you means your recognition of the United Synagogue as an integral part of the Anglo-Jewish community in the same way as our recognition of your congregations.

'I cannot recall a time when the United Synagogue was not an integral part of Anglo-Jewry, and not recognised as such by you. I can very well recollect a time when you were not so recognised and when you clamoured for such recognition, which I have now helped to confer upon you, as the very assumptions in your letter make clear.

'At this point, I am afraid we shall have to rest our cases. Perhaps the next meeting of the Teff Committee will enable us finally to determine whether any useful purpose is being served in what to you is an exercise in reciprocity already existing, and what to me is a so far futile effort to build a community in which unity and goodwill are more than empty slogans.'[56]

In a concluding message, Rayner responded: 'The only last comment I should like to make is this. In order to build "a community in which unity and goodwill are more than empty slogans", the only changes of policy necessary are changes of policy in regard to "inter-sectional" relations, not in regard to the internal teachings and practices of one section or another, although changes in the latter regard may also be desirable.

'Therefore, if in the past Section "O" has been lacking in co-operativeness towards Section "P", but not vice versa, it is indeed a fact that co-operation requires a greater change of policy on the part of "O" than on the part of "P". I myself think that these exchanges have achieved some measure of clarification, and I hope that this in turn may yet prove fruitful.'[57]

CHAPTER THREE

1970–1980

Disputes and Divisions

Within eighteen months of his taking office, the clouds were already darkening over Jakobovits' Chief Rabbinate, and in a Rosh Hashanah message to 'the leadership of Anglo-Jewry' in September 1968, he spelled out some of his woes. 'I am fully aware,' he declared, 'of the depth of feeling and anxiety on the important matter of communal unity among the great majority of Anglo-Jewry.

> The Six-Day War, and the extraordinary upswell of Jewish identity resulting from it, no doubt gave even further impetus to this desire to underscore what binds us together as Jews rather than what divides us. If it were not for the misrepresentation of a press often interested in featuring the excitement of dissension rather than the tedium of harmony, it would be more widely appreciated that we have, in fact, made some very considerable strides towards the improvement of inter-communal relations since my assumption of office.
>
> Already in my installation address, I laid down the principles which would guide me. I offered the hand of friendship to all sections of the community, and I pleaded for calling an end to the acrimony and sterile strife of the past.
>
> At the same time, I made it abundantly clear that co-operation with those who grievously rejected fundamentals of Jewish belief, law and tradition could extend only to areas that did not impinge upon our religious differences. This obviously excluded the joint conduct of religious services. Any other course would be a contemptible betrayal of what we hold more precious than life

itself, and represent but a fraudulent façade of unity where there exists, alas, no unity.

And, above all, I solemnly averred that I would dedicate whatever strength and abilities I possessed to attempts at narrowing the differences which had produced our painful disunity in the first place. For what, after all, is the 'disunity' of conducting two separate Israel Independence Day services compared with the disunity of basic belief and action, threatening to divide us into two peoples who cannot marry into one another!

Consonant with these cardinal principles, I set out to do my best to relax the tensions of the past. During the Israel crisis, I convened two conferences of spiritual leaders from all sections of Anglo-Jewry, the first time that such diverse assemblies had ever taken place here. I set up and maintained numerous personal and official contacts with Progressive leaders. I raised no objection to the certification of a marriage secretary at the New London Synagogue by the Registrar General. I accepted an invitation to lecture at the Leo Baeck College, and I persevered in establishing a University Chaplaincy Board representing the entire spectrum of the community.

Short of recognising, or appearing to recognise, non-Orthodox leaders as spokesmen or teachers of authentic Judaism in any sense – which, had I done so, would make a mockery of the sacrifices and discipline demanded by Orthodox teachings – I did all I could to open up lines of communications and to heal some of the wounds of the past through friendliness and understanding.

In some respects, this spirit of friendliness has been reciprocated, and the quest for preserving unity where unity is possible has been mutual. The communal atmosphere today is certainly far more temperate than could have been anticipated only a short while ago, and this could not have been achieved without the contributions of goodwill from many quarters.

But I must now admit that my policies have not so far proved an unqualified success. While I was and remain convinced that the détente I was seeking would ultimately serve not only to promote communal harmony, but also to strengthen Orthodox interests – through improving the image of the traditional elements and their ability to concentrate on constructive endeavours – many of my Orthodox friends felt otherwise, some of them opposing my policies with great passion and bitterness.

Nor was this exposure to Orthodox suspicion and attack in any way rendered more worthwhile by any compensating response from the Left, or indeed by any recognition of the strides made from the rest of the community. In fact, I am still awaiting the first meaningful counter-gesture by the Progressives designed to relieve Orthodox anxieties and susceptibilities, as well as to help bridge the chasm of disunity created by their defection from traditional Judaism.

If the Liberals and Reformers, though a small and dissident minority in Anglo-Jewry, really expect equal rights within the wider community, they must be prepared to accept equal responsibilities, too. They cannot be rebels and partners at the same time. This means, first, their recognition that reconciliation cannot be achieved through unilateral gestures on one side only, through taking without giving; and, secondly, their acknowledgement that there can be no beginning in reducing the painful rift between us so long as they continue to wreak havoc in Jewish life by their indiscriminate conversions, marriages and divorces, often in blatant defiance of biblical and rabbinic law, and with disastrous consequences which have already disrupted entire communities and not merely families.

Always sensitive to the charge of hypocrisy, they should not expect rabbis faithful to traditional Jewish teachings and observances to accept as equally or also authentic the denial or subversion of these teachings and observances. They should not preach unity and practise disunity by demonstratively announcing the appointment of their own 'independent' spokesman, as if they had not always been free to speak for themselves.

Nor should those who demand tolerance refuse to extend it to others. To belabour traditional Jews for insisting on the conduct of religious services by traditional Jews is surely an act of intolerance no less objectionable for turning unity into a fetish and principle into an expendable trifle.

Jakobovits concluded: 'In recent exchanges with Progressive leaders, I have therefore left them in no doubt that I could not persist in my efforts at reconciliation in the face of growing opposition and frustration unless there was to be soon some tangible evidence of reciprocity, particularly to show that the search for a rapprochement with traditional Judaism in matters of marriage and conversion would be translated from words, which were pledged to me at the very beginning of our encounter, into significant deeds. I know that even larger Jewish communities than Anglo-Jewry, including important Orthodox as well as Conservative and Reform elements, anxiously and hopefully await our lead in what may prove to be one of the most momentous contributions to Jewish solidarity and unity the world over.'[1]

* * *

Months into the new decade, the Chief Rabbi's perplexities were aggravated by two controversies that, in time, had a permanent impact on the opposing forces. The first, relating to non-Orthodox representation on the Board of Deputies, had begun in November 1966 when, in advance of Jakobovits' incumbency, Brichto wrote to Teff regarding 'the possibility of establishing an advisory ecclesiastical committee of the Board, on which religious representatives of all the different sections in Anglo-Jewry would have an opportunity for contact and discussion of mutual problems'.

Linking his name to that of the Haham, Brichto added: 'Both of us feel that the Jewish community is worn out by the conflict which it has been suffering, and that the establishment of such a committee might well create goodwill and understanding between all Jews in the community.... Only if my own community can see some indication of progress can they be discouraged from taking any action, together with other sympathetic communities or even unilaterally, if necessary. I do not want this to happen, as I feel that under the leadership of the Deputies, the entire problem of community relations could be solved amicably.'[2]

Alongside this unproductive approach, but independently of it, representatives of the Reform movement met honorary officers of the Board that same month with a view, *inter alia*, to amending Clause 50 of its constitution to include the ecclesiastical authority of the Reform Synagogues of Great Britain (RSGB). However, the Board's officers believed that, for a variety of reasons, 'the political climate of the time would not favour such a change'.[3]

No advance was made until April 1969, when a further proposal was put to the Board's officers that the Council of Reform and Liberal Rabbis – established a year earlier – should become the ecclesiastical authority of the Board for Reform and Liberal Jews, which involved amending Clause 50 of the Deputies' constitution.

A memorandum to that effect was considered by a sub-committee, and a second meeting with the honorary officers was held some six months later, when they handed down their view that there was 'no possibility of the Board accepting an amendment to Clause 50'.

They added, however, that a similar result could be achieved by an amendment to Clause 43, which protected the rights of action of any congregation not under the Board's ecclesiastical authority, but 'did not require the Board to recognise and consult with the ecclesiastical authority of any such congregation'. The honorary officers then put forward proposals of their own sub-committee, which were regarded by the Reform as 'more limited than Clause 43 as it then stood' and were therefore rejected.[4]

* * *

Further wrangling over the precise wording of an amendment dragged on for two years until, in October 1971, the Board's president, Alderman Michael Fidler, sent the following letter to each of its members:

> Deputies will be aware of the efforts which the Hon. Officers have been making on the Board's instructions to find a generally acceptable formulation of Clause 43 of the Constitution.
>
> The Liberal and Progressive Deputies have requested that the right of consultation be granted on religious matters which concern them. On the other hand, representatives of the Orthodox groups of Deputies, whilst not pressing any objections to this, have been anxious that the Board should continue to be guided by its Ecclesiastical Authorities (the Chief Rabbi and the Haham – Clause 50 of the Constitution) on all religious matters.
>
> The Hon. Officers were of the opinion that it was in the best interest of the community that both these requirements should be provided for in the Clause, not least because the alternative might well have been withdrawals from the Board on one side or the other. In that spirit and in all circumstances, the Hon. Officers felt that it became their duty and responsibility to put forward their own recommendations. Our recommendation is in the following terms:
>
> *'The Board shall be guided on religious matters* (inclusive of matters relating to marriages and matters involving questions affecting the religious customs and usages of the Jews) by the Ecclesiastical Authorities to whom all such matters shall be referred; but without prejudice to the position of Congregations, groups of Congregations and Institutions not under the jurisdiction of the

Ecclesiastical Authorities, or either of them which may be represented on the Board, in regard to which Congregations or groups of Congregations and Institutions nothing in this Clause contained, nor any decision given under it, shall be taken to represent the opinion of any such Congregation, or group of Congregations or Institutions, nor shall abridge the rights of action of, or affect in any way, such Congregations *or groups of Congregations or Institution, and the Board shall consult with those designated by such groups of Congregations as their respective religious leaders for this purpose on religious matters in any manner whatsoever concerning them*.'

The words italicised indicate the two changes which this will achieve. 'The Board shall be guided on religious matters .... by' clarifies the existing situation; while the words in the last four lines clearly set out the rights of consultation accorded to those groups of Congregations on religious matters which concern them.

The Hon. Officers recently met the Chief Rabbi and the Haham again to consider the position. The Ecclesiastical Authorities were concerned to ensure that their present status would remain unaffected, which indeed was also the desire of the Hon. Officers. After consultation with the Chief Rabbi and the Haham at that meeting, a letter was sent to them. They have since indicated that they accept the assurances given in that letter.

The Hon. Officers thereupon placed this amendment before a joint meeting of the Executive Committee and Law & Parliamentary Committees and, after a full discussion, both endorsed this recommendation. In the Executive Committee, twelve voted for, and none against; in the Law & Parliamentary Committee, seventeen voted for, and none against. There were two abstentions.

The proposed amendment will now be placed before the Board at a Special Session on Sunday, 24 October, backed by both Committees as well as the Hon. Officers. It is earnestly hoped that you will make a special effort to be present then, and give your support to this, the result of so much consultation and deliberation, so that this matter which has been of so much concern in the Community for so long may finally be settled, by approval of all – certainly we hope not opposed by any.[5]

Days later, proposing the amendment's adoption, Fidler repeated an assurance he had made to Jakobovits and Gaon that 'we have always assumed that the words "the Board shall be guided on religious matters (inclusive of matters relating to marriages and matters involving questions affecting the religious customs and usages of the Jews) by the Ecclesiastical Authorities to whom all such matters shall be referred" are mandatory and mean, inter alia, that the Board cannot act contrarily to the guidance it receives from the Ecclesiastical Authorities. The Board, however, must always reserve the right to decide for itself what course it should take in the light of that guidance.'[6]

The motion was put to the delegates and adopted by 228 votes to seven, in the absence of members of an ad hoc Orthodox Group who, the previous week, had addressed a protest to Fidler:

> The letter dated October 15th addressed by the President to members of the Board of Deputies implies that he has met the objections of the Orthodox Group who were concerned to ensure that the revised Clause 43 shall contain safeguards to preserve the overriding authority of the Chief Rabbi and the Haham. This the Clause does not do.
>
> The President has apparently allayed the fears of the Chief Rabbi and the Haham by a letter which, apart from being self-contradictory, has no legal or constitutional significance. It will be binding on the present honorary officers as a matter of honour only, but it will be meaningless so far as their successors are concerned.
>
> Insofar as their words are meaningful, the Hon. Officers have served notice, for the first time in its history, that the Board is no longer bound by Jewish Law. It would seem advisable for the Chief Rabbi and the Haham to consider whether they have any further useful purpose to serve in the Board, and for the Orthodox Jews to consider the establishment of other machinery to guard Judaism, while leaving the Board to defend the civic rights of all Jews.

Of the eighty or so Orthodox delegates who then resigned from the Board, many from the Federation of Synagogues returned some two years later, while the Union of Orthodox Hebrew Congregations (Adath) remains unrepresented to this day.

Offering his resignation, Bernard Homa – an honorary officer and trustee of the Machzike Hadath movement – told Fidler: 'The amendment to Clause 43 put forward by you and your colleagues, which has now been passed by the Board, gives consultative ecclesiastical status for the first time, inter alia, to the religious leaders of the Reform and Liberal communities and thereby recognises these bodies as legitimate movements within authentic Judaism. This is emphasised by the fact that no constitutional provision has been made that decisions by the Board on religious matters shall always be in accordance with the halachah, such as we had previously envisaged.

'You must of course be aware that your explanatory letter to the Chief Rabbi and the Haham of 27 September, in which you set out your assumptions as to the meaning of *the guidance on religious matters* to be given by the Ecclesiastical Authorities, is of no legal or constitutional significance either for you or for your successors in office. It is only that which is written into the Constitution that is binding. Moreover, your claim that "the Board, however, must always reserve the right to decide for itself what course it should take in the light of that guidance" indicates quite clearly that the final arbiter in religious matters will be a lay body, namely the Board.

'It is my opinion, therefore, that in the new circumstances that have now been created, the Board can no longer be entrusted with any religious affairs, such as shechitah, Jewish education and, perhaps above all, with matters concerning personal status (marriage, etc.). After the fullest consideration of all the factors involved, I feel compelled, on grounds of religious principle, albeit with the greatest reluctance, to resign from the Board and, in consequence, from the shechitah committee of which I am chairman. I am handing a copy of this letter to the press.'[7]

Apropos of his imminent resignation, Homa received a letter of admonition from a 'shocked' and 'dismayed' Jakobovits: 'I am even more profoundly shocked by your reported statement that you took this step because the amended Clause 43 "gives consultative ecclesiastical status ... to the religious leaders of the Reform and Liberal communities, and thereby recognises these bodies as legitimate movements within authentic Judaism".

> The amendment implies nothing of the sort. The recognition of these communities, to the extent to which it exists, derives from their long-standing membership of the Board, on which you have sat for many years without protest.
>
> By claiming, without the slightest foundation, that they now enjoy recognition as legitimate movements within authentic Judaisrn, you provide the most effective ammunition which the Progressives could have desired, while the amended clause in

fact clearly stipulates that their religious leaders are acknowledged as such by no one except themselves, and that the Ecclesiastical Authorities retain the exclusive right to guide the Board as hitherto.

Having reached the end of this unhappy episode with last Sunday's vote. I can only express my utter consternation at the inconsistency, disloyalty and ineptitude of the Orthodox Group throughout these negotiations.

From the beginning, the Group at no time expressed its opposition to the grant of consultative status to the Progressives. In fact, the Group is on public record as having stated that the agreement to confer consultative status was never in dispute. Moreover, the Group's agreement was indicated well before the Haham and I were formally drawn into the discussions.

What was then argued was that the amendment must not use any phrase which might imply the Board's official recognition of the Progressives' religious leadership. When this was eliminated by rewording the draft to restrict such recognition to the Progressives themselves, the Orthodox Group — on the insistence of the Haham and myself — pressed a new demand.

We wanted it to be made absolutely and bindingly clear that our guidance of the Board would be mandatory, and that under no circumstances would the Board take any action or make any statement conflicting with Jewish law as determined by the Ecclesiastical Authorities.

This was secured by rewording the opening phrase of the clause to read 'The Board shall be guided...', which the Board's Honorary Officers assured us covered our demands. However, the Orthodox Group regarded this assurance as inadequate and urged us to secure its endorsement by a formal decision of the Law and Parliamentary Committee.

This, too, was duly obtained, in accordance with the terms agreed upon at our last meeting with your Group. True, the Group suggested that we moreover ask for an unconditional assurance that the Board would always act as advised by us. But I pointed out that, while we would aim at obtaining such additional safeguard, I could not regard it as a matter of vital principle, so long as the Board could not do or say anything which violated Jewish law.

It is clear therefore that, despite the Group's erratic conduct in constantly asking for new revisions as soon as existing demands were fully met, we succeeded in securing those safeguards which represented essential principles to us, leaving the Progressives with nothing more than the right to be consulted, which was conceded to them in the first place.

A further example of the Group's curious inconsistency is its reversal on the proposal to secularise the Board. When the Haham and I originally sounded you out on this proposal several months ago, you were vehemently opposed to any such suggestion and prevailed on us to discard it. Now that we have managed to obtain the vital assurances properly authenticated, this very suggestion is once more aired by the Orthodox Group itself – like all your other statements, again without any consultations between us.

I also cannot conceal being greatly irked by several personal embarrassments in this sordid story, such as your public reference to private correspondence between us and your request for halachic guidance from the London Beth Din and others without even the courtesy of so advising me beforehand, not to mention the damaging and misleading statements now so hastily circulated to the press.

Finally, on the broader issues involved, I have every respect for an *Austritts*-attitude which refuses to acknowledge the corporate existence of non-Orthodox Jews, or to engage in any cooperation with them. But logically, this should have precluded you from sitting on a Board which includes any representatives of non-Orthodox congregations.

What you evidently overlook, in complete disregard for the spiritual responsibilities imposed on me for the tens of thousands of 'middle-of-the-road' Jews within mainstream Orthodoxy, is that the expulsion of the Progressives now, by disrupting the vaunted unity of the community, is bound to alienate these Jews from our cause and to help the Progressives as 'martyrs' and 'underdogs' to secure far more strength than any clause in the Board's constitution could ever give them.

Religious decisions involving the careful weighing of such pros and cons are traditionally the prerogative of rabbis, and I cannot allow this prerogative to be usurped by others without abdicating my responsibilities. I need hardly quote to you chapter and verse to prove to you what are the duties of observant Jews in accepting such rabbinic decisions, whether deemed right or wrong.

By your publicly denying this loyalty to me, you undermine the very halachic authority which you claim to defend. Having secured the Board's submission to the sovereignty of halachah, I am confident I will not fail in securing yours.

I do hope that you will review your position in the light of the above, and in particular that you will see your way to reconsider your intended resignation from a body which you have served with such distinction and irreplaceable skill and expertise.[8]

Having failed in his plea to Homa, and addressing a closed-door meeting of the United Synagogue's Chief Rabbinate Council in the aftermath of the controversy, Jakobovits declared that the issue had 'blown up out of all proportion.

'I would like to assure the Council that when the future history of Anglo-Jewry and the Jewish community is written, Clause 43 will feature in a very small form. There are far more important challenges to face within our community, and it is a thousand pities that we have had to be sidetracked by such matters as Clause 43.'[9]

For his part, on behalf of the Reform movement, Harold Langdon begged to differ. 'I believe,' he later wrote, 'that this was a battle that had to be won if we were to remain on the Board of Deputies and play our full part in the mainstream of Jewish life. It shows that we are no longer second-class members of a secular organisation claiming to represent all Jews. We are no longer "congregations of Jews" only for the purpose of communal activity. Our synagogues are Jewish synagogues, and our rabbis are religious leaders.

'Above all, it has been shown to be in the best interests of the whole Jewish community, both religious and secular. None of the fears that were voiced have been realised. On the contrary, it has been found possible for the Chief Rabbi of the United Hebrew Congregations and the chairman of the Council of Reform and Liberal Rabbis to meet rabbinic and lay colleagues to discuss matters of common interest, to their mutual advantage.

'The Board of Deputies has not changed overnight, but neither has it been bedevilled by religious sectarian differences. It is much more truly representative now, and perhaps, shorn of religious strife, it may attract more of that 36 per cent of Jews who, alas, have no synagogue affiliation. It is, I believe – or at least I hope – inconceivable that the Board would in future select any broad delegation or representation without including a Reform or Liberal Deputy.'[10]

* * *

Another 'important challenge' faced the Chief Rabbi some two years later, after a further series of barbs between the opposing forces. Exasperated by growing attacks from both the Left and the Right, Jakobovits had earlier given vent to his frustrations in the columns of the *Jewish Chronicle*, one of his loudest critics. 'While one journal raps me for my "bigoted" and "perverse" opposition to Reform,' he had written, 'another (issued the same day) accuses me of "betraying" Orthodoxy by "appeasing" Reform!

'Orthodox Jews are always belaboured for being "intolerant", yet when they seek tolerance for the dictates of their conscience – for example, in not attending Reform services – they are met with misrepresentation and abuse. Future historians might be grimly bewildered by a community fiddling with such contradictions while its soul is burning with Jewish ignorance and drift.... Communal harmony will be advanced not by paying lip-service to it, but by co-operating in, and highlighting, what unites us rather than what divides us.'[11]

To that end, in July 1973, Raymond Goldman, representing the Reform and Liberals' Standing Committee on Relationships within Anglo-Jewry, wrote to the Office of the Chief Rabbi seeking a meeting between the two parties. Moshe Davis, the Office's executive director,[12] replied: 'The Chief Rabbi readily responds to your suggestion that a meeting should take place between one or two of your representatives and the Chief Rabbi. May I suggest 20 September, at 5 p.m., at the home of the Chief Rabbi? The Chief Rabbi suggests that the meeting also be attended by Sir Samuel Fisher [the newly elected president of the Board of Deputies] and Mr Harold Langdon.'[13]

Confirming the arrangement, Goldman wrote: 'The members of the Standing Committee were happy to hear of the Chief Rabbi's agreement to the suggested meeting. The representatives of the Committee on 20 September will be Rabbi Hugo Gryn, chairman of the Council of Reform and Liberal Rabbis, and Rabbi Sidney Brichto, executive director of the Union of Liberal and Progressive Synagogues.'[14]

Thus began a sequence of clandestine meetings between the conflicting parties – held mainly at 85 Hamilton Terrace, the Chief Rabbi's official residence in St John's Wood – that ultimately spanned more than two decades.[15]

* * *

The impetus for these meetings was a long-standing dispute regarding the Council of Christians and Jews (CCJ). Three times in recent years – 1965, 1968 and 1971 – unsuccessful attempts had been made to appoint the chairman of the Council of Reform and Liberal Rabbis as a second Jewish president of the CCJ, founded in 1942 by Chief Rabbi Hertz and William Temple, Archbishop of York, 'to work against all forms of discrimination and to promote the fundamental ethical teachings which are common to Judaism and Christianity'.

The Council had five Christian presidents, representing its various strands, but only one Jewish president – the Chief Rabbi. Despite the number of Reform and Liberal rabbis and lay persons involved in its work, opposition from Brodie and Jakobovits, as well as lack of support from other Jewish members of the CCJ executive, had stymied these earlier attempts.[16]

The appointment of a joint Jewish president, or rotating president, had been the subject of correspondence in late 1966 between the various Jewish parties, including Brichto, Gaon, and Lord Cohen, president of the ULPS. Reporting to Cohen on a meeting at the time with Gaon, Brichto had written: 'The Haham expressed to me his very strong feeling in regard to the presidents of the Council of Christians and Jews.

'He feels that it is wrong for a non-Jewish community to be given the impression that the Jewish community has a religious hierarchy.... The Haham would like to have the opportunity of discussing the matter with you, and I have agreed to arrange a mutually convenient time for the three of us to meet.'[17]

Supporting the proposal, Cohen told Brichto in a handwritten note: 'Of course I should be pleased to meet the Haham. Would you and he come to lunch with me here [at his home in Porchester Terrace] on Friday the 9th [December]? I would order a fish lunch, but if he prefers not to meet over lunch, I could manage a morning meeting at any time that suits you both.'

Cohen added: 'Have you reported to the Reformers the result of your talk with the Haham? I think it is important that whatever we decide, we try to carry them with us. I prefer a rotating to a second Jewish president, but I think we shall find it difficult to explain to the Christian side of the CCJ why, after twenty years, we suddenly want to alter the setup.'[18]

Replying a day later, Brichto wrote: 'The Haham ... will be glad to come to your home on the morning of Friday, 2 December. Neither he nor I would wish to take too much of your time, so that our visit to you should not interfere with any luncheon arrangements you have made. Both the Haham and I also would prefer a rotating president rather than another president. I have not contacted the Reform, but I will do so following our meeting with the Haham.'[19]

That same day, Cohen wrote again to Brichto: 'I have just been reading the last minutes of the executive committee of the Council of Christians and Jews on 20 October, from which I note that the Chief Rabbi-Elect had acknowledged the congratulations and good wishes sent on behalf of the Council on his appointment as Chief Rabbi, saying that he would be honoured and happy to serve as joint president of the Council of Christians and Jews.

'We shall have to bear this in mind when we meet the Haham. It would be difficult, I think, for the Council to undo what it has already done. Please treat this letter as confidential as the minutes of the executive committee are of course confidential, but the Haham has, I am sure, received a copy of the minutes as he is a member of the executive committee.'[20]

* * *

As Cohen had feared, this and further efforts to expand the presidency were rejected by both the Chief Rabbi and the CCJ executive. Seven years later, justifying a similar outcome to a meeting of the Chief Rabbinate Council, Jakobovits asserted that a joint presidency from the Jewish community 'would be inadvisable not only because it would possibly undermine my Office, which is my personal concern, but because I felt it would give the seal to a final break in the unity of our community in the very area in which I have always maintained there should be complete unity'.

Inter-communal co-operation in the field, the Chief Rabbi declared, 'is highly desirable insofar as the outside world is concerned and where it does not impinge on existing religious divergencies. The Progressives have argued that the religious diversity of the Jewish community is well known to the outside world. Although the non-Jews on the CCJ have three spiritual leaders among its presidents, were we to appoint two Jewish presidents, it would give public confirmation of a schism.

'If there are arguments within the Jewish community, they must be internal arguments, and I am concerned that there should be no arguments when it comes to relations with Jews and Christians vis-à-vis the outside world.' They had therefore 'all accepted the idea that, rather than press for a separate person to represent the Progressive sections of the community, they would agree to work together with me in consultation on policies to be adopted with the Council of Christians and Jews, or with agencies connected with Jewish and non-Jewish relationships'.

The Chief Rabbi added: 'I hope shortly to have in operation such a consultative committee on lines agreed to by all the parties concerned.'[21] At this stage, he had not revealed to the Chief Rabbinate Council that concrete decisions had already been taken towards finalising the committee's formation.

Over a period of months, following Goldman's approach to the Chief Rabbi's Office the previous July, representatives of the various religious groupings had confidentially drawn up a list of 'proposals', including that 'the Committee shall be appointed initially for a period of two years'; that 'the Convenor (who shall preside at meetings) shall be nominated by the Council of Reform and Liberal Rabbis'; and that 'the Convenor will liaise directly with the Chief Rabbi, and will be recommended by the Chief Rabbi as a Vice-President of the Council of Christians and Jews'. The proposals also included the possibility of 'extending invitations to representatives of other interested organisations as circumstances require'.[22]

The committee's formation became public knowledge in March 1974, with the *Jewish Chronicle* disregarding a Chief Rabbinical embargo on a statement that 'Orthodox and Progressive religious leaders in Britain agreed this week to establish a Consultative Committee on Jewish–Christian Relations.... Agreement came at a meeting of the interested parties held at the Chief Rabbi's Office.'

Alongside Jakobovits and Gaon (or his Sephardi representative), members of the committee would include rabbis and laymen from the United Synagogue and Reform and Liberal movements, under the chairmanship of Hugo Gryn, senior rabbi of the West London (Reform) Synagogue and chairman of the Council of Reform and Liberal Rabbis.[23]

Commenting on the committee's formation and composition, the *Jewish Chronicle* wrote:

> This week's brief but significant announcement that Orthodox and Progressive leaders in Anglo-Jewry have combined to establish a 'consultative committee on Jewish-Christian relations' heralds a positive new development in this community. It is not often, outside of the sphere of direct action for Israel (and then mainly in the field of fund-raising), that the rabbinic leadership of the two wings of Anglo-Jewry have come together for some common purpose.
>
> In this instance, the origin of the new-found co-operation derives from the concern of the Progressive community to enjoy fair representation on the Council of Christians and Jews, where the Chief Rabbi holds senior office. The Consultative Committee

provides a means of avoiding damaging competition and of a strengthening of the Jewish contribution to the Council.

It is a healthy sign of the goodwill of the Orthodox section of the community that the Chief Rabbi has agreed to serve on the Consultative Committee under the chairmanship of a Progressive rabbi. It also bodes well for the greater health of Anglo-Jewry as a whole, since contacts of this sort have a dynamic of their own, no matter what their original motivation.

In the long run, the problem of this community lies not between those who are faithful to different shades of Judaism, but between those who uphold the Jewish heritage and those who disavow any allegiance at all. The new committee provides a small beginning to that greater community-wide co-operation which Anglo-Jewry so sorely needs.[24]

A fortnight later, Goldman, public-relations spokesman for the Committee, told the JC that one of its aims was 'to ease any friction which might at present exist between the religious sections of Anglo-Jewry'.[25] This was confirmed by Gryn when, presiding over the committee's initial meeting, he described it as 'a step in cordial relationships within the Jewish community itself'.[26]

Elaborating on the 'small beginning' at a meeting of the Chief Rabbinate Council the following month, Jakobovits stated that the committee's formation was 'in accordance with my oft-stated principle affirming co-operation with the non-Orthodox segments of the community in all matters of common concern which do not impinge on our religious differences'.

The terms of reference, he added, related to such matters as Jewish/non-Jewish relations, parliamentary legislation, and 'possible contacts with the Moslem community'. No mention was made of what was to become its main preoccupation – 'easing any friction' within the ranks of Anglo-Jewry.[27]

* * *

In July 1970, twelve months after their fruitless exchanges on issues of divorce, marriage and conversion, the opposing parties had reconvened and, following their brief encounter, Brichto had written to Jakobovits:

> I enjoyed meeting with you, the Haham and Rabbi Rose, and I hope that something constructive will result from our discussion.

I was asked to draw up a memorandum based on our discussions and I would like you to treat the contents of this letter as such. While I am not in the position to promise any agreement without consulting the Rabbinic Conference, I am of the opinion that for the sake of communal harmony, and in order to prevent personal hardship to future generations whenever this could be avoided without compromising our principles, it would agree to take necessary steps. I feel that the state of *gittin* is such an opportunity for agreement between us.

The Rabbinic Conference might agree to rule that couples who have married either religiously or civilly should not be remarried unless they have obtained a *get* from the Beth Din. Their agreement to do so, of course, would depend upon the details being worked out in such a way that no inconvenience was caused to the parties who are members of our movement. This might be accomplished by our Rabbinic Conference acting as agents for the parties, or by a Liberal rabbi accompanying the parties in their appearance before the Beth Din.

However, in those cases where the Beth Din could not issue a *get*, the Rabbinic Conference would still have the liberty to remarry without such a *get* if, in their opinion, there are humanitarian and ethical grounds for doing so. Were there to be such an agreement, the Rabbinic Conference of the ULPS would wish to make it known that, while they in principle did not feel that a *get* should be necessary, it is taking this course of action for the sake of unity, and it does not feel that its new ruling imposes any hardships or any ethical compromise upon the parties involved.[28]

The Chief Rabbi responded: 'I am having a copy of this forwarded to the Haham, but I fear that my impending departure for Israel will make it impossible to consult with him properly until after my return early in September. Meanwhile, I do appreciate your prompt effort to set out your thinking in writing.'[29]

Nothing constructive, however, resulted from the meeting, or from Brichto's memorandum, and it was left to the newly formed Consultative Committee, five years later, to try again, boosted by radical proposals from Marmur as vice-chairman of the Council of Reform and Liberal Rabbis.

Advocating a joint Progressive and Orthodox approach to conversions, Marmur cited the views of two United States rabbis – Eliezer Berkovits

(Orthodox) and Theodore Friedman, a past president of the Rabbinical Assembly of America—that non-Orthodox conversion procedures 'can be acceptable to Orthodox Jews since differences in interpretation of the halachah are not permitted to rupture the unity of the Jewish people. We appeal to the leaders of British Orthodoxy to heed this principle, lest the unity of our people be ruptured.'

Marmur added that, 'in view of recent conciliatory and eminently sensible comments about the separation of politics and religion made by the Chief Rabbi, is it not reasonable to expect Dr Jakobovits to take a leaf out of Dr Berkovits' book and give a lead to Anglo-Jewry?

'Our commitment to Jewish unity can induce us to further changes in our conversion procedure. Let one example stand for many. Although Reform Jews may have serious reservations about *tevilah* as a necessary requirement for conversion, if such a requirement would make possible Orthodox acceptance of our conversions, surely we could demand it from our converts.

'With a measure of goodwill, it would be possible to come to an understanding ... and I believe that I speak for the vast majority of my colleagues in the RSGB when I say that we are ready to talk and ready to act. If for us the unity of the Jewish people is of paramount importance, then we must be prepared to modify our conversion procedures in the service of that principle.'

'However', Marmur cautioned, 'we are able to do so only if Dr Jakobovits and his colleagues indicate their willingness to accept the approach of a Dr Berkovits and forgo Orthodox intransigence and "halachic" imperialism'.[30]

In response to the proposal, the Chief Rabbi's Office stated: 'At a time like this, far from accentuating and perpetuating our differences, we ought to make a supreme effort to narrow and eliminate them. If only to find strength and comfort through unity, can we not now draw closer to our common heritage and repair the tragic rifts in our ranks, whereby we cannot worship together, we cannot eat in each other's homes, and sometimes not even marry each other's children?

'Whether the arguments advanced by Dr Berkovits are tenable, and whether they bear the construction placed upon them, is open to debate. The Chief Rabbi has always favoured continued research and consultation on all matters concerned with conversion, including sociological and contemporary aspects, as well as historical and religious implications. He has been particularly concerned to avoid family tragedies resulting from the present divisions and the estrangement from traditional practices.'[31]

The exchange brought immediate condemnation from the strictly Orthodox community, not least from the Chief Rabbi's own Beth Din. 'There can be no possibility of any discussions with the Reform on the question of conversions,' said the senior dayan, Morris Swift. 'The Reform and, in many ways, the Conservatives have rejected the Divine revelation of the Torah, the Written and the Oral Law. The admission into the Jewish faith of a convert by religious procedure, even it includes *tevilah*, is not sufficient. The convert must accept completely that the Torah was divinely revealed.'

Others from the Orthodox spectrum took a more lenient view. Expressing 'full support' for the Chief Rabbi, the Haham said: 'He has taken the right attitude, and we must come closer together. The time has arrived for really serious discussion.'

Hendon Synagogue's Leslie Hardman, a member of the Chief Rabbi's 'Cabinet', asserted: 'However unbridgeable the chasm dividing Orthodox Judaism from Reform Judaism, no one should say "Never the twain shall meet". I therefore recommend high-level – albeit secret – talks between the Chief Rabbi and the Reform rabbinate on such fundamental issues as divorce and conversion, for the sake of family happiness and communal unity.'

For the Conservatives, Jacobs stated: 'I should have thought that any move for greater unity in this area is well worth while, especially since there are so many cases of injustice practised by the Beth Din in this field.'[32]

The Liberals, on the other hand, rejected the approach. 'We freely chose to go outside the Law wherever the law clashed with our dictates of reason and justice,' wrote Rabbi David Goldberg in *Pointer*.[33] 'It would be a sad reflection on our courage and our sense of mission if we choose now to creep back within a legal framework we cannot totally accept....

'We would say that the founders of Progressive Judaism did away with ritual immersion as a symbol of conversion because it is ethically unedifying, spiritually irrelevant, and in modern times it has, ironically, Christian rather than Jewish connotations. Their reasons are still valid today.'

Writing in the *ULPS News* the following month, in a personal capacity, Brichto took issue with Goldberg, urging his Liberal colleagues to 'keep an open mind on the possibility of rethinking our principles, if the Orthodox are prepared to do the same.

'They would have to accept as Jews converts who are not taught to be Orthodox and who, from their point of view, would be Jewish sinners from the outset of their Jewish life. I find it difficult, however, to imagine that the Orthodox, with their numerous and often differing rabbinic authorities, would be able to overcome this hurdle.

'We should not close any doors, but wait in the hope that the Orthodox will open theirs, so that discussions can begin between us which could lead to all Jews being part of a united people.'³⁴

Paying heed to this appeal, both Reform and Liberal rabbinical authorities reluctantly decided 'to open a dialogue with our Orthodox counterparts, in an attempt to heal the sectarian schism within Anglo-Jewry, especially in the fields of conversion, marriage and divorce.'

Their initiative was reported to have Jakobovits' consent, and Brichto began sending out invitations to (among others) the Chief Rabbi, the Haham and the acting Rav Rashi of the Federation of Synagogues, Michael Fisher, for 'immediate and joint discussions'.

Fisher, however, in line with the dayanim of the London Beth Din, strongly opposed the move, telling the Aguda-controlled *Jewish Tribune* that 'the strength and stability of the United Synagogue lie in its adherence to Jewish law and practice', and suggesting that 'those who make overtures to the Reformers' were lacking in such characteristics.³⁵

* * *

In the event, the invitations were reversed. On the first Monday in July 1975, Jakobovits, Gaon, Brichto and Marmur held a closed-door meeting at the Chief Rabbi's home to begin exploring the issues involved.

At the outset, the parties agreed that 'no individual, or individual organisation, will issue a statement about these talks, their progress, or their conclusions. When a conclusion has been reached, an agreed statement will be issued by Moshe Davis from the Office of the Chief Rabbi. If no agreement is arrived at, the final statement should be designed so as to effect minimum harm within the community. It should be on the lines of "an agreement to disagree". The door should be left open for future discussions.'

Jakobovits opened the talks by stating that 'three areas need to be discussed – the issues of *gerut*, *kiddushin* and *gittin* – and the wider ramifications of communal unity and community relations.' He added that the last point 'would include instructions to ministers regarding participation with, and relations between, the various groups'.

Marmur pointed to the interconnection between these areas and said that 'they may require reciprocal compromise.... The issue of conversion is more important than that of divorce.... While an agreement on *gittin* would help the Chief Rabbi, an agreement on *gerut* would considerably help me in relations with my movement.'

Supporting the view that 'gerut is of wider concern than gittin', the Chief Rabbi conceded nevertheless that 'the issue of gittin is more immediate and more serious, as the consequences are greater.... There is a need to create a psychological climate: if success can be shown in one area, there is a greater chance of narrowing differences overall. It is important to show that distrust and pessimism are misplaced.'

Brichto pointed out that the Liberal movement had originally been prepared to send its members to the Beth Din for gittin, 'but the Chief Rabbi had wanted an agreement that the Liberal movement would not marry parties unless such gittin had been obtained. The Liberals had been unable to agree to this and, as a result, had gone to the Federation.'

The meeting concluded with 'a general feeling that discussions should range freely over the whole area, and only at a later stage might it be necessary to deal with individual issues item by item.'[36]

Six weeks later, Jakobovits opened a further meeting of the committee – attended by the same five participants – with a declaration that 'at the root of the problem gnaws the bitterness occasioned by the feeling that there are two communities within our people gradually moving apart, and eventually millions might be involved. There is an appreciation of a calamity in the making.'

There was also, he added, 'the aspect of the humanitarian approach of the Reform, whereby it is felt that grievous tragedies are occasioned, and hence halachic modifications and concessions ought to be made. In my view, the tragedy today is becoming wider because concessions were made in the past: mamzerim[37] are being created in their hundreds within this country, and in their tens of thousands in the United States.'

The Chief Rabbi added that 'it is important to see and accept facts as they are. It is unlikely that major halachic changes will occur in the next few decades. The gedolei hador [sages of the generation] are immune to pressures, whether from the Right or the Left. They have sustained the major losses of the Holocaust and have sought to preserve their strength and rebuild their community, which they are successfully doing. Hence, they will not accept change.'

Brichto pointed out that 'this strengthens the extremes, and the middle is being weakened', to which Marmur added: 'While the extremes present insurmountable problems, it may be possible to achieve something in the middle. The Reform and Liberal movements are not concerned with fighting Right-wing Orthodoxy, but want to be within the broad middle of the spectrum.'

On the question of gittin, said Marmur, 'if these are dealt with centrally by Adler House [the London dayanim], then it is to be hoped that subsequent marriages would not be so closely scrutinised and "researched". The hostility in the Reform movement by individuals is frequently because of their experiences with the Orthodox Beth Din. Our attitude on this matter is influenced by the fact that we have our own Beth Din which grants *gittin*, but I understand the argument that by abdicating our rights over this, other rights might accrue to our community.'

Jakobovits conceded that 'the rulings of the Beth Din do sometimes create hostility. Occasionally, it is possible to help individual cases, and changes within the Beth Din would be conducive to creating changed attitudes. This, however, will still be the fringe of the problem.

'In my view, there is no dichotomy between Torah and humanity, but in any law and its administration there are difficult cases, and some individuals will suffer. The *mamzer* pays a fearful price, but the gain has been the sanctity of Jewish life within the community.

'If people knew that they cannot rectify acts of negligence, that there were no exit doors, they would not act irresponsibly. Hence, a united front in the future on this crucial issue will make people aware of their obligations.'

Under certain conditions, Marmur responded, 'the Reform Beth Din might hand over *gittin* entirely to the Orthodox Beth Din. In return, marriages of each community should be accepted without question. This will necessarily involve the question of conversion and this, too, needs to be examined. Ideally, I would like the *kiddushin* of each movement to be accepted by all, and *gittin* to be carried out by the one Beth Din.'[38]

The following spring, referring to 'the religious monopoly' of the Orthodox community, Marmur conceded that 'both the machinery of consultation and the agreement to differ are now possible, since we are developing channels of communication based on mutual respect and in a spirit of civility. However, at no time should we ignore the fundamental differences between Progressive and Orthodox Judaism: these must be articulated and acted upon in the interests of a vibrant and pluralistic Anglo-Jewry.'[39]

At the same time, backing up these assertions, Marmur sent Jakobovits what the Chief Rabbi's Office acknowledged as 'the thoughtful formulation of the aims and suggestions, as you see them, pertaining to our prolonged discussions on marriage, divorce and conversion procedures'.[40]

* * *

On the question of accepting *tevilah* for converts, the RSGB Assembly of Rabbis had established a working party to study the issues involved and had considered its findings. Immediately after its initial report,[41] Marmur had written to Jakobovits with his 'aims and suggestions,' although the Assembly's decisions were far from agreed.

A subsequent recommendation in favour was based on four considerations: '1. that it would bring Reform procedure in line with rabbinic tradition; 2. that it would allow applicants to be accepted "in the time-honoured manner of Jewish tradition", and be a more meaningful ceremony; 3. that it would be a positive step towards the long-term goal of Jewish unity; and 4. that it reflected the more traditional stance of the Reform movement, both in Britain and abroad.'[42]

The proposals, however, proved highly controversial. The rabbis themselves were divided, with opponents arguing that it was a regressive step, that the ritual carried 'offensive connotations', and that the hope it would lead to Orthodox acceptance of Reform converts was illusory. It would also have the effect, said some, of separating Reform procedures from other Progressive bodies, including the ULPS.[43]

After lengthy consideration for and against, the matter was eventually passed – by eighteen votes to four – at the annual meeting of the Assembly of Rabbis a year later.[44] A resolution that *tevilah* should be optional for a period of two years, intended to 'allay the fears of opponents and to restore unity among the rabbis', was defeated on the casting vote of the chairman.

At the same time, the Assembly introduced changes to the movement's policy on *gittin*, reintroduced in 1946 following its nineteenth-century dispensation by the early Reformers.[45] The rabbis agreed that the writing, witnessing and delivery of their *gittin* would follow rabbinic tradition, as part of a general move towards the harmonisation of procedures.

Women would no longer be witnesses, but this did not prevent female rabbis being members of a Beth Din that permitted the *get* to proceed. Many in the movement hoped that the changes might make the Reform *get* acceptable to the Orthodox authorities; others regarded it as 'necessary for internal reasons', and in conformity with the movement's developing policy of combining tradition with modernity.

Marmur's support for this policy was enunciated some months later in a volume of essays he had edited on the Reform approach to religious issues:

> We are now looking [he wrote] for an alternative building; that is the purpose of our search. There is no evidence whatever that the revolutionary approach in religion, on its own, leads to

religious revival, but it does lead frequently to chaos and loss of self-confidence.

We are in search of a Judaism that is both authentic and relevant. We are not prepared to destroy the old only for the sake of air and light, because we know that without shelter we may die from exposure. However dissatisfied we may be with what we have, we should beware of destroying it unless we know what we want to replace it with.

This search should not be misunderstood as a disguised return to Orthodoxy. For to believe that the problems of today can be solved by returning to an earlier state of affairs, or by retaining such a state and merely dressing it up in modern garb, is to delude oneself.

Thus, neither rigid Orthodoxy nor mild liberalism, nor minor innovations and marginal beautifications of services, deserve the name authentic; they do not provide a proper framework for a genuine search for new ways. Like revolution, mild reform does not bring about religious revival.

For such a revival, a radical approach is required, as an alternative to both revolution and mild reform. For the radical, persons are always more important than principles. He is an insider who – as the word suggests – goes to the roots of *his own* tradition. He must love that tradition: he must – as the prophets did – 'weep over Jerusalem, even when he has to pronounce its doom'. There is never any question of heresy.

Like the biblical prophets, the radical must be a man of passion, an insider, a man of deep faith, a person who dares to question, even to mock at, himself as well as others. With the prophets in mind, we know that this kind of radicalism can bring about religious revival. However bombastic and pompous it may sound, it must be stated that it is this kind of radical mood we strive for, this kind of radical certainty we seek. Only thus can we undertake that genuine search for new ways which will make for authenticity.

The old ways do not solve the new dilemma. They offer either personal freedom without Judaism, or a kind of Judaism without freedom. But we need both. Our search for new ways may therefore bring us to an attitude normally associated with community decisions, of letting the group, the extended family, the individual congregation shape its halachah in the light of its search for the meaning of revelation, under the guidance of the rabbi who, by virtue of his training, is the expert, though never the sole authority.

We must seek a system of Jewish practice that each community takes upon itself, and which is binding on its members as long as they remain in that community. What they do outside it must be a matter of their discretion, although it is reasonable to assume that they are likely to live by the same standards. Inevitably, standards would vary from congregation to congregation, but it is not a tidy and uniform RSGB platform that we should be striving for. Our concern is to make Judaism active in the lives of our members.

Jewish law provides ample support for this community halachah. Not only would the rabbis refrain from imposing laws which the community was not able to keep, but the concept of *minhag*, law created by local custom, is a version of community halachah. In the words of Solomon Freehof, the greatest living authority on halachah in Reform Judaism, 'the people themselves, by their rejections and their acceptances, by their neglect and their observances, have largely determined their own religious practices'.

Our quest for authenticity must lead us along these paths. For Judaism without a halachah is impossible, but Judaism on the basis of the halachah of Orthodoxy is unsatisfactory; hence the search for new ways. But this search is open to grave misunderstanding. It can easily be seen as justification for a halachah decided on the basis of expediency and mere relevance, divorced from the notion of revelation and the real needs of a living community.

The search for the authentic may thus lead to its opposite. Let us therefore heed the warning of another of our contemporary teachers, Emile Fackenheim, when he writes that the problem of a living halachah 'cannot be solved by committees that simply formulate codes of religious practice. It is a useless – more, a dangerous – procedure to ask for a code of practice without at the same time inquiring into the foundation and ultimate significance of such practice. If revelation is in principle impossible, all such practices, no matter how inspiring, become in the end indistinguishable from folklore.'

Questions concerning the nature of community bring further considerations: our involvement in inter-faith dialogue, and our attitude to conversion to Judaism. The various inter-religious projects in which we are engaged need never be empty public-relations gestures, although in the inauthentic manifestations of Judaism they often are; they can be true expressions of our religious convictions....

Another consequence of the open society is intermarriage. The threat it presents to Jewish survival in the diaspora is beyond dispute. But we also know that it brings many marginal Jews back into the community when their non-Jewish spouses seek conversion.

Our search for new ways should bring us to a new understanding of conversion, and our role in it. And when I say 'our' role, I do not mean the rabbis only. For the greatest obstacle to proper integration of converts is the non-co-operation of many congregations and congregants. In characteristic inauthentic fashion, we form our opinions on the basis of the invective of our opponents. The quest for authenticity points, therefore, to a much more open and positive attitude to conversion.

The RSGB has, in recent months, sought to bring its conversion procedure more in line with traditional halachah. This has been done consistently with the notion of community halachah, but in no way to make it more difficult for those who wish to embrace Judaism under its auspices. On the contrary, by providing a halachic structure, it is hoped to make it easier for proselytes to be acceptable to Klal Yisrael, the Jewish people as a whole.

But will not a possible influx of converts dilute our Judaism? Not if what we bring them to is strong and vibrant and authentic. If it is none of these, our chances of survival are small, irrespective of whether our members are born Jews or are converts to Judaism. By what criterion do we seek to meet this enormous challenge of the open society? The answer is both simple and almost impossibly difficult. In the same way as we Jews have met every challenge: with Torah.[46]

* * *

In thanking Marmur for his 'thoughtful formulation', as expressed in his April letter to Jakobovits, Moshe Davis wrote on behalf of the Chief Rabbi: 'The points you make will certainly be studied and considered with great care. While a few of them seem to afford some basis for progress in our efforts, others clearly indicate the width of the gap still separating us. As agreed, and quite independently of your assessments, I am herewith setting out a kind of "position paper" on what should and could be achieved in the light of our discussions, from our point of view:

We should seek to reach agreements designed, above all,

(a) to restore and preserve the unity of the Jewish people now gravely and increasingly imperilled by the consequences of diverse norms in the attitudes to marriage, divorce and conversion whereby admissibility to Jewish status and/or Jewish marriage is disputed for a large and ever-growing number of people who are recognised as Jews and/or eligible for marriage in the eyes of some congregations, and denied such recognition by the rest: and

(b) to avert the personal tragedies often inflicted on individuals, or their descendants for all future times, arising from their disputed status, in the event that they or their children should ever seek acceptance, or the right to marry, within the traditional community.

Long-term solutions

Ideally, our problem would be solved by adopting the pattern which prevailed in German-Jewish *Grossgemeinden*. While Orthodox and Reform congregations naturally differed widely on religious services and other observances – perhaps even more widely than they do here – and despite the Orthodox often being in a minority, both sections were united under a common community administration and jointly submitted to the jurisdiction of an Orthodox Beth Din in matters normally within its purview, such as kashrut and shechitah, as well as divorce and conversion....[47]

Any agreement on such lines to be eventually reached here could not be retroactive, and existing marriages or conversions of doubtful halachic validity would remain unaffected. But at least we would prevent any new cases being added to the grievous toll of communal bitterness, personal tragedies and national disunity afflicting our people today.

Intermediate measures

Pending such admittedly drastic restructuring of our inter-communal relations and organisation, it should prove possible progressively to introduce a number of measures aimed at the above objectives in the spirit of our discussions. Some 'concessions' will have to be made on both sides. But it lies in the very nature of the conflict between Traditional and Progressive Judaism that the custodians of the former claim – and can assert – far less liberties in this respect than the latter.

Altogether, it would be an abdication of our trust, and offensive to the sanctity of the issues under discussion, if we were to think in terms of *quid pro quo* and conduct our parleys as if they were some trade-union negotiations or political bargaining between nations, in which there must be a calculated balance of 'give and take'.

Accordingly, we believe that the following proposals would substantially advance the cause which has united us in our deliberations:

1. For members of Orthodox synagogues, the exclusive jurisdiction of Orthodox rabbis should be upheld. Such members, or parties applying for conversion with a view to marriage to such members, should under no circumstances be admitted for remarriage or conversion if such acts would not be sanctioned by Orthodox authorities. Progressive synagogues should never be used as a haven for 'rejects' of the Orthodox community.
2. Non-Orthodox divorcees applying for remarriage should also be advised that they must first obtain a *get* universally accepted by all rabbinic authorities, so as to preserve the unity of the Jewish people and to prevent the tragic disabilities of any children who may be born within the second marriage. Should efforts to obtain such a *get* prove unavailing, such exceptional cases should not be further considered until the lapse of at least two years.
3. Similarly, all applications for conversions should in the first instance be referred to Orthodox *batei din*, so as to give them unquestioned validity, and not be entertained for acceptance under non-Orthodox auspices for at

least two years following the original application. The strictest enforcement of these provisions would substantially reduce. if not altogether eliminate, the incidence of *mamzerut* and the admission of persons whose Jewish status would be in dispute. It would also remove the principal cause of bitterness and dissension between our respective communities.
4. On the Orthodox side, undertakings should be given to deal with all applications with the utmost despatch, courtesy and sympathy. Appeal procedures should be set up to take effective action on any complaints of undue delay, alleged lack of civility, etc. Representatives of the Progressive ministry should be entitled to pursue such complaints on behalf of their members.
5. Such representatives, including laymen if desired, should also be invited to join or constitute a consultative board charged to advise and make representations on applications lodged with Progressive synagogues, as well as on instruction programmes.
6. Consideration should be given to the suggestion of the Marriage Authorisation Bureau registering marriages at Progressive synagogues which do not encounter any halachic impediment. But this would be contingent on some agreement being reached on the preceding proposals.

It is, of course, appreciated that the positions now before us still reveal considerable differences in approach and substance. But, together with the discussions that have inspired them, they do constitute some significant narrowing of the gap between us.

Perhaps even more important, they demonstrate the common will to solve the agonising problems bedevilling our community and our people, and from them may well emerge at least a meaningful start on the road to reconciliation and real unity. This certainly is our hope – to heal the wounds of the past, and to promote trust and co-operation consistent with our halachic commitments.[48]

'Despite our best intentions', Jakobovits was later to declare,[49] 'as in 1969 so again in 1976, our efforts proved abortive. On both occasions, the extended discussions had to be abandoned, as the proposals were in the end not acceptable to the Progressives.' However, surveying – as Davis put it to Marmur – 'the width of the gap still separating us', at least one Progressive rabbi, ten years on, did not desist from trying again.

* * *

Despite Jakobovits' hope 'to heal the wounds of the past, and to promote trust and co-operation', consultations gradually dwindled within the Consultative Committee, and 'the road to reconciliation and real unity' proved ever-more difficult. But, even as a blanket of uncertainty shrouded the communal scene, the Chief Rabbi remained optimistic over the longer term. Discussing Anglo-Jewry's religious differences in the wider context,[50] he put it this way:

> I seek to adjust my reasoning power to the heritage bequeathed to me. But I can recognise certain problems, and I think we are not expected blindly to commit ourselves to unreason or to irrationality, but are meant to apply our intellectual faculties in an endeavour to understand.
>
> We have to relate our reasoning power to the supranatural. I readily admit that I do not always find adequate or satisfying answers, or that I have had to wait for years until I have found them. All in all, I don't find it too difficult.
>
> But I realise, of course, that others do not see life in that light. The ideal alternative to going to the synagogue by car, if you are not able to go except by using transport, is not to go at all. My answer categorically is, 'Say your prayers at home, because the sanctity of the Sabbath is superior to the sanctity of the synagogue.'
>
> On the other hand, I certainly prefer a person who leaves the car around the corner to the one who parks it in front of the synagogue door. That is not hypocrisy, but a recognition that there are standards, even if you do not live up to them. That recognition is all-important.
>
> My argument with Reform is less that they allow individual liberties to their members than that they legitimise that which is illegitimate. I want members of a congregation, observant or not, to accept their rabbi as the custodian of absolute values without compromise.
>
> The majority of Anglo-Jewry recognises this. It is a tremendous asset to our community that, although we all fall short of the

ideal, at least we recognise both the ideal and the fact that we fall short of it. Leaving the car round the corner is a recognition of it. It is a virtue rather than an hypocrisy.

In itself, the disunity implicit in Reform is not important. This obsession with unity is an Anglo-Jewish fetish. After all, for generations past we have had different forms of prayer, slightly different forms of worship, different pronunciations. Nobody has ever suggested that, unless we all pray together, we destroy the unity of our people. This whole notion is based on false premises. I do not see that the holding of occasional joint services – to which I am totally opposed – has any bearing on unity. What we need is unity of purpose.

My policy is to work together in all areas which do not impinge on our religious differences: Israel, Soviet Jewry, Jewish–Christian relations. But where the Progressive element has chosen to dissent – we are not the dissenters – to reject something extremely sacred to us, we cannot work together, because we have no common ideals to unite us.

I do not believe that you must have the monolithic structure of leadership or organisation after which Anglo-Jewry seems to be hankering. It is not a cardinal principle of faith. Often it is through the tensions of diversity and conflict that you generate the energy for dynamic activity. In the Middle Ages, the Karaites [who rejected the Oral Law] created enormous conflict, but to the Karaite challenge we owe much of what Saadya, Maimonides and other immortals have contributed to Jewish thought.

The very origin of our people is its division into twelve tribes and then into two kingdoms, and then came all the different schools of the Talmud. But I cannot legitimise the teachings of Reform: it is not part of authentic Judaism.

I do not see it as another form of Judaism. I see it as a challenge to Judaism. Reform will not prevail. It is self-liquidating. Their birth-rate is so low, and their defection rate so high through assimilation and intermarriage, that in two or three generations there will be none left. The problem will solve itself through natural processes. Call it the survival of the fittest.

But I still regard Reform Jews as Jews. I do not deny their Jewish status as long as they are Jews according to the halachah. But I do not regard their beliefs as authentically Jewish.

For all that, Jakobovits concluded, 'I see a regeneration of Jewish life the likes of which we have not seen for one hundred years. It is on a colossal scale and is creating an unprecedented intensity of Jewish learning and living. We in Britain have today thousands of homes where there is daily study of the Torah. In two or three generations, it will be a massive movement.

'Vast numbers will be lost in the process, as the gap between the observant and the non-observant Jew widens. But what is being salvaged today will be of higher quality and faster relative growth than in the past. The survival of Jewish life in this country is no longer at stake.'

* * *

What was clearly at stake, however, was 'the common will to solve the agonising problems bedevilling our community and our people'. A series of controversies and misunderstandings over the coming months foretold of growing tensions at both ends of the spectrum, presaging unforeseen consequences in the coming decade.

In March 1979, more than 100 rabbis and ministers from across the communal spectrum met in London for a conference on solidarity with Israel; among the topics discussed were ways of bringing Israel Independence Day into the religious calendar. Towards the end of the session came news that Cyril Harris, minister of the St John's Wood (United) Synagogue, and Sidney Brichto, in conjunction with the Jewish Agency office in London, had prepared a 'Hagadah' for the Independence Day celebrations two months later.[51]

As the event drew close, however, Jakobovits circulated a letter to ministers under his jurisdiction expressing 'strong misgivings' about the 'Hagadah'. Declaring that he had had 'no prior knowledge of, or connection with, this publication', he added: 'I cannot approve of it on the following grounds:

1. Traditionally, the term 'Hagadah' is used exclusively for the statutory text of the Hagadah shel Pesach, and it is entirely inappropriate to use this title for any other order of service, particularly when it includes purely secular texts.
2. The suggested readings include items which clearly violate the halachah, such as a 'Kiddush', not recited for halachic reasons even on long-established semi-holy-days like Chanucah, Purim and *chol hamoed* [the intermediate days of festivals], and

a new formulation of a formal benediction, in breach of an halachic rule; and

3. The sponsorship by the Rabbinic Advisory Council, with which I have no connection, of a quasi-religious enterprise is inconsistent with the clear line of demarcation I have always drawn between strictly religious and secular areas to define the fields in which co-operation with non-Orthodox leaders is possible.[52]

This statement drew a strong response from Brichto, who wrote to Jakobovits: 'For the record, it is important that you and others know that there exists no disagreement between us on the demarcation lines as you have set them out, and that it is on this basis that the Rabbinic Advisory Council was established.

'You know that without the assurance of your blessing and co-operation, I would never have initiated the two one-day ministers' solidarity conventions, nor the Advisory Council itself. Indeed, I always viewed Rabbis Harris's position on our Council in a double capacity – as chairman of the Assembly of United Synagogue Ministers and as the member of your Cabinet for the Israel portfolio.

> As to the Hagadah itself, you may recall that, at the request of the Solidarity Committee which wished to promote home celebrations of Yom Ha'atzmaut, I – in consultation with Moshe Davis – drew up a short service which appeared in the *Jewish Chronicle* two years ago in the form of a half-page advertisement.
>
> The following year, at Moshe's request, I did the same, but in consultation with Rabbi Harris. This year, the main Yom Ha'atzmaut committee of solidarity encouraged the youth and hechalutz department [of the Jewish Agency] to prepare a hagadah and agreed to finance it. This proposal was reported to the main Solidarity Committee meeting and, as there was no disapproval voiced, acted upon.
>
> Once the text was prepared, it was shown to Rabbi Harris and myself. We ourselves made only minor corrections and suggestions, some of which (I might add) were not even accepted. The idea that the RAC was responsible for this publication was disavowed by me in a letter to the *Jewish Chronicle*.
>
> As to the halachic objections to the Hagadah, I know that you will believe me when I say that I had assumed that Rabbi Harris

felt confident in your agreement to those parts of the Hagadah which may have been open to dispute. What is unfortunate now is that the community may feel that the Solidarity efforts of the ministers may have lost your support and caused division in the community, when the problem arose out of a failure of communication between you and Rabbi Harris.

I know that the pressures of your Office are very exacting, and it happens at times that our lines become crossed, even with those with whom we work closely; and I appreciate, therefore, that it is your intention to make it clear that you support the work of the Rabbinic Advisory Committee and accept that it was not its intention to go beyond your lines of demarcation.

'You know of my high personal respect for you,' Brichto concluded, 'in your effort to keep the community united in its efforts for Israel. Without it, I could not continue in my own efforts towards this end within the ranks of rabbis and ministers.'[53]

'Your letter just received,' retorted the Chief Rabbi, 'calls for some comments. My statement on the "Hagadah" was circulated as a letter to my colleagues, in response to insistent requests that I make it clear whether I approve of the booklet or not.

'It was not intended for publication, and no copy or other notice was communicated to the press by my office. Any further statement from me on the matter would therefore also be addressed to my colleagues and I do, in fact, intend to dispose of any possible misunderstandings at next week's Conference of Anglo-Jewish Preachers.

Rabbi Harris himself appears to have been misled. He tells me that he was simply asked to go through the English text, making such corrections as he saw fit. He was not asked to give his or my approval to the publication itself, nor told that comments or corrections would be elicited from anyone else, least of all that the entire project would appear under the aegis of the Rabbinic Advisory Council. Hence I cannot see any justification for your assertion that 'the problem arose out of a failure of communication between you and Rabbi Harris'.

Still on the 'Hagadah,' I gather that the Jewish National Fund education department have also voiced their protest, since they were not consulted, despite assurances that they would be, and having regard to the fact that they issued a very similar publication for distribution in this country a couple of years ago. It seems to me, therefore, that it is Rex House [head office of the JNF] rather than my office, or any other body, which should be charged with a 'failure of communication'.

On my contacts with the Rabbinic Advisory Council itself, my recollection is also somewhat at variance with yours. I recall no consultation with me prior to its establishment, nor was I ever told that Rabbi Harris was to represent my Office on it, though he did report to me about it from time to time. I was advised post facto that this body was set up by agreement and in co-operation with the United Synagogue Council of Ministers, which is of course an entirely independent body that neither claims nor requires my endorsement for all its decisions.

I certainly was not aware that either of our two ministers' conferences had been convened under auspices other than the Solidarity Committee itself.

Quite frankly, even without my direct involvement, I have never been too happy over the formation of the RAC, and I voiced my misgivings through Moshe Davis on more than one occasion. But I admit that I never expressed any disapproval once it was established.

My fear was precisely that it might lead to blurring the line of demarcation as has now occurred. No disclaimer can really rectify this, as subsequent events have shown. Moreover, I always preferred 'ministerial' to 'rabbinic' for any joint endeavours, including conferences, if only because so many spiritual leaders on our side were not in fact rabbis.

Summing up, I reaffirm that the Solidarity Committee itself has my blessing and support, enjoying my co-sponsorship together with such Orthodox bodies as the Office of the Rav Rashi, the United Synagogue and the Mizrachi, among others. But this 'blessing' never extended, either directly or by representation, to the 'Hagadah' or to the RAC.

To avoid confusion or misunderstandings, I felt duty-bound to communicate this to my colleagues, though I never had any intention to turn this into a public issue between us. As for any further statement, I will consult, as promised, with Rabbi Harris, who is as anxious as I am not to be misunderstood.

'I certainly hope,' the Chief Rabbi concluded, 'that this unfortunate episode will eventually join others in the limbo of oblivion, making room for the pursuit of less contentious endeavours.'⁵⁴ That it would 'eventually join others' was to be realised far sooner than expected, though not in 'the limbo of oblivion' for which Jakobovits had hoped.

* * *

Early the following month, the *Jewish Chronicle* reported that 'the Chief Rabbi has refused to join the Beth Din of the Union of Orthodox Hebrew Congregations and a large group of roshei yeshivah and rabbis of independent Orthodox congregations in a blanket denunciation of Reform and Liberal Jews.

'The independent Orthodox rabbinate, headed by Rabbi Henoch B. Padwa and including Rabbi M. M. Schneebalg, the rav of the Machzikei Hadass community in Manchester, as well as the Stanislower and Sassover Rebbes and the rosh yeshivah of Gateshead, joined last week in a statement. The target of their wrath, although at least three of the rabbis are known to have been reluctant signatories, was presumed to be the Chief Rabbi, who recently participated in a "Solidarity with Israel" conference with representatives of the non-Orthodox communities.'⁵⁵

> In the light of recent events [read the statement], we feel it our duty to declare that, according to the Torah, the Reform, Liberal and all kindred movements bear no relationship whatever to Judaism. Their followers have rejected Divine Authority, their beliefs are heretical, and the very existence of such groups is a denial of the Written and Oral Law given to us at Sinai.
>
> Furthermore, any participation with these movements and their leaders gives them moral support and undermines our own firm adherence to Torah. Anyone who imagines that these dissenters can be brought back into the fold by consorting with them is deluding himself and misleading others. Instead, such contact will repel the Orthodox and those awaiting proper spiritual guidance.
>
> May the Almighty give His counsel to those who err and help them to return to the path of Torah and traditional faith.⁵⁶

In response to an inquiry from the JC, Jakobovits commented: 'I respect the honour of the Torah too much to enter into a public dispute with rabbis whose commitment I share. But their jurisdiction or sympathy is limited to 'Independent Orthodoxy', and I cannot adopt their policies, certainly not without alienating the bulk of Anglo-Jewry from Orthodoxy.

I cannot exclude non-observant Jews from my concern and co-operation. This would gravely damage Orthodox interests, as well as communal unity and the endeavours based on it, notably in the support of Jewish education.

My experience convinces me that what drives waverers to Reform is Orthodox intolerance and divisive agitation, rather than any 'legitimacy' allegedly conferred by sharing secular platforms with its leaders. All Jews are authentic Jews, but neither Judaism nor rabbis can be authentic, in the Orthodox view, unless they embrace the totality of Jewish belief, law and tradition.

Therefore, my own policies have consistently been guided by the principle I clearly spelled out in my installation address twelve years ago: I cannot join with Reformers in areas affected by their dissent from our traditions, but I will work with them on matters on which we are united, such as Israel, Soviet Jewry, welfare and Jewish defence.

In this, I follow the example set by my father, my predecessors and even such a distinguished pioneer of 'Independent Orthodoxy' as Rabbi Ezra Munk of Berlin, who collaborated with Dr Leo Baeck, the Reform leader of German Jewry. I believe that these policies are overwhelmingly understood and supported, and have resulted in the intensified loyalty of our community to the values we cherish.[57]

In a brusque response to the rabbis of the Union of Orthodox Hebrew Congregations[58] – 'Not to be made public', and sent to each of the signatories – the Chief Rabbi wrote:

Only because of the strict honour due to the Torah have I desisted from creating a public outcry against my persecutors, and from taking a stand against those who cast aspersions on me and my community. I prefer to be counted among the insulted who do not repay in kind, who hear rage but do not respond.

I am not complaining about the attack on my honour – for who am I? Nor do I argue over the incitement that serves to fan the flames of the current atmosphere. However, the stronger – indeed, the worst – aspect of this matter is the publication of a slander on the basis of a *da'at Torah* [Torah pronouncement] without any research or inquiry into the nature of the issues, into the facts and circumstances, and lacking any contact or personal consultation – clearly not the way such matters should be handled within our tradition....

What is difficult to understand is the claim of the *gedolei haTorah*, the rabbis and the heads of yeshivot, that contact with the Reform – even on secular matters – damages our faith in the Torah. Could it be that your faith is so weak? And is not more logical the argument that as a result of such contacts we are giving them, or their views, moral support? The opposite is true. And who more than I upholds the sages' instruction in such matters as these, in order to know what strengthens, and what weakens, their influence?

What I lament most, however, is the insult to the Torah and the aspersions cast on so many, in your camp and in mine. Even the most observant individual recognises that the *kol koreh* [public voice] became a *kol korei'a* [divisive voice] when you sought to embarrass me – and, in consequence, the institution of the Chief Rabbinate – in the eyes of the vast majority of our community, and of those who identify with us.

What is the point of attacking the Reform if it results, among those who fear the word of God, in weakening their faith in the Torah scholars among us; in reducing their support of Torah institutions; and, among those less committed, in distancing themselves from their Maker? Anyone who is out to destroy and defame the Orthodox need not look for a greater spur or a more potent 'blessing' or vehicle than this so-called *kol koreh*....

There is no such thing as a *da'at Torah*; in reality, there is only a *din Torah* [a Torah ruling]. Consequently, I fail to see, in your public declaration, either *da'at* or *Torah*, only a stirring of conflict and a lack of respect for Torah, lessening people's love of it and forcing them away from observance of the mitzvot.

The halachah that my fathers passed on to me was based on the general principle that the dayan has [as his tools] only that which his eyes can see. Now, gentlemen, you should know that my eyes see far more of what is happening among the rank-and-file than those eyes that have limited vision in the sanctuaries we all occupy.

I see thousands of Jews, dejected and rejected, who are striving for the right path, who are disturbed, disconcerted and disappointed by the *da'at Torah*, which does nothing to draw young Jews closer to their Father in heaven. On the contrary, it pushes away so many simple Jews – as is proven by the attached letter from a young man expressing himself from the depth of his heart.[59]

Appended to his own letter was another from one of these 'thousands', who had written to the JC in support of the Chief Rabbi:

'Having been for a number of years involved in the activities of the student Jewish Society in Cambridge,' declared Benjamin Chain, 'I feel compelled to comment on the recent pronouncements of a Beth Din concerning the Reform movement, and in particular the incredible advertisement published in your paper, signed by many of our leading rabbinical authorities.

'I feel that, while this controversy will undoubtedly harm the whole community, the brunt of the damage will fall on its younger members, and indeed, for us, such behaviour of the Beth Din of the Union of Orthodox Hebrew Congregations amounts to a real catastrophe.

'There can be no doubt that there has taken place in recent years a real revival of interest in traditional Judaism. I have, indeed, been personally involved in this remarkable phenomenon. This revival has manifested itself not just as a vague awareness of "Jewish consciousness", but as a genuine and sustained effort on the part of many young people to study and try to reassimilate the very complex and intricate structure of Orthodox Judaism.

'Marvellous as this revival has been, however, it has remained so far merely a spark: it would require the most unremitting effort and encouragement from the whole community to blow this spark into a real blaze of "Torah Judaism" which would provide a basis for a thriving Anglo-Jewish community in the future.

'In particular, the people who should have been enthusiastically leading this movement could only be our religious scholars, whether they be rabbis, dayanim or roshei yeshivot. It is only they, in fact, who have the profound learning and intimate involvement with Orthodox culture which such a role would require.

'It is the tragedy of our community, therefore, that so many of these people have singularly failed to take advantage of this opportunity. Far from enthusiastically leading the campaign, they have on every possible occasion adopted a negative, insensitive and rigid attitude calculated to repel even the most ardent and motivated inquirer.

'Worse still, in this latest outburst of virulent obscurantism, they have openly demonstrated their obvious state of total insecurity, and a pitiful unwillingness to devote themselves to the problems facing modern

Orthodox Jewry. I fear it will only be with the greatest difficulty that even the most committed among us will be able to remain associated with a community whose spiritual leaders are capable of making a statement so remote from the spirit of Judaism.'[60]

The final public words on the controversy came from John Rayner during a Shabbat sermon at the Liberal Jewish Synagogue, it being also the second day of Shavuot, which he and his congregants — as throughout the Progressive movement — did not observe.

Referring to the dispute, Rayner described Emeth, the organisation that had blazoned the letter, as 'just a very small group in Leeds which until recently nobody had ever heard of, and its motivation seems to be largely negative: not to commend Judaism to Gentiles, or even to unaffiliated Jews, but to denounce those religious movements within the Anglo-Jewish community which it does not approve of — that is to say, all that are not strictly Orthodox.

> Why such an organisation should have been formed at this particular time is something of a mystery. The answer seems to be that, although Progressive Judaism has been growing rather slowly of late in terms of membership, it has secured for itself a more respected status in certain communal bodies such as the Board of Deputies, the Anglo-Jewish Association, the Council of Christians and Jews, and the World Zionist Organisation, and that it has done so with the acquiescence of the Chief Rabbi of the United Hebrew Congregations, Dr Immanuel Jakobovits.
>
> Not that he is favourably disposed towards Progressive Judaism. On the contrary, he is the most Right-wing Chief Rabbi Anglo-Jewry has ever had. But he is a man of eloquence, dignity, urbanity, courtesy, integrity, humaneness, moral earnestness and courage; and his sense of justice does not permit him to discriminate against fellow-Jews in those areas of communal life in which his religious scruples do not compel him to do so....

Referring to the teachings of Rabbi Israel Meir Kagan, of Poland,[61] and to the volume that carries his pseudonym — *Chafetz Chaim*, 'He Who Desires Life' — on the necessity to avoid slander, gossip and tale-bearing, Rayner asked: 'Are the rabbis of the Union of Orthodox Hebrew Congregations unaware of these teachings? Surely not.

'How, then, could they so flagrantly disregard them? The answer is, of course, that they were carried away by their zeal. But then we must add: it is a strange kind of zeal which defends the Torah by violating the Torah!

'The statement of the UOHC is not merely a lie: it is an example of the notorious "Big Lie". How shall we account for it? Ignorance? Yes, it may be safely assumed that the signatories know next to nothing about Progressive Judaism. But is that an excuse? Not if one accepts the teachings of our sages, that we should not judge without knowledge (*Avot* 2:4), and that even then we should judge l'*chaf zechut*, "by the scale of merit" – that is, charitably (*Avot* 1:6). No, the real explanation is not ignorance but, once again, zeal: the kind of zeal for the little truth which blinds people to the "Big Truth".

'It is indeed ironic that an organisation calling itself Emeth [Truth] should resort to the "Big Lie", and that the leading rabbis of ultra-Orthodox Jewry should so misrepresent the spirit of the tradition which it is their task to uphold.

'But let us say these things in sorrow, not in anger. For the growth of Progressive Judaism will not be impeded by their denunciation. On the contrary, it will almost certainly be accelerated. Though this episode may therefore turn out to our sectional advantage, it is still sad, because the good name of Judaism as a whole – which is even more important – has been gravely damaged by it.'[62]

* * *

Differences of opinion between the opposing parties continued to escalate, with another clash occurring over remarks in the Chief Rabbi's opening address to the Conference of Anglo-Jewish Preachers. 'The Orthodox view on Reform and Liberal Judaism,' he declared, 'is no different from the ultra-Orthodox standpoint. Where we do differ, however, is in how we deal with them.

'I operate a clear line of demarcation. On matters on which we are united – Soviet Jewry, Israel, Jewish defence, and Jewish–Christian relations – we cannot write them off. If we refused to share a platform on such matters, we would alienate the bulk of our own members and create a situation that would spell the end of the United Synagogue, the Chief Rabbinate and the hegemony of Orthodoxy in our community.

'Recent attacks on the Reform movement by ultra-religious groups have done more harm than good. If anything, these attacks have promoted Reform. They have never had so much publicity during my twelve years in office. Nor have they received so much sympathy. A policy of non-co-operation could easily be undertaken in Gateshead or Stamford Hill, but I believe it is we who are doing more to stop the growth of Reform.

'It is patently wrong to say that Anglo-Jewry is moving from Orthodoxy to Reform. There has been an incipient reawakening of Orthodoxy, especially among the young, and a rise in the numbers attending Jewish dayschools. Nothing can be more damaging to the cause of Orthodoxy than the denigration of advancement and the exaggeration of failures.'[63]

Once again, the Chief Rabbi's words led to a spat with Reform. 'The report in last Friday's *Jewish Chronicle*,' wrote Marmur to Jakobovits, 'has caused me considerable unease and prompted this letter; I even spoke about it to my congregation last Shabbat. However, rather than publish the text of that sermon, and thus perhaps add further fuel to the already heated debate, I have decided to write privately in search of clarification.

> Primarily, it is two issues that trouble me. First, am I right in understanding the report to say that you agree with the assessment of Reform and Liberal Judaism, as expressed by the group of rabbis on the 'extreme Right' and promulgated by the Emeth advertisement, that 'Reform, Liberal and all kindred movements bear no relationship whatever to Judaism'?
>
> Ever since I interviewed you for Living Judaism, shortly after you assumed office, the Reform movement in Britain has been aware of your views that, on the one hand, you reject it as 'organising a defection from Jewish law', while, on the other, you recognise that it 'has helped to stem the drift from Judaism'. Working with you since that time, we thought it had been proved that 'we could not only build bridges, but walk on them too'.
>
> However, in the light of this recent attack on us, the opening sentence of the JC report – 'The Orthodox view on Reform and Liberal Judaism is no different from the ultra-Orthodox standpoint' – has serious implications. It would be helpful to know whether my understanding of that report, as an endorsement of the 'extremist' view, is correct. If it is not, what is it that you really wanted to say to the community?
>
> Secondly, am I now to understand that the co-operation that exists at the moment is only a function of expediency and, from your point of view, lacks any intrinsic merit? The direct quote in the JC report – 'Where we differ is in how we deal with them' – seems to be saying precisely that.
>
> The same report further suggests that, 'to stop the growth of Reform', your approach is more effective than that of the

'extreme Orthodox'. I have always thought that the purpose of co-operation was to strengthen Judaism and support fellow-Jews. My colleagues and I would have to be masochists to engage in co-operation in order to curb our own progress.

To some extent, we have learned to accept the fact that in order to hit each other, you and the 'extreme Right' have to fire shots over the heads of Reform. But when the bullets begin to hit us, I feel constrained to react, even if such a reaction has political repercussions.

My concern is practical. If your view is not, in substance, different from that expressed by the 'extremists' – if you co-operate with Reform and Liberal Jews only for tactical and not for intrinsic reasons – I find it difficult to remain as Convener of the Consultative Committee.

Since the nature of the next meeting makes it impossible to discuss this matter, I am taking this opportunity to write to you. Once I know your views better, I shall be able to decide whether or not I can continue as a member of that committee.

To avoid any misunderstanding, let me make it clear that I am fully committed to co-operation, and anxious that it should continue, but I see no value in it unless, within the limitations we both recognise, the dialogue is mutual and not a camouflage for disdain and manipulation.

I have found it very difficult to write this letter for many reasons, one of them being the personal affection that my colleagues and I have for you, and the esteem in which we hold you. It is shocking to contemplate the prospect, which the JC report opens before us, that we have so profoundly misunderstood your attitude.[64]

So speedily – and publicly – was the Chief Rabbi anxious to respond that he wrote to Marmur in these terms:

Your letter has just reached me, erev Shavuot afternoon, and although I know that my reply will not be typed until Monday, I am dictating it now so as to give you my immediate reaction.

The JC report to which you refer is substantially correct as far as it goes, but consisting only of brief and sometimes truncated excerpts of my address. The effect is like evidence which tells the truth and nothing but the truth, but not the whole truth. For instance, I did say 'Where we differ is how we deal with them', but I added 'and how we relate to them'. This sounds, and is, a little different from the published account.

In reply to your main question, you can take it that I have not changed my views or attitudes in the slightest over the years or in recent weeks. When I stated at the Preachers' Conference that our view on Reform Judaism (not Reform Jews!) was the same as the ultra-Orthodox standpoint, I went on to explain that all Orthodox Jews subscribe to the Oral Law, accept the Shulchan Aruch as binding, etc., and that therefore there were no differences among us on our attitude to Reform teachings.

I even added that it would be sheer hypocrisy for Jews who held traditional beliefs and practices as sacred to regard doctrines denying these commitments as equally authentic. By this I stand, and I have never made a secret of this stand.

Yet this does not prevent me from working conscientiously with non-Orthodox groups and their leaders in areas on which we are united. I do so both as a matter of conviction, in as much as I believe in the causes on which we work together – and as I regard all Jews as authentic members of our people – and as a matter of 'expediency', realising that any other policy would alienate the great majority of Anglo-Jewry from Orthodoxy.

I am not engaged in any game 'to hit each other' with the 'extreme Right', as you suggest, nor even with the Left. I never initiate an attack on anybody, but when both sides occasionally snipe at me, I have to defend myself and the community I represent. And I do so with as little rancour as I can.

But those happily only intermittent occasions apart, I seek to concentrate my energies and resources on constructive endeavours, above all on putting our own house in order. I believe this will keep me busy for the rest of my tenure, and I have no plans to engage in any destructive attacks or denunciations in the future any more than I did in the past.

I hope these have answered your questions. Whether they satisfy you, only you can decide; but I can assure you that they are honest and consistent – so much so that I have no objection if you show them to anyone who shares your 'considerable unease' and is likewise 'in search of clarification'.[65]

Drawing this correspondence to a close, Marmur replied after Shavuot: 'I am most grateful for your letter, for it did clarify the two points that troubled me most – namely, that your statement to the Preachers' Conference is not an endorsement of the Emeth position, but a reminder that all Orthodox Jews share the same views with regard to Oral Law, the Shulchan Aruch, etc.; and that, in addition to whatever political advantages there may be, you recognise intrinsic merits in co-operation.

'I believe that there is here enough of a basis for working together in the spirit of unity in diversity and for the good of the Jewish people, and I am greatly relieved to know this. I am also grateful for your permission to make your letter known to others; I would obviously have to share my letter, too, to explain your reply.'[66]

New London Synagogue

Dec. 30th 1965

Dear Rabbi Brichto,

I am looking forward to the meeting on January 20th and shall bring one of my Hon. Officers along with me.

Percy Selwyn Goldberg telephoned me today and I told him that I had had your letter and intending communicating with you. In fact, I telephoned the Synagogue but you were out.

On reflection I cannot see the point of a special preliminary meeting with Rabbi Swift. He is absolutely sold on the idea and requires no persuasion. May I suggest that you telephone him and invite him to come to the meeting on the 20th, with one of his Hon. Officers. Or if you prefer it you could call in to see him and invite him.

As for Rabbi Rew, frankly, I think it would be best if the invitation came directly from you. I do not know him

Rabbi: Dr Louis Jacobs, Secretary: Simon Wilsack
33 Abbey Road NW8. Telephone: Maida Vale 3739

Louis Jacobs to Sidney Brichto, 30 December, 1965, on the possibility of joining the proposed British Council of Synagogues/National Rabbinical Council (Chapter Two, page 15)

FOUNDED IN 1657
ק״ק שער השמים
Office of the Haham
of the
Spanish & Portuguese Jews

4, Ashworth Road, Maida Vale
London W.9.

Telegraphic Address:
GAON, LONDON - W.9
Telephone:
CUNNINGHAM 4189

7th Elul 57 26
22nd August 19 66

Rabbi Sidney Brichto,
Unionof Liberal & Progressive Synagogues,
28 St. John's Wood Road,
London, N.W.8.

Dear Rabbi Brichto,

It was nice speaking to you last week, and I enjoyed our talk very much indeed.

Mr. Teff is at present away on holiday, but I shall be seeing him as soon as possible after his return, probably towards the beginning of September. I shall, of course, contact you in order to inform you of what transpires at our meeting.

I entirely agree with the suggestions put forward in your letter, and trust that we may see their fulfilment.

With kindest regards,

Yours sincerely,

Solomon Gaon to Brichto, 22 August, 1966, following a meeting to establish 'a deeper relationship' between their respective synagogal bodies (Chapter Two, page 15)

PERSONAL

ROYAL COURTS OF JUSTICE,

LONDON.

8th November 1966

Rabbi Sidney Brichto,
Union of Liberal & Progressive Synagogues,
28, St. John's Wood Road,
LONDON, N.W.8.

Dear Rabbi Brichto,

Thank you for your letter of yesterday enclosing the draft letter to be sent to The Times.

So far as the draft is concerned I think the letter is very good and I have no suggestions to make. What however does worry me is whether or not this letter should be sent before we have tried out the new Chief Rabbi and ascertained his reactions towards the non Orthodox sections of the Community. I ventured at our last meeting to emphasise the importance of timing with regard to our future relations with him. My fear is that if we sent a letter of this kind to a national newspaper now, we shall antagonise the new Chief Rabbi as well as those whom he directly represents, thus causing a further and possibly fatal split in the Anglo-Jewish Community.

It is my considered view that no letter of this kind should be sent until the new Chief Rabbi has been in office for at least six months and his attitudes and conduct closely considered.

Yours sincerely,
S.E. Karminski

S.E. KARMINSKI

West London Reform's Sir Seymour Karminski to Brichto, 8 November, 1966, advising against a premature welcome from the non-Orthodox to the Chief Rabbi-elect (Chapter Two, note 32)

March 9, 1967.

Dear Rabbi Brichto,

Just a line to acknowledge with many thanks your letter of March 6 just received. I now look forward to continuing our "dialogue" in person once I am a little settled in London.

You are right in your assumption re my participation at the Liberal Jewish Conference. At this early stage in our search for a détente, I am most anxious to avoid anything which may be construed as provocation by those who still have to be conditioned to the new climate we seek. I know you will understand.

Reciprocating your good wishes and reassurances,

Sincerely yours,

I. Jakobovits

P.S. During my recent wide travels, especially also in Canada, I met several friends of yours who remember you from your American days. They will be remembered (though, alas, with the thousands of people I met, I cannot remember all their names).

Jakobovits to Brichto, 9 March, 1967, after their preliminary 'dialogue' in London, declining an invitation to participate in a ULPS conference (Chapter Two, note 29)

המרכז ליהדות
בתאור האום

MEMORANDUM

TO: Mr. Raymond Goldman   FROM: Rabbi A.M. Bayfield
    Mr. Maurice Michaels   (wearing the Council of
    Sir Sigmund Sternberg   Reform & Liberal Rabbis
    Rabbi Hugo Gryn   hat!)

DATE: 27th February 1985

RE: Meeting of Consultative Committee - 4th March

----

1. Hugo Gryn and John Rayner, and John Rayner and I have had private meetings with the Chief Rabbi over the last few days. The mood is one of conciliation. We have impressed upon him the need to build good personal relationships and trust and to tackle certain basic issues. Both of these points are accepted.

2. Rabbi Maurice Unterman has been acting as an 'elder statesman' and has put forward the enclosed draft statement.

3. The Executive of the Council of Reform and Liberal Rabbis met last night and came to the following conclusions:

    (a) The Unterman statement should be warmly welcomed

    (b) The last two lines should be elaborated. We would like to see established a small ecclesiastical liaison committee of six - myself, Hugo Gryn and John Rayner on our side, the Chief Rabbi and two of his nominees on the other, to meet on a regular basis

        (i)   to try to build up relationships of understanding

        (ii) to explore a number of important issues such as what the Chief Rabbi's representation of us means, how rabbis from either side work together, how public statements on religious issues are best made, etc.

        (iii) to act as a monitoring body

        (iv) to develop personal contact to a point where problems could be dealt with on the telephone rather than in the columns of the Jewish press

                                              cont.....

Tony Bayfield, 27 February, 1985, setting out the agenda of the Consultative Committee meeting (4 March) on 'the need to build good personal relationships and trust' (Chapter Four, page 134)

The Sternberg Centre for Judaism
The Manor House · 80 East End Road · London N3 2SY · Tel: 01-346 2288

מרכז ליהדות
במאנור האוס Director · Rabbi A M Bayfield MA

DS.120/1   August 9th 1988

Mr. Raymond M. Goldman
R.S.G.B.

Dear Raymond,

I write to thank you very much for returning the reply slip and to
let you know that the first meeting of the new group to
monitor/improve Orthodox-Progressive relations in Anglo-Jewry will
be held at Rabbi Unterman's home (Flat 67, Wellington Court,
Wellington Road, London NW8 9TB, Tel: 01-722 1331) at 4.00-5.30
p.m. on <u>Tuesday, October 18th</u>.

Yours sincerely,

Dot Swarc

THE CENTRE FOR JEWISH EDUCATION · THE ADVANCEMENT OF JEWISH EDUCATION TRUST · AKIVA SCHOOL · COUNCIL OF REFORM AND LIBERAL RABBIS
THE LONDON MUSEUM OF JEWISH LIFE · LEO BAECK COLLEGE · MANOR HOUSE SOCIETY · MICHAEL GOULSTON EDUCATIONAL FOUNDATION
NEW NORTH LONDON SYNAGOGUE · PRO-ZION · REFORM SYNAGOGUES OF GREAT BRITAIN

Notice on behalf of Bayfield, 9 August 1988, to participants in the first meeting of the Unterman Committee 'to monitor/improve Orthodox-Progressive relations' (Chapter Four, pages 155-157)

Union of Liberal & Progressive Synagogues

The Montagu Centre, 109 Whitfield Street, London W1P 5RP   Tel: 01-580 1663   Fax: 01-436 4184

Our Reference:
Your Reference:

President
Lord Goodman C.H.

Chairman
Harold Sanderson

Vice-Presidents
Rabbi Dr. Sidney Brichto
(Exec Vice-President)
Geo. Davis
Douglas Gluckstein
Rabbi Bernard Hooker
Greta Hyman
David J. Lipman
Edgar Nathan
Cecil Reese
Clive Winston

Vice Chairmen
Neville Lewisohn
Rose Segal

Hon Treasurers
Terry Benson
Tony Sacker

Director
Rosita Rosenberg

Youth Director
Tony ...

Administrator
Sharon Silver-Myer

Past Presidents
Dr. Claude Montefiore
1902-1938
The Hon. Lily Montagu
1939-1962
Rabbi Dr. Leslie Edgar
1962-1965
Lord Cohen of Walmer
1965-1972
Eva, Marchioness of Reading
1972-1973
Malcolm Slowe
1983-1987

STATEMENT ON THE APPOINTMENT OF THE CHIEF RABBI OF THE UNITED HEBREW CONGREGATION

In view of the procedure now being implemented to appoint a successor to the present Chief Rabbi, we feel it important to clarify our own relationship to the Office of the Chief Rabbi.

The Chief Rabbi of the United Hebrew Congregation of the British Commonwealth is elected by a committee appointed by the Officers and Council of the United Synagogue. All the members of the committee are members of constituents of the United Synagogue and associated Synagogues. No other synagogue body is formally consulted in the election of the Chief Rabbi.

Accordingly it is appropriate for us to say on behalf of The Union of Liberal and Progressive Synagogues that the Chief Rabbi to be elected has no authority over our own Rabbis or lay people, nor does he represent us or speak on our behalf.

Our community appoints its own rabbinic and lay representatives and spokespersons.

This statement does not seek to detract from the status of the Chief Rabbi of the United Hebrew Congregations or his authority over his constituents, but only to reaffirm that the Jewish community is not monolothic but pluralistic in nature. In Judaism, as in other faiths, there is much diversity of belief and practice, even though the common ground far exceeds the differences.

We make this statement before the forthcoming appointment to make it clear that our relationship to the office of the Chief Rabbi is not dependent on the person who fills it. We will respect the views of the new appointee and seek to co-operate with him in our mutual efforts towards the strengthening of the Jewish Community. We hope that he too will respect the differences between his views and ours, and that those differences will not be allowed to diminish co-operative endeavour in areas of common interests and objectives.

Harold Sanderson
Chairman

Rosita Rosenberg
Director

ULPS statement on the appointment of the Chief Rabbi of the United Hebrew Congregations, 16 December, 1989, 'clarifying our own relationship' (Chapter Four, pages 166-167)

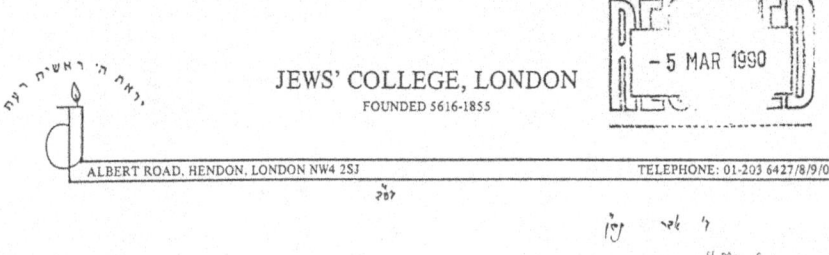

Jonathan Sacks to Brichto, 4 March, 1990, congratulating him on *Halachah* with Humility, 'the most courageous statement by a non-Orthodox Jew this century' (Chapter Five, page 176)

CHAPTER FOUR

1980–1990

Dissent and Disunity

Early in the new decade, the Chief Rabbi called upon Dayan Isaac Lerner, of the London Beth Din, to spearhead a definitive halachic response to the Reform and Progressive stance on conversion, marriage and divorce, and other religious issues.

> There is a tendency [Lerner subsequently wrote[1]] to regard the present-day reform movements benevolently as acceptable sects within Judaism. With a rather poor perception of historical perspective, they are sometimes likened to earlier sects such as the Samaritans, Sadducees and Karaites, as if this comparison confers some measure of respectability.
>
> It is imperative to recognise two basic facts. First, whatever differences those early sects may have had with those who maintained the chain of true Jewish tradition, they all alike accepted the Divine sanctity of the Written Law.... The same, unfortunately, cannot be said of Reform today. It will be shown beyond a shadow of doubt that the Scroll of the Law is for them nothing more than a ceremonial relic whose contents, far from being regarded as sacred, are subject to change and abrogation to suit every whim and fancy of social convenience.
>
> Furthermore. in spite of their common allegiance to the written word of the Torah, those early sects were all utterly and absolutely rejected by the main body of Jewry in their time.... Needless to say, the objections to those earlier sects apply with greater force to the modern Reformers, who do not accept the validity of either the Written or the Oral Law....

> The Torah law that the marriage bond can be severed only by the giving of a *get* is clearly stated in the Book of Deuteronomy (chapter 24). Without *get*, the original marriage bond remains in force. Thus, if a woman remarries without a *get*, not only are her children of the second marriage condemned to the ineradicable stigma of *mamzerut*, she and her second husband are also in constant and continual violation of this supreme prohibition of adultery, obedience to which ought to be more sacred than life itself....
>
> According to halachah, anyone who is even suspected of immoral conduct, or is professedly lax in such matters, is unacceptable as one of the two formal witnesses whose presence is essential for a valid Jewish marriage or divorce. The negative attitude of Reform clergy to the basic requirement of Torah law that divorce can only be effected by *get*, and their active condoning of the violation of this halachah by performing second marriages without *get*, apart from other considerations, is a serious reflection upon their credibility as officiants at any marriage or divorce proceedings they may conduct.
>
> The doubtful validity of Reform marriages in Jewish law was publicly pronounced by leading Orthodox rabbis more than a decade ago, and clearly in view of Reform opposition to the *get*, there is ample justification for this ruling.

Citing examples of Sabbath desecration and disregard for kashrut – 'laws that could be multiplied many times over' – Lerner then asked: 'How are we to confront Reform encroachments and alarming manifestations of militancy in demanding an ever-increasing place and voice in communal affairs?

> Certainly, we must at all times be mindful that Jewishness requires that we emulate the *middot*[2] of our Maker: 'As He is merciful, so be thou.' Every individual, however far removed, must be received with kindness and compassion: 'A sinful Israelite remains an Israelite.' Our attitude must be to explain, and hopefully to welcome back the erring ones of Israel.
>
> Whenever competent Orthodox authorities broach this theme, we may be sure that it is not motivated by a desire to castigate or condemn. For them, it is a matter of conscience. They are charged with the solemn and sacred duty to give guidance: their sole desire is to warn the unwary that Reform is not the true Jewish way of life.

While misguided individuals must be warmly welcomed back to the fold, when confronted with a collective claim for recognition of the Reform movement and its institutions as 'holy congregations' within the House of Israel, we have no alternative but to direct them to the origin of that term in the nineteenth chapter of Leviticus.

That famous passage, containing the Golden Rule of Judaism – 'Love thy neighbour as thyself' – commences with the words: 'Speak to all the *congregation* of the children of Israel, and say unto them: Ye shall be holy.' This is followed by the Torah definition of a 'holy congregation'. Among its specifications are the exhortations 'Ye shall keep my Sabbaths' (19:3); 'refrain from violating the holiness of marriage by committing adultery and kindred immoral acts' (20:10); and 'separate between the clean beast and the unclean.... Then shall ye be holy unto Me' (20:25-26).

Reform religious leaders must be reminded of the saying of the sages that Torah can be acquired only by 'faith in the wise'. Countless sages and rabbis in every age have laboured and toiled in piety and purity of heart to preserve our glorious heritage and hand it down in an unbroken chain from generation to generation. To scorn and set aside their sacred teachings by labelling the ancient rabbis as fallible, and their teachings as fanatical, calls into question the worth of the selfsame rabbinical title and authority claimed by those who do so.

To those who sincerely believe in the Divine origin of the Torah, it seems the height of human arrogance and conceit that men, however intellectually accomplished, should abrogate to themselves the right to pick and choose what they will or will not accept as valid in the teachings of the Torah. To assume such a right is surely an absolute denial of the divinity and the sanctity of the Torah.

To argue, as some do, that it is necessary to change laws to suit the conditions of the times in which we live is not only a denial of the Divine origin of the Torah, but is contrary to our whole historic experience.... Moreover, to suggest that our sole criterion must be the need to adapt to the times and climes in which we live is a complete rejection of the concept of the uniqueness of our people, which is precisely what is meant by being a 'holy congregation'.

Lerner's article brought a delayed and forceful response from Reform's Tony Bayfield, in his capacity as chairman of the movement's Assembly of Ministers: 'I accept,' he wrote,[3] 'that Orthodox Judaism finds it very difficult to view Reform as an equally valid interpretation of Jewish tradition. For Orthodox rabbis to argue passionately against the intellectual and religious assumptions of their Reform counterparts is, therefore, both reasonable and to be expected.

> However, gratuitous vilification and outrageous misstatement of fact borne, presumably, of sheer lack of knowledge is indefensible. It reduces what could be a serious and beneficial exchange of views to the level of trading insults, with all of the accompanying dangers which the history of other religious traditions so sadly exhibits.
>
> The article by Dayan Lerner is a classic example of the kind of mixture of insult and misrepresentation of fact, rather than reasoned argument, to which I refer. Let me cite just one example out of many. He states: 'The negative attitude of Reform clergy to the basic requirement of Torah law that divorce can only be effected by *get*, and their active condoning of the violation of this halachah, by performing second marriages without *get*....'
>
> This is absolutely untrue. No Reform rabbi in this country would dream of performing a second marriage without a *get*. Surely the position of Orthodoxy is not so weak that its exponents need to resort to smear tactics and veiled hints about "invalid marriages" as the only way of arguing their case.[4]

Accounting for the year's delay in publishing this rebuttal, Lerner wrote in a footnote to Bayfield's comments: 'Further to the discussion at a recent meeting of the Chief Rabbi's Cabinet regarding the letter received from the chairman of the Reform Minister's Assembly criticising my article, I most emphatically insist on the accuracy of the facts as stated, which are amply confirmed by evidence made available to the London Beth Din. Furthermore, I understand that Dov [sic] Marmur, Minister of the North Western Reform Synagogue, London, in an article in the *Journal of Reform Judaism* (USA, 1978), states that the Reform Synagogues of Great Britain allows remarriage without *get*.'

* * *

Despite Marmur's acknowledgement to Jakobovits of a 'basis for working together in the spirit of unity in diversity', tempers reignited when, in late 1982, Manchester's Beth Din issued a statement branding the Reform movement as 'a serious hazard to the identity and future of the Jewish people'.

'Recent experiences,' the dayanim declared, 'have demonstrated that a large proportion of the Jewish public is unaware of the basic differences that exist between authentic Judaism and the Reform movement. We feel that it is incumbent upon us to clarify the situation and to explain why the Reform movement cannot be considered a legitimate branch of Judaism.' Highlighting 'those areas of everyday life affected by Reform Judaism's disregard for halachah and traditional Jewish practice,' the Beth Din specified four points:

1. 'Conversions carried out by the Reform movement are not in accordance with Jewish law and are, therefore, not recognised by the Orthodox rabbinate.'
2. 'The Reform movement does not adhere to halachah as far as gittin are concerned, and a get carried out by Reform is not considered valid.'
3. 'The Reform movement carries out marriages prohibited by Jewish law.'
4. 'The Liberal movement has, without any basis in halachah, redefined the term "Jew" to include children born of a marriage where only the father is of the Jewish faith.'

The statement concluded: 'Anyone facing a dilemma regarding their personal status would be well advised to contact the Beth Din or an Orthodox minister, who will naturally treat such an inquiry both confidentially and with sympathy.'[5]

Not unnaturally, spokesmen for both the Reform and Liberal movements were quick to respond. 'The dayanim of the Manchester Beth Din,' declared Reform's Raymond Goldman, 'take it upon themselves to make pronouncements upon the validity of the Reform movement in Judaism. Is it not time that such bodies ceased sitting as judge and jury in their own cause? Should they not try following the halachic principle of "go down and see what the people do"?

> They would discover that in today's Jewish world, the vast majority of religiously affiliated Jews belong to synagogues

that variously describe themselves as Reform, Liberal, Conservative, etc. This is understandably an uncomfortable and threatening situation for those who see themselves as bastions against change.

That there are now no fewer than three established and flourishing Reform congregations in Manchester may not please the dayanim, who try to stem with words the tide which they fear may sweep them away. But it is this absence of change that places Jewish law increasingly out of touch with the real world in which the majority of Jews live, and it is the intransigent attitudes of such institutions that undermine the authority of the very Law they seek to protect. Thus it is that growing numbers of their people alter their allegiance, having realised that, for them, fossilisation is not the road to Jewish survival.

If, instead of tilting at windmills by issuing empty denunciations against those who have already rejected their authority, the dayanim were to ask themselves why this is happening; if they were to question their own confident assertion of a monopoly of all Jewish religious truth, then we might begin to create the possibility for dialogue between the various standpoints in the religious life of the community.

Such a dialogue would enhance rather than detract from the dignity of all concerned. More importantly, it would genuinely benefit the long-term health and future of Judaism and the Jewish people. Surely at a time when so many are leaving the ranks of the religiously affiliated, it is that which should have priority among our concerns.[6]

In a rabbinical response to the dayanim, Edgware Reform's Michael Leigh wrote: 'In spite of their assumptions of superiority and correctness, one wonders whether this very attitude indeed reflects authentic Judaism, their Establishment situation notwithstanding. To hide behind the Law's immutability is an easy answer, but it fails to capture the spirit of halachic Judaism which was shown by past rabbinical authorities – not least, I believe, in Anglo-Jewry.

'It so happens that the Manchester Beth Din's statement is not even correct. Reform conversions are in accordance with Jewish law, including *milah* [circumcision], *mikveh*, and a prolonged period of instruction. Furthermore, in cases where a *get* is executed amicably, great pains are taken to ensure that the procedures are halachically correct. In both cases the

Beth Din can, of course, nonetheless refuse to accept them and look for technical excuses. But Reform and many, many Jews have come to accept this situation with resignation.

'In other areas, where the husband unreasonably refuses to give a *get*, or a marriage between a Cohen and a divorcee, Reform tries to operate in the "spirit" of the Law – a spirit it, too, considers authentic – to include, not exclude, hundreds of Jews who are penalised unreasonably through no fault of their own and want so much to continue their lives in a full Jewish way.

'Reform rabbis could tell of many cases where they have had to restore faith in Judaism itself with good upstanding Jews who were shattered by the Beth Din. Anglo-Jewry must recognise that no longer has the Beth Din the monopoly as the "authentic" interpreters of Judaism, especially when it pursues a hard-line policy of exclusion rather than inclusion.'[7]

Days later, the London Beth Din's Morris Swift entered the fray when, during a Shabbat study session in Golders Green, he spoke of his 'solemn duty to state that not only the London Beth Din, but any recognised Beth Din in the world, would uphold the Manchester Beth Din's statement.

'Conversions, divorces and marriages performed by ministers of the Reform and Liberal movements have absolutely no validity under the halachah. Even if their conversions are performed with *milah* and *tevilah*, the formal acceptance by the applicant of the procedure is secondary to the admission into the faith.

'First and foremost, there must be absolute and unconditional acceptance by an applicant of the Divine authority of the Written and Oral Law. These conditions have been rejected by the Progressive movements and, equally, their marriages and divorces do not conform to the laws of Moses and Israel.'[8]

Strong support for this view came from Cyril Harris, minister of the St John's Wood (United) Synagogue, following a heated dispute on the subject with Hugo Gryn during the radio programme 'You Don't Have to be Jewish'.[9] 'If it is an offence to be indignant at those who threaten the values one holds dear,' Harris declared, 'I gladly plead guilty. Is one to remain impassive while Reform and Liberal spiritual leaders belittle so much that is precious to observant Jewry?

'During the past six months, their disparagement has reached new levels, including highly offensive and misleading statements on Jewish status, boasting in the non-Jewish press about eating non-kosher food, and injurious claims concerning the halachic validity of their marriages.

'Moreover, they are redefining vital concepts in an insidious way. Thus "unity" necessitates the co-operation of groups with opposing aims; "tolerance" implies the condonation of homosexuality; and "compassion" demands that potential converts comply with convenient rather than essential requirements. Most hurtfully, anyone who dares to challenge them out of cherished principle is, instead, immediately accused of causeless hatred.

'What is at stake in this controversy is nothing less than the future religious complexion of the community. Anglo-Jewry has always been traditional – the individual who parks his car round the corner of the synagogue blames himself for his shortcomings; the individual who parks in front blames Judaism – and only a determined fight will keep it so.

'The Jewish public must be made aware that Progressive Judaism, with its vacillating sources of authority and mutilated forms of practice, is – as the late Chief Rabbi Hertz forecast in 1925 – "a moving staircase carrying those who have taken their stand on it out of Judaism". For those, rabbis and laymen alike, who seek a Jewish future for the community, this is a time to speak out.'[10]

Speak out the *Jewish Chronicle* did, in the immediate wake of Swift's 'solemn duty':

> If there is one renewed controversy Anglo-Jewry does not need at this particular time in its history it is that of Orthodoxy v Reform and Liberal Judaism (and even in the use of nomenclature there is need for care, since some Reform leaders would be averse to a linkage with Liberal Judaism, and vice versa).
>
> The subject has surfaced from time to time – usually in proof of the old adage that to ask a *she'elah* is *treif* – but not in recent years with the intense degree of heat which has been aroused by the statement from the Manchester Beth Din, issued, it was said, because 'a large proportion of the Jewish public are unaware of the basic differences that exist between authentic Judaism and the Reform movement'.
>
> It is without question legitimate for an Orthodox Beth Din, or rabbis, to set out those practices in the Reform and Liberal tradition which are unacceptable to them because they do not conform with the halachah. It is even acceptable that they feel duty bound to do so. The question, then, is whether they should go to the further point of declaring non-Orthodox 'illegitimate'

and 'a serious hazard to the identity and future of the Jewish people'.

By doing so, is not the Beth Din moving on to very dangerous ground indeed – that of proclaiming any and every Jew who does not accept the commandments of the Torah to be 'illegitimate'? By this test, what proportion of that great mass of middle-of-road Jewry which in Britain regards itself as 'traditional', and nominally adheres to an Orthodox synagogue, might not also be condemned as 'illegitimate'?

The great Jewish Code of Laws sets out all the requirements for conversion, divorce, marriage and the conduct of Jewish life. What it does not do is proclaim any formula for those Jews who do not observe the laws as they are set down.

This, then, becomes a matter to be dealt with by Jewish ethics, and here, surely, the rabbis have to grapple with the basic Jewish principle of *Klal Israel*, the community of Israel and its unity, and *Ahavat Israel*, the love of Israel which, in this context, has traditionally been expressed by going to the utmost lengths not to exclude one group of Jews from community with another.

Would it not be more positive, within the terms of both *Klal Israel* and *Ahavat Israel*, to call on Reform and Liberal Jews to enter into a dialogue with the Orthodox community in an endeavour to close the breach in those vital matters of conversion, divorce and marriage which will strengthen our unity and love rather than, by declaring a sizeable part of Anglo-Jewry "illegitimate', thereby seeking to excommunicate it? The painful fact with which Orthodoxy has to grapple, which is indeed its primary challenge, is that – in Orthodoxy's terms – the great majority of Jews throughout the world, including the State of Israel, are not *mekablei mitzvot*, observant of the commandments of the Torah. They are not likely to become more so by being proclaimed a danger to the future of the Jewish people.[11]

Allied to his 'spirit of unity' agreement with the Chief Rabbi, Marmur added his voice to the growing controversy. 'Those who have shaped the way of the Beth Din of the Reform Synagogues of Great Britain,' he asserted, 'never set out to seek the approval of the Manchester Beth Din, Dayan Swift or their likes.

'Our aim has been to do what is right in Jewish law and Jewish tradition. We are obviously succeeding. Otherwise Anglo-Jewry would not be repeatedly subjected to the pathetic invective by those who realise that their monopoly on authenticity can no longer be maintained. The sense of panic in their statements reflects an insecurity which should trouble every truly Orthodox Jew.

'For another kind of response *is* possible. The Chief Rabbi pointed to it when he spoke at the recent conference of Jewish leaders from the Commonwealth. In the presence of rabbis from all groupings, he stressed the need for tolerance and mutual understanding. Is this a case of the right hand not knowing, or not understanding, what the head is thinking?'[12]

In an attempt from the Liberals to add action to words, Rayner offered a possible path to 'concessions', asserting that 'the recent series of unprovoked outbursts against Reform and Liberal Judaism by certain Manchester and London dayanim will have dismayed many, and done little to enhance their respect for any kind of Judaism, least of all theirs.

'We submit that no one group of rabbis is any more competent than another to judge what is and what is not "authentic" in contemporary varieties of Judaism, and that the most "authentic" are not necessarily those which preserve most precisely the legal technicalities of a bygone age, but those which express most faithfully the eternal religious and moral values of our heritage.

'In any case, religious pluralism – within the Jewish world, as well as without – is here to stay. Therefore, for everybody's sake, we had better learn to live with it by practising mutual understanding, respect and tolerance.

'To this end we invite our Orthodox colleagues to enter into a genuine dialogue with us. They will find us very respectful of their position and even willing, for the sake of unity, to make any concessions consistent with our own sincerely held convictions, if they will show a similar spirit.'[13]

A further attempt to cool the atmosphere came weeks later from King-Hamilton, whose own committee he described – not too accurately – as 'dormant, because for the last sixteen years there has happily been little call for it to meet. I am dismayed, however, at the resurgence of unjustified criticism and the puerile attacks on Progressive rabbis, both Reform and Liberal, coming from some rabbis and others in Orthodox Jewry.

'There was reason to hope that this nonsense had been finally buried when, after seemingly interminable negotiations, the Board of Deputies amended its constitution with the acquiescence of the Chief Rabbi and the

Haham, requiring it to consult the chairman of the Council of Reform and Liberal Rabbis on religious matters affecting their movements.

'Since then, the Consultative Committee on Jewish–Christian Relations, which is convened by Reform or Liberal rabbis, is regularly attended by the Chief Rabbi and other Orthodox and non-Orthodox rabbinic and lay readers, who take part also in other matters of joint concern. These meetings have taken place in an atmosphere of total amity and courtesy.

'It would seem that, in a desperate attempt to arrest the growth of the Progressive movements, some Orthodox rabbis are prepared to attack, in a most undignified manner, their Progressive colleagues in public, while acknowledging them in private behind the scenes.

'Two facts need to be stated emphatically and unequivocally: these attacks on the Progressive movement do nothing but harm to Anglo-Jewry as a whole; and, after 140 and eighty years respectively, Reform and Liberal Jewry are here to stay. The more they are attacked, the stronger they will become.'[14]

* * *

As 1982 drew to a close, and in light of the mounting disputes, Jakobovits told a closed meeting of the Chief Rabbinate Council that 'we should now for a few moments look at communal relations both outside our synagogue community and within the community as a whole.

'I have made it my policy since my installation address to draw a line – a clear line of demarcation – to indicate where we could not work with those who dissent from our religious views and who do not recognise the validity of Jewish Law and the origin of the Torah at Sinai by Divine revelation.

'There are areas where we are not in dispute, but where we are bound together by common problems and on which I have maintained that we ought to work together so as to maintain the essential fabric and cohesion of Anglo-Jewry and, by extension, of the Jewish people. It has been strongly argued, however, that by adopting this policy I have helped in the process of the erosion of the Orthodox community.

'I am the first to acknowledge that such an argument is plausible, but it needs very careful investigation to see whether there is any substance to it – which, if true, would greatly influence me in revising my guidelines and attitudes. But, as far as I can see, these arguments cannot be sustained.

Wherever I have made specific inquiries, I have invariably been given the answer by the spiritual leaders of those communities that they are not losing any members.

'I have tried to avoid public battle with the Progressives because it would otherwise give them cause to hit back, with the consequent publicity to them. I have tried to keep the situation quiet. Our job is to put our own house in order: we do not have to attack anyone, and we do not want to denounce anyone.

'There are, however, elements in the community that pick upon this approach and who believe that the strength of the Reform element is directly attributable, in part, to my neglect in fighting them. On the present situation, they have no doubt gained enormously in public exposure, and it is a source of profound anxiety and regret to me that their public spokesmen are to be found on the media – on television and radio, and in the press – disproportionately to their number.

'We are not projecting the proper position either to the Jewish community or outside. This causes me great anxiety, and I hope soon for some remedial action on our part.'[15]

Action – of a kind – was soon to follow, in the form of a Consultative Committee meeting at the Chief Rabbi's home, attended by rabbis from United Synagogue, Sephardi, Reform and Liberal congregations, and devoted mainly to 'recent unhelpful developments between Orthodoxy and Progressives'.

While Gryn – who presided – expressed ignorance as to 'why this controversy has emerged at this particular time', Jakobovits averred that 'while one may regret the fact that there are divisions in the community, they are nevertheless facts of life. There are many occasions when the Progressives make statements that are offensive to me as an Orthodox Jew, but to which I personally choose not to react.

'It is unrealistic to think that controversy will not arise from time to time: it is in the nature of religion to arouse strong and even violent emotions. While the more reasonable members of both camps will always be prepared to discuss, it is equally certain that there will always be the more extreme elements that wish to condemn.'

In a remark destined to have a practical, though by no means immediate, outcome, Kenton (United) Synagogue's Jeffrey Cohen suggested that 'there is no point in covering over cracks that exist, and there is value in airing differences in responsible debate. The problem is to find a proper forum for such discussions.'[16]

* * *

Late in the following year, during a *Jewish Chronicle* series on 'The Changing Face of British Jewry', the Chief Rabbi tackled what was headlined 'The quiet revolution':

'I realise full well,' he wrote,[17] 'that we live in an age in which pluralism is an accepted fact of national life, and in a community in which the slogan of pluralism is used by the non-traditional element in questing for religious legitimacy and acceptance.

'We now hear a persistent clamour for such legitimation under the cloak of American-imported pluralism. But let it be acknowledged by all who seek communal harmony that in this quest there can never be complete mutuality and reciprocity, and that there are inherent limits to the tolerance within pluralism.

'There is no problem for those who feel no longer constrained by the dictates of traditional Jewish law in recognising the legitimacy of those who live by its discipline. But the converse is not tenable. Those who regard the integrity of the Law as sacrosanct can hardly accord legitimacy to those sanctioning its violation; such legitimation would be making a mockery of their innermost convictions. Keeping the Law and ignoring the Law cannot be equally valid.

'In the face of the likely trends of polarisation, followed by the renewed ascendancy of the most committed elements in the community, our communal statesmanship will have to be exercised to preserve the essential cohesion of Anglo-Jewry by preventing a form of confrontation in which a single section will make demands upon the rest of the community such as it cannot as a matter of conscience meet.

'If the community is not to be riven by irreconcilable communal conflicts spilling over into areas at present at peace, we must uphold a form of tolerance which extends to recognising the fact of dissent, deems every Jew an infinitely precious brother whom we will always join in defending common Jewish interests, and encourages goodwill and solidarity, but which retains the right of traditional Jews refusing to accept, and rejecting, the claim that the beliefs of other segments are equally authentic.

'To demand equal legitimacy for all in a predominantly traditional community would brand those making the demand as intolerant, and those ready to grant it as hypocritical – since fulfilment and non-fulfilment of religious conscience can never enjoy equal status.'

A month later, addressing a gathering at the Yakar synagogue and community centre in London,[18] Jakobovits remarked that Reform Judaism today 'regards itself as a kind of halfway house to retain some Jewish loyalties among Jews who would otherwise be completely lost... The whole thrust of the rebellion has changed radically from defiant betrayal to halting compromise; from opening exit doors to making corridors and lobbies more attractive for those who feel alienated in the interior....

'At many levels, polarisation and mutual antagonism have reached a new peak. Yet in many ways we may be optimistic. Signs can already be clearly discerned that the most committed, the hardest hit in the Holocaust, are powerfully in the ascendancy.

'With this newly emerging sense of security, the community of the observant is beginning to reach out to the non-observant. The process of building bridges has begun. The *baal teshuvah* movement is a notable symptom of this significant change. The day schools are already making an ever-widening impact on the quality and direction of Jewish life. The estranged are coming home.

'But so far this welcome new phase touches only individuals, albeit now counted in thousands the world over. Meanwhile, the gap and tension between the opposing camps remain as great as ever. True bridges through dialogue and mutual understanding will be built only in the next phase, when self-assurance will have completely replaced the former fear of extinction or attenuation.

'What is needed is the capacity of a section of the community to see what makes the other side tick, what accounts for their dissent, which often arises out of ignorance. There must be an openness of mind that can come to terms with the existence of a difference of view.

'Such understanding of the views of others does not mean compromising one's own stand. It simply allows for honest and open discourse, eventually to enable those who have been alienated to be restored by argument and conviction to the common heritage of all Jews – and those who have held fast to our traditions to resume their leadership role in guiding the destinies of our people.'

Even as these words came forth, the first shots of open warfare were being prepared by the Progressives. The perceived *casus belli* was a sequence of events as detailed by Rayner and unfolded in correspondence between him and Jakobovits, and in a statement before the Council of Reform and Liberal Rabbis, the chairmanship of which Rayner had just relinquished in favour of Bayfield.

Delivering his farewell address at the Council's annual meeting,[19] Rayner prefaced his remarks with an historical perspective:

> The appointment [of Chief Rabbi Jakobovits], which opened a
> new chapter in Anglo-Jewish history, occurred at a time of rising

self-confidence on the part of the Reform and Liberal sections of the community, which had grown substantially, forged closer bonds with each other through their joint sponsorship of Leo Baeck College, and were in no mood to go on tolerating second-class citizenship in Anglo-Jewry.

The purpose of the King-Hamilton Committee, set up in 1966, was both to grasp the opportunities and to ward off the dangers of the new era: opportunities because Rabbi Jakobovits had experienced pluralism in New York, dangers because he was known to be theologically more 'right-wing' than his predecessors. But it soon became apparent to the Committee that any attempt to assert the rights of Progressive Jewry would be seriously hampered as long as it did not have a figurehead who could, when necessary, act as spokesman and representative of both movements, and it was for this reason that our Council was created.

A constitution was drawn up, amended and approved by the two rabbinic bodies, and the first meeting was held at the West London Synagogue on 11 February, 1969, with Rabbi Werner Van der Zyl as chairman and myself as vice-chairman.

In the past two years, Hugo Gryn has been chairman of the Consultative Committee on Jewish–Christian Relations, and here I must pay tribute to him for the consummate skill and the disarming bonhomie with which he has conducted the meetings of this body in the Chief Rabbi's house, by which he has won not only the respect but the trust of the motley collection of Orthodox and Progressive rabbis and lay leaders who attend the meetings.

I must say that I am not sure to what extent this set-up serves our interests – or a useful purpose; but in these days of sharpened conflict in the community, each channel of communication across the great divide ought, if possible, to be kept open, and I will do what I can.

The 'great divide' I have just referred to is, as I indicated, what brought our Council into existence in the first place. Unfortunately, the divide has grown wider in recent times, and therefore the original purpose our Council – to defend Progressive Jewry against Orthodox intolerance – has not diminished in importance. It is the least pleasant and the least productive part of the work of our Council, and we would happily give it up if we did not know that that would be the greater evil.

The present spate of attacks on Progressive Judaism began in 1982, when Dayan Chanoch Ehrentreu, then Av Beth Din in Manchester, refused to join a delegation of Manchester Jewry to greet the Pope because a Reform rabbi, Bobby Silverman, was a member of the delegation. The resulting controversy prompted the Manchester Beth Din to issue a statement condemning the Reform movement as 'a serious hazard to the identity and future of the Jewish people' which 'cannot be considered a legitimate branch of Judaism' and whose conversions and *gittin* have no validity'.[20]

This was followed up by Dayan Morris Swift, who used a Shabbat shiur at the Golders Green Synagogue to endorse the statement of the Manchester Beth Din and to add, for good measure, that 'conversions, divorces and marriages performed by ministers of the Reform and Liberal movements have absolutely no validity under the halachah'.

In December 1982, the Chief Rabbi was reported as having made a strong attack on Reform Judaism when he spoke at a rabbinic ordination and graduation ceremony at Jews' College, in the course of which he suggested that 'traditional Judaism is the only way of life for members of the community who genuinely want to consider themselves Jews'.

This prompted me to write to the *Jewish Chronicle*[21] as chairman of our Council, saying that if the Chief Rabbi 'persists in making public statements intended to be understood as denying the legitimacy of any but Orthodox Judaism, he will not only lose much of the goodwill he has won, but forfeit any right to act as spokesman or representative of British Jewry as a whole. For it is self-evident that leadership of a pluralistic community presupposes respect for the principle of pluralism.'

The Chief Rabbi replied: 'By the convictions I hold sacred, and by the authority vested in my office, I am unable to confer legitimacy on any form of Judaism which denies the divine origin of the Torah and the binding character of Jewish law';[22] and I responded by saying that we were not seeking his hechsher, but only that he should accept the fact of diversity and refrain from making denunciatory statements. I reiterated that we would welcome 'serious, sober, polite discussion of our agreements and differences... both because we think that we have a strong case and because we endorse Ben Zoma's teaching that wisdom consists in learning from all men.'[23]

Another recent episode indicative of the exacerbation of communal disharmony relates to the Jewish Welfare Board, which has always drawn a very large proportion of its support and leadership from the Progressive sector of the community.

In spite of that, its 125th anniversary was celebrated earlier this year with a commemorative service in an Orthodox synagogue (the New in Egerton Road) and conducted by an Orthodox rabbi and an Orthodox cantor, with another Orthodox rabbi, Sir Immanuel Jakobovits, giving the address. The only concession to us was that, with the consent of the Chief Rabbi, I was invited to be one of the Ark openers, an invitation which, *mipnei darchei hashalom* [because of the ways of peace] I accepted.

But when the news got out, a number of leading Orthodox rabbis, including one or two who had previously been considered relatively moderate, became so incensed against the Chief Rabbi for having made such an outrageous concession that it looked (so I was told) as if he might be toppled, and I was therefore asked to withdraw. To which I replied that I would withdraw only if the Welfare Board, which had invited me, requested it. Eventually, I received a phone call from the chairman of the Welfare Board saying, in so many words, 'We wouldn't dream of asking you to withdraw, but will you?' – which, after requesting that the matter be put in writing, I did.

But that is not quite the end of the story. For it was then suggested that I should, instead, recite *birkat hamazon* [Grace after Meals] at the dinner; whereupon the chairman of the dinner committee, Mrs Gail Ronson, came to see me to beg me to withdraw from that honour also. My reply was: 'If you are asking me to decline an invitation I have not received, I can hardly refuse; but if you are asking me to say nothing of this to the press, I can make no such promise.' Within a few hours, I received a phone call from the Welfare Board inviting me to say the berachah before the dinner; and once more, for the sake of shalom, I agreed.

The dinner took place at the Guildhall on 6 March, in the presence of the Prince and Princess of Wales. I was duly introduced as chairman of the Council of Reform and Liberal Rabbis, and *birkat hamazon* was recited by Moshe Davis, executive director of the Chief Rabbi's Office – entirely in Hebrew, by the way, presumably on the grounds that the prayers were not addressed to the royal guests but to the Supreme King of kings, the Holy One, blessed be He, who, as is well known, is a monoglot and capable only of understanding Hebrew.

'These are just a few examples [Rayner concluded] of the new aggressiveness which has manifested itself recently among the Orthodox and which prompted us, as you may recall, to hold a public meeting under the auspices of our Council here at the Manor House Centre on 31 March this year for the purpose of restating the Progressive point of view and reaffirming our commitment to it.'

* * *

The day after this address, Rayner sent Jakobovits a copy of the text, because (as he wrote in an accompanying letter) 'it contains references to you and to matters of mutual concern.... I am also writing to let you know that, on the basis of the "tradition" that the convenorship of the Joint Consultative Committee on Jewish–Christian Relations devolves on the past chairman of our Council, I was elected to take on that office in succession to Rabbi Hugo Gryn.

'I therefore wonder whether you consider that, in the present communal atmosphere, it is possible for this Committee to carry on? Maybe that makes it all the more desirable that it should. If that is your view, would you kindly let me know in due course when you feel that the Committee should be reconvened, and what its agenda should be? I am, of course, very willing to come and see you to discuss this matter if you wish.'[24]

Jakobovits replied that 'it is always illuminating to see a candid appraisal of oneself and one's world through the eyes of others. Naturally, there are assessments on which we would differ quite substantially, notably your conclusion that "the divide has grown wider in recent times". I am not sure that this is so, but if it were, I think the fault is not on one side only.

'As for the Consultative Committee, I see no reason why this should be discontinued. If you prefer to change the venue, I would be quite ready to consider any alternative suggestion. As for the agenda, this is usually set by the convenor – and, indeed, by current events.... If you feel that the very usefulness of our Committee should first be reappraised, by all means let that be done.'[25]

Expressing 'delight', in his response to the Chief Rabbi, 'that you do not think the divide has grown wider in recent times', Rayner added, however: 'I devoutly hope that you are right. I am also quite willing to believe that, in so far as there has been deterioration, the fault is not on one side only, although I cannot immediately recall any instance of public discourtesy to Orthodoxy on the part of spokesmen of Progressive Judaism. (If and when such incidents occur and the matter is brought to my attention, I will gladly take up the matter with the person concerned.)

'With regard to the Consultative Committee, I am very glad to know that you see no reason why it should not continue. That being the case, I am very willing and anxious that it should. Regarding the venue, I have sometimes wondered whether we were not imposing unduly on Lady Jakobovits by meeting at your home; but if that is no problem, I am sure I speak for all members of the Committee in saying that we could not conceive of a more agreeable setting.'[26]

* * *

In the closing days of 1984, the Chief Rabbi wrote ('in deep sorrow') to Reform's life president, the philanthropist Sir Sigmund Sternberg, querying his donation of £300,000 towards the cost of the movement's Manor House Centre in north-west London, on the condition that it was renamed the Sternberg Centre for Judaism.[27] 'Sometimes the mind will not accept what the eyes see,' Jakobovits declared, 'and I am still rubbing them in disbelief and acute distress. The questions are baffling, and seem to defy my understanding.

> Was the new Jews' College – catering for the remaining four-fifths of Anglo-Jewry – unworthy of such support? Or the CCJ, struggling to be consolidated under your stewardship with but a fraction of this amount? Or are these major bulwarks of Anglo-Jewish stability yet to receive similar benefactions? And would not prior discussions have been indicated, at least for friendship's sake?
>
> Even if these questions remain unanswered, may I at least prevail on you to use your newly earned naming rights to one constructive end? The present 'Centre for Judaism' is clearly a deliberately misleading misnomer – for reasons which are obvious and which I recently spelled out, without challenge, in a different context before the Board of Deputies.

'Centre for Progressive Judaism' or for 'Non-Traditional Judaism' would at least be honest, and would avoid affronting the bulk of a community which continues to cherish as 'Judaism' traditions and beliefs quite openly discarded by the dissidents in their official doctrine and teachings.[28]

In a three-page response, Sternberg replied, *inter alia*: 'As you know, I have been a member of the Reform movement, and Alyth Gardens [North-Western Reform Synagogue] in particular, for many years. The Manor House project is considered of the utmost importance by that synagogue.

'What is more natural than for a member of a synagogue to support its most urgent appeal? Why prior consultation should have been required, I cannot imagine. My charitable foundation has supported, and will continue to support, institutions from all quarters of Anglo-Jewry....

'Perhaps you are not aware that, although the Reform movement has played a major part in the establishment of the Manor House, the Centre is owned by an independent group of trustees, and the tenants include an Orthodox synagogue. The trustees' avowed intention is to establish a broadly based Jewish Centre.

'The omission of a qualifying adjective in the name of the Centre now becomes clear. "Progressive" would instantly associate the Centre with the Union of Liberal and Progressive Synagogues, and "Non-Traditional" is simply bizarre. The Manor House Centre is there to serve the Anglo-Jewish community as a whole, and does so in a number of ways.'

Listing the Akiva School, the Leo Baeck College, the Museum of the Jewish East End, the Spiro Institute for the Study of Jewish History and Culture, and 'an Orthodox synagogue' among its many occupants, Sternberg then added: 'What I am trying to indicate is simply that the Manor House cannot be dismissed as the work of dangerous "dissidents" attempting to subvert our community.

'Rather it is the work of deeply committed Jews with a passionate commitment to the needs of Anglo-Jewry, and a real desire to circumvent sterile political divides. Seen in these terms, it should be clear that I would want to be associated with such a project, and am now deeply proud that it will bear my name.

'I can only hope that, in the not-too-distant future, you will come and see the Centre and accept that you and I have identical interests at heart – namely, the welfare of the Jewish people in this country – and not further the division which is so apparent at present. You and Lady Jakobovits have been a reconciling force for many years, despite the bricks that have been thrown at you.'[29]

In an equally extensive response, the Chief Rabbi began by 'appreciating the care and thoughtfulness with which you have now given me your considered reply to my earlier letters.

> While I realise I will now have little chance to influence your decision, or even to elicit a response to my particular request regarding the misleading name of the new Centre, I nevertheless feel I owe you a detailed answer, and I will give it to you point by point on the items as listed in your letter.
>
> You start 'As you know, I have been a member of the Reform movement....' Frankly, I did not know, at least not until after the announcement of your donation appeared. But my ignorance or knowledge of this makes little difference, certainly not to friendships I have cherished with several Reform Jews for many years....
>
> You then continue that your Charitable Foundation has supported institutions from all quarters of Anglo-Jewry, and you proceed to list [some]. These causes, worthy as they may be, are hardly institutions of Anglo-Jewry.
>
> Next you mention the inclusion of 'an Orthodox synagogue' in the Manor House complex. You surely know yourself that if the leaders and members of that particular synagogue branch were truly Orthodox, they would not be associated with a Reform venture.
>
> Then you argue that 'Progressive' is unacceptable as honestly defining the orientation of the Centre because of its association 'with the Union of Liberal and Progressive Synagogues'. The meaning of this argument completely escapes me.
>
> After all, they are associated with the Union, Leo Baeck College and several other joint enterprises, including Manor House. So why not openly admit the association? That the Centre wishes 'to serve the Anglo-Jewish community as a whole' I do not dispute; what I do challenge is that its 'Judaism' represents, or even seeks to represent, that of anything but a small minority within the community.
>
> On the Akiva School, you tell me that 'many of the pupils come from non-Reform homes'. I wonder what kind of homes they do come from? But even that is irrelevant. What matters is, what kind of Judaism is taught there other than Reform Judaism?

Once again, honesty demands that this be made clear, and not covered up by a façade of semantic pretence.

The library (among other amenities) at Jews' College is also used by Reform Jews; does that make the college any less Orthodox, or more worthy of your support by your own criterion of 'serving the whole community'? As for the other activities you list, I do not doubt that many Orthodox Jews come there to see exhibitions, etc. Doubtless they also go to events sponsored by other denominations. All this does not alter the *religious* outlook and aims of the Centre as other than those of Reform Judaism.

I do not question the sincerity or commitment of those who support the Centre. But I do question both their integrity and their motives when they call it a 'Centre for Judaism' without any qualification – in order to procure the very participation by Orthodox elements which you mention to justify the claim that the Centre serves the whole community.

Finally, you invite me to come and see the Centre. I have had an official invitation to lecture there. In principle, I might have done so, consistent with my belief that the Torah was not given to Orthodox Jews only. But the moment I had reason to suspect that such an appearance would be used only as an Orthodox endorsement of the Centre, to vindicate the very claims you are now making for it on the grounds of Orthodox participation, I could not consider lending my name to such exploitation.

This has nothing to do with 'political divides', as you allege; my religious convictions, beliefs and practices are not a matter of politics. Nor should this be a political matter to Reform members, as it now turns out to be, if I read your letter correctly. In a nutshell, wool is being pulled over someone's eyes, either by the Progressives over yours, or by you over mine. I prefer that we both keep our vision clear.[30]

* * *

Weeks after this episode, in quick succession, two letters from Bayfield reached the Chief Rabbi's desk – one a so-called 'draft' (revealed by a third-party confidant), and the second the definitive text, sent by Bayfield himself in his capacity as chairman of the Council of Reform and Liberal Rabbis.

In the former, Bayfield wrote that he was 'profoundly saddened by the apparent deterioration in relations between the United Synagogue and our section of the Jewish community. Your reported letter to your rabbinic colleagues;[31] recent events at the Board of Deputies; frequent intemperate outbursts from Rabbi Harris and others – all give the clearest possible evidence of a concerted attempt to isolate and undermine the institution of Progressive Judaism in Britain.

'I have been led inexorably to the conclusion that the claim of the Office of the Chief Rabbi to represent all of Anglo-Jewry is now a fiction. It would seem to be more honest to face the fact that you, as leader of the United Hebrew Congregations, represent only indiscriminate opposition to everything that I and my colleagues stand for.

'Accordingly, and with much regret, I intend to write to *The Times* and the *Jewish Chronicle*, informing them that you do not represent all sections of Anglo-Jewry, and inviting people and institutions wishing for representation from our section of the community to contact the chairman of the Council of Reform and Liberal Rabbis. I further intend to seek representation by the chairman of the Council as president or patron on all communal bodies where this situation does not already obtain – for example, on the Council of Christians and Jews.'[32]

In a message to his confidant, the Chief Rabbi wrote: 'Since you were thoughtful enough to send me a preview of the draft Bayfield letter, I want to reciprocate with a preview of what I would consider replying if I would ever receive such an ill-tempered missive.

'That the gentleman feels highly irritated I can understand. After all, he invited me to lecture at Manor House. As he knew, I had no objection in principle and had spoken on Reform platforms in the past, consistent with my belief that the Torah was not given to Orthodox Jews only. But I suspected that political capital would be made out of my acceptance, and hence had to decline. My fear of such exploitation has now been proved....

> Now [Jakobovits continued] some comments on points made in his planned letter: '... the apparent deterioration in relations'. I dispute this. On the contrary, in the whole of Anglo-Jewish history, the Reformers have never enjoyed the consideration and communal acknowledgement they now have, thanks to policies I have consistently pursued. Any blame for lately disturbing this relationship rests entirely with them, now making inflated demands and claims which the Orthodox majority cannot accept with resignation....
>
> '... the claim... of the Chief Rabbi to represent all of Anglo-Jewry is now a fiction.' Four-fifths of all Jews and most non-Jews are likely to think otherwise, and that is good enough for me.

The only true sentence in the letter, except one word, is this: '... you, as leader of the United Hebrew Congregations, represent only indiscriminate (?) opposition to everything that I and my colleagues stand for.' In that capacity, that is obviously so, and I have never claimed differently, just as I expect you to represent opposition to everything that I and my colleagues stand for.

The suggested letter to *The Times* – this is a free country. If you now intend to drag our internal religious arguments into the public, and dispute my spokesmanship for the whole community on matters over which we have been and continue to be united (on other matters I have never professed such spokesmanship), I cannot stop you. But the community will draw its conclusions as to who promotes unity and who destroys it. And readers of *The Times* will hardly see my role differently from what it has been for the past eighteen years. So this is a threat to their reputation rather than mine.

'Council of Christians and Jews.' The Progressives are quite at liberty to put up a rival Jewish president for election. Indeed, they can be sure that I will stand neither with nor against them, for I will be redundant and simply bow out. It will not affect my personal rapport with Church and Government leaders, but it may well mean the collapse of the CCJ, and once again the community will know whom to blame.

It was precisely when such a second Jewish CCJ president was last suggested, and the enormous damage was realised in such a proposal, that a discreet Consultative Committee was set up under Progressive convenorship, and high-level spiritual and lay representation from all camps. It has worked usefully and on friendly terms over the years. I cannot see why these channels should not again be used to iron out any avoidable causes of conflict, as we have so successfully done in the past.

The Progressives will have to accept that it was not the Orthodox who either started religious dissension in Anglo-Jewry or now consider wrecking communal unity in areas on which we were hitherto united; that traditional Jews continue to make up the great majority of the community and, if challenged, are bound to set a limit to the demands of the Progressives, already grossly over-represented in the media and on the Board [of Deputies] and its committees; and that I am not only 'Chief' speaking for the whole community on general matters, but also 'Rabbi', even more concerned to preserve the religious stability of the community than its external unity. For, without that stability, Jewish survival is both questionable and meaningless.[33]

In place of his 'draft letter' to the Chief Rabbi, Bayfield rephrased aspects of his 'personal and confidential note' – sent, he added, 'because I am confronted by a growing problem' – and concluded that he was 'now under considerable pressure, as chairman of the Council of Reform and Liberal Rabbis, to write to *The Times* and the BBC publicly stating that you no longer represent our section of the Jewish community.

'I am obviously very loathe to take such a step, which would have far-reaching consequences. I would very much like to have an opportunity of discussing the matter with you – if not personally, at least in a small and private gathering which can look with some degree of calmness before irrevocable public steps are taken.'[34]

Jakobovits' response was brief and pointed: 'My most effective response to your astounding threat would be to ignore it and let you act as you wish. But since I do not share your apparent indifference to the interests of Anglo-Jewry, I enclose herewith a copy of a detailed reply prepared when I first heard of your intention.

'I will add only this. You mention two key questions: first, "How can anyone who is so publicly opposed to us still represent us?" I never knew I had, or required, your mandate to speak for the whole community. I believe the proportion of my support among the entire community is larger than the Prime Minister's among the people she represents! Second, "How can we tolerate an increasing number of public statements with which we disagree... ?"

'No one has asked you to "tolerate" anything I state. Any public statements I make on behalf of the community I do my best to ensure they represent all sections. But in statements on Judaism I claim no communal endorsement, and I am accountable only to my conscience – and certainly not to you, so long as we subscribe to fundamentally opposed beliefs and practices.

'My stand has remained consistent for the past eighteen years, and you can be sure it will so continue, however sharply you may vary yours, as you have done in recent months. Withal, I am always ready to discuss personally any matter troubling you and your colleagues.'

Attached to this letter was a note, 'for your information, with the compliments of the Chief Rabbi:

'1. If I shared your indifference to the communal weal, I would not reply but simply tell you "Go ahead!" 2. I am always ready to discuss problems troubling you and your colleagues, including your "two key issues". 3. I would have thought you have enough problems in your own ranks at this time other than threatening me with blackmail for being loyal to traditions which some of your fraternity have betrayed!'[35]

Five days later, after a meeting with the Chief Rabbi aimed at reducing tensions, Hugo Gryn wrote to Jakobovits: 'Again, many thanks to you and your wife for your hospitality – in every sense. I have already contacted those of my colleagues most directly involved in present and future discussions.

'All of them are looking forward to a meeting of the Consultative Committee and are as hopeful as are you and I that that meeting, and subsequent get-togethers, will have the effect of improving that part of the climate which it is in our power to improve. I hope that my role as a "dove" may result in actual and refreshing oil, and not just in mouthing a symbolic branch.'[36]

On the same day, Bayfield replied to the Chief Rabbi's letter in plaintive terms.[37] 'I am most distressed,' he began, 'that you should have seen a letter which it was decided not to send, and I am equally sorry that you should be so obviously upset. However, I am pleased that you wish to see the Consultative Committee reconvened, and I know that Rabbi John Rayner is in the process of fixing a meeting. I won't try to answer each of the points raised by you, but rather to define a brief agenda for such a meeting.

> At the outset, however, I should like to clarify two issues. First, this is not in any way a personal matter. Both letters reflect the real concerns of the entire executive of the Council of Reform and Liberal Rabbis and would be endorsed by almost every Reform and Liberal rabbi in this country. It isn't a matter of personal self-seeking or hot-headedness, but of widely felt and deep anxieties.
>
> Secondly, I have the distinct impression that events are being coloured by your perception that we are seeking legitimacy. Such a perception has no basis in reality whatsoever. The Progressive movement sees itself as part of the mainstream of Judaism – as an important branch within the tree of Judaism – and seeks legitimacy from no other branch. Incidentally, our reason for calling the Manor House a Centre for Judaism, with no qualifying adjective, is a direct reflection of that view of ourselves as part of the mainstream of Judaism.

May I now try to clarify three issues which I believe should form the agenda of our meeting or series of meetings:

1. Acrimony

It would be very helpful if we could arrive at an effective agreement to try to eradicate generalised abuse and gratuitous insults from sermons, letters and public statements on both sides. If we can restrict discussions to specific issues, we would go a long way to avoid the deep personal wounds that unnecessary remarks cause. While there are faults on our side which we must work to eliminate, I wonder whether you realise just how much 'alien religion and its priests' and 'the affliction of Reform' hurt. They are unhelpful in the mouth of anyone; they are impossible to accept from someone who, at certain levels, publicly represents us.

Issue I: Can we replace invective by reasoned discussion?

2. Co-operation

When I spoke to you about the possibility of your coming to the Manor House to speak on an area of medical ethics, I had in mind a seminar on different attitudes to the profound religious and moral questions raised by the Warnock Report.[38] Rabbi Rayner's evidence to that committee and your differing views pave the way for a vital discussion. In trying to develop a major Jewish Centre at the Manor House, nothing could be more important than ensuring that we undertake discussion on the most important issues of Torah.

While understanding your response that other people might make capital out of your visit, I am still concerned that platforms for discussion and co-operation should exist. A number of Orthodox rabbis do contribute to our work and we do not, as a rule, disclose their names in order to further the process of dialogue unhindered.

I believe that we have a great deal to learn from each other. I also believe that it is vital for the future of Anglo-Jewry that we are able to work together. How can we do so without giving rise to the fear that such co-operation is bestowing some kind of legitimacy upon us? How can we meet without such meetings always having to take place 'away' or on neutral territory?

Issue II: How can we discuss, debate and work together as rabbis without compromising each other's positions?

3. Consultation

Perhaps the most vexed of the three issues is that of consultation. The Council of Reform and Liberal Rabbis represents a substantial body of rabbinic opinion. We believe that we speak not only on behalf of Jews, but in the name of Judaism, if indeed that distinction is valid.... We do not expect you to voice our views when they differ from yours. We certainly would not expect you to give credence to opinions which you regard as a breach of halachah, but which we regard as an expression of halachah. But when we wish to express views, how do we do so?

How do we deal with Government bodies and others wishing to consult the Jewish community? How do we deal with public expressions of 'the Jewish point of view'? We do not wish to paralyse the community, and we certainly have no right to impair your ability to speak on behalf of Orthodox Judaism. By the same token, as spokesmen for the non-Orthodox sector, we must feel free to express what are the legitimate views of our sector of the community.

Issue III: How do we deal with the issue of consultation and the public expression of diverse Jewish points of view?

'May I conclude [wrote Bayfield] by saying that if we can resolve these three matters to everyone's satisfaction, then I honestly believe that considerable good will have come out of the present tense situation. The security and stability of a family is not secured by a pretence of spurious unity, but rather by being able to accept the existence of differing views and opinions and still remain a cohesive, caring unit. Such is our sincere aim, and I hope that the above agenda can pave the way for a higher degree of communal harmony than presently exists.'

* * *

The outcome of these conciliatory efforts was the establishment of what came to be known as the Unterman Committee, named after its first chairman, Marble Arch Synagogue's Maurice Unterman,[39] and operating as a close-knit branch of the Consultative Committee. Again gathering at the

Chief Rabbi's home, its meetings were destined to be conducted in utmost secrecy, not revealed to the outside world until well after Jakobovits had left office – and then in only the briefest of terms.

Even before the ink had dried on the formal agreement that launched the committee, a background account, an interview with Jakobovits, and a strong appeal for unity appeared in the national and Jewish press. Under the heading 'More kosher than others', *The Economist* wrote:

> Imagine the Archbishop of Canterbury telling *The Times* that non-conformists had caused 'grievous damage' to the most sacred Christian beliefs, had published things 'grossly offensive' to Anglicans, shown 'utter disregard' for the well-being and reputation of Britain's Christian minority, and had brought 'untold misery' to individuals through a lax approach to marriage and divorce. Then for 'Christian' read 'Jewish', change a few other words, and you have the highlights of a *Jewish Chronicle* interview with the Chief Rabbi, Sir Immanuel Jakobovits, which has set religious Anglo-Jewry by the ears.
>
> Only the highlights, yes. The Chief Rabbi's main point was the sober truth that, as leader of the Orthodox – the largest segment of Britain's Jews – he is happy to work with the Progressive (Liberal and Reform) minorities on issues of common Jewish concern, but that he cannot sacrifice fundamental beliefs to make that easier. Yet even this, compared with the brotherly syrup of church ecumenism, measures the divisions in the Jewish community....
>
> A compromise is probably near. That, though, will not resolve a much sharper argument. The Chief Rabbi chose the moment to give new advice to Orthodox rabbis not to join Progressive ones in activities that might seem to validate their varieties of Judaism as legitimate.... The Progressives do not expect him to abandon his beliefs. But if they are to go on recognising him as spokesman for the whole community, they argue, he must behave like it.[40]

In an interview the previous week,[41] Jakobovits had asserted that 'it is a perversion of the truth to allege that the Orthodox side in recent months has introduced a degree of bitterness or divisiveness that has accelerated the polarisation of the community. Yes, I will admit, there is polarisation, not just in this country. It is worldwide. It is a sad feature of Jewish life, and I have often publicly taken a stand to try and strengthen the middle ground and build bridges of understanding.

'But this is not something you can lay purely at the feet of the Orthodox, let alone the central Orthodox. What has happened in very recent times has been an aggressiveness on the part of the Progressives, making claims on the rest of the community, including my Office....

'The community should know that if there is any threat of stirring up communal disunity beyond the truly internal religious confines, such a threat comes solely from the Progressives. They have recently published in the national press articles and letters grossly offensive to the Orthodox community; some of their leaders have called for breaking up such co-operation as has for years existed; and, in utter disregard for the well-being and reputation of Anglo-Jewry, they now warn that they may carry the battle into the public arena – and into areas on which we have been, and continue to be, united as Jews.'

Alongside these remarks came a forceful leading article in the *Jewish Chronicle*.[42] Opening with a comparison to disputes within the churches, it added: 'The likelihood of their ever agreeing remains remote, but the effort is at least being made to establish a *modus vivendi*.

> In Anglo-Jewry, at the moment, we seem bent on tearing apart what measure of co-operation exists. We are in real danger of being riven by a war of religion more damaging in its implications than the so-called 'Jacobs Affair' of twenty years ago.
>
> What is threatened is not only the splitting of the community into at least two bitterly hostile camps, but the opening of a communal divide which will paralyse joint action beyond the religious sphere in support of causes vital to all of us, including Israel, Soviet Jewry and communal defence.
>
> Advocates on both sides are barricading themselves behind superstructures of words from which they will find it difficult to extricate themselves. The no man's land opening up between them is fertile ground for mischief-makers on the peripheries of both camps who would take a delight in turning the divide into an unbridgeable void. Anglo-Jewry cannot be carved up in this way without fragmenting the whole.
>
> The arguments on both sides have been rehearsed in these columns over the past few weeks, and the position of the Chief Rabbinate is made crystal clear in the interview on another page with Sir Immanuel Jakobovits. It should surprise no one that the Chief Rabbi cannot accept that there are two or more brands of

authentic Judaism and that, as someone dedicated to upholding the code of Jewish law as enshrined in the halachah, the permissiveness of non-Orthodox Judaism is an affront to the belief he proclaims.

At the same time, it must also be accepted that those who practise the Progressive form of Judaism do so with no less sincerity than their Orthodox brothers. It is only to be expected that, as they begin to feel their muscle in terms of numbers and participation in Anglo-Jewish organisations, they will demand the recognition they feel is their due, especially at a time when the major organ of central Orthodoxy, the United Synagogue, is assuming a much more vigorous role in many areas of communal activity.

The *status quo* to which the Chief Rabbi refers has worked because both sides have accepted it. It has broken down when one of the parties to it rejects it. What is needed now, and speedily, before the barriers hastily being constructed become fortresses, is some new formula for the secular expression of religious divergence which, while it will not demand of halachically-motivated Jews that they renege on the deeply revered tenets of their faith, will permit a sizeable minority in Anglo-Jewry to give formalised expression to its view.

It should not be beyond the wit of religious and lay leaders of goodwill to come up with a form of understanding which, while it will not blur the fundamental differences between the two sides, will preserve the sense of *Knesset Israel*, the whole congregation of Israel, in which alone lies the strength of Anglo-Jewry to tackle the many problems which it confronts in the wider arena.

In response to these challenges, the rabbinical heads of the Reform and Liberal movements set out their stalls. As chairman of the Council of Reform and Liberal Rabbis, Bayfield wrote:[43]

Responsible communal leadership surely demands a positive reaction to last week's excellent editorial when it contends that 'it should not be beyond the wit of religious and lay leaders of goodwill to come up with a form of understanding which, while it will not blur fundamental differences... will preserve the sense of *Knesset Yisrael*.

To begin to espouse that principle requires, however, the acceptance of certain realities without which the seeming common-sense nature of the statement is unlikely to be translated into the reality of communal unity. Orthodoxy, whether it be Orthodox Judaism, Roman Catholicism or Islam, is prone to see any departure from its central body of dogma as heresy. That is the dichotomy which lies at the heart of the office of Chief Rabbi.

It makes it extremely difficult, even for someone as moderate by inclination as Sir Immanuel Jakobovits, to speak on behalf of a community where one in five synagogue members belongs to a Reform or Liberal congregation, and where a far greater number, while paying their subscriptions to the United Synagogue, find themselves more in sympathy with non-Orthodox views than with an establishment that has moved substantially to the Right.

Indeed, it is not strictly accurate for Sir Immanuel to speak of 'polarisation', as he did in his interview, because, in fact, the movements we represent have come steadily to occupy more of the middle ground.

The dichotomy at the heart of the Office of Chief Rabbi is also expressed in the dual role of 'head of majority party' and 'head of state'. What may or may not be acceptable in the mouth of the religious leader of the United Synagogue can be totally unacceptable in the mouth of someone who seeks to represent us all. Precisely those actions which sit more easily with the former than the latter role have precipitated the constitutional crisis which is now upon us.

What, then, is to be done to avoid creative energies being dissipated in sterile dissension? Is it possible for the Orthodox (the United Synagogue and other bodies to the Right of that venerable institution) and for the nonconformists (Reform, Liberal, Progressive, Conservative or other adjectival flag) to accept that there are, and will continue to be, a variety of ways in which the members of this community choose to serve God and to make their varying contributions to Jewish survival and revival?

Your interviewer last week rightly dismissed the possibility of Progressive Jews taking the unlikely course of embracing Orthodoxy. In that situation, can we preserve the institution of the Chief Rabbinate, the undoubted value of an authoritative and respected voice, able to address the non-Jewish world in the name of the whole Jewish community and, in doing so, can we also prevent that other great institution, the Board of Deputies, from being diverted from its central function into destructive internecine strife? In order to do this:

1. The Jewish community must accept, as has the Christian world, that in an irreligious world, both Orthodoxy and non-conformity are on the same side; their battles bring comfort only to those who deride religious faith.
2. Having accepted this reality, we have to develop ways of expressing ourselves with mutual respect, and the recognition that neither side has a monopoly of sincerity.
3. Surely there has to be a choice as to whether the Chief Rabbinate is to be used primarily as representing the whole of British Jewry, or is to be solely the official voice of the Orthodox in the community.

There are a few specific points made by the Chief Rabbi last week that should not go unchallenged, and one asks why it is that certain misrepresentations are constantly repeated to bolster the Orthodox argument against the Progressives.

If 'it is a perversion of the truth to allege that the Orthodox side... has introduced a degree of bitterness or divisiveness', why did the United Synagogue, exhorted by the Chief Rabbi, suddenly move to reduce that limited measure of recognition accorded under Clause 74 [the former Clause 43] to the Progressives by the Board of Deputies in 1971 after years of negotiations?[44]

Why is it necessary to pressure Orthodox rabbis to toe the line in following a policy of 'non-fraternisation'? Given that Reform and Liberal reasoning is grounded in a rejection of Orthodox fundamentalism, and wholly committed to pluralism, it really is standing reason on its head to suggest that Reform leaders might feel some sense of endorsement if Orthodox Jews contribute to our journals or debate on common platforms.

One is left with the conclusion that Orthodox leaders derive an illusory comfort from telling themselves that the Progressives are anxious for their 'hechsher'. Since it is not true, abandoning this particular illusion would remove the fear of guilt by association and allow normal discussion to take place between groups of differing viewpoints, as it would in any other discipline.

The so-called 'aggressiveness of the Progressives' is a reference to the fact that as one-quarter of synagogue-affiliated Jews in this country, we have the chutzpah to believe that we are no longer an insignificant voice in the community and, having both a viewpoint and a substantial constituency, are entitled to be heard. The desire of a minority to be heard is a belief in democracy and should not be construed as aggression.

The interview contained two pieces of gross misrepresentation. First was the suggestion that we are less concerned than any other section for the freedoms of Jews. The mischievous example given was that we might require the Board [of Deputies] to state that 'a minority don't care for a second day [of the festivals] and don't mind if your schools require children to attend on the second day'.

It isn't true that we 'don't care' about the second days of yomtov on the *shalosh regalim* [three foot-festivals]. We conscientiously believe that they are as much an anachronism here as in the State of Israel, but we believe with equal passion and conscience in the right of Orthodox Jews to observe such days.

The derisive wording used in the example shows the lack of mutual respect which continually bedevils the possibility of serious debate. Furthermore, as repeatedly stated by our spokesmen in your columns, we have not asked – and we do not ask – that the Board of Deputies actively puts forward the opinion of the minority. We simply ask that the Board lets it be known, when and where necessary, that the view provided by the Board is that of its ecclesiastical authorities, but that the Board also represents those not under their aegis.

Lastly, we reject absolutely the charge of 'reckless irresponsibility' in matters relating to divorce and conversion. The statement that those who use our rabbinic bodies 'act in ignorance and are being misled' is false. All who come to us for our help are required to sign a document declaring that they are fully aware, and have fully understood, the implications of the fact that most Orthodox authorities do not recognise our procedures even when they follow Orthodox halachah.

The challenge of 'irresponsibility' might well be thrown back at those who seemingly feel no need to react to the rate of intermarriage. Many of those who seek our help are affiliated to Orthodox synagogues and are directed to us by their rabbis.

Bayfield concluded 'by responding to your call for unity, and pledging our support for all statements and actions which bring such unity to our community, while recognising and respecting its diversity'.

Brichto likewise responded to the *Jewish Chronicle* challenge. 'The Chief Rabbi,' he wrote, 'will confirm that I was instrumental in forging those links between the Progressives and the Orthodox which have allowed the community to enjoy a "gentleman's agreement which has worked splendidly over eighteen years".

> The essence of this 'gentleman's agreement' was to avoid confrontation and not to cause unnecessary and gratuitous offence. We avoided doing what your constructive leader astutely notes is happening today – that is, that 'advocates on both sides are barricading themselves behind superstructures of words from which they will find it difficult to extricate themselves'.
>
> Of course there were lapses in good taste. On occasion, the Chief Rabbi would insult Progressive Judaism at a shiur. Equally, a leading Liberal rabbi would condemn Orthodoxy as medievalism. Generally, however, we kept our negative thoughts about each other away from the public arena.
>
> In a spirit of mutual respect, we Progressive Jews stopped demanding that our rabbis officiate at Yom Ha'atzmaut services in Orthodox synagogues, and the Chief Rabbi agreed that there should cease to be a central service to mark the occasion.
>
> In this same spirit, we agreed to what is now Clause 74 of the constitution of the Board of Deputies, which gave the chairmen of the Reform and Liberal Rabbinic Assemblies consultative status without threatening the role of the Chief Rabbi.
>
> We also had numerous private meetings in which we attempted to overcome the problems posed by our different attitudes and practices in regard to Jewish status and marriage and divorce. These talks did not succeed, but they were motivated by a love for *Klal Yisrael* and were conducted with great respect for each other's views.

'Unfortunately', concluded Brichto, 'the "gentleman's agreement" has been broken because we have ceased to be sensitive to each other's cherished convictions, and we doubt each other's sincerity. I, for one, would be prepared to start again and come up with what you in your leader so wisely urge – "a form of understanding which, while it will not blur the fundamental differences between the two sides, will preserve the sense of *Knesset Israel*, the whole congregation of Israel.'[45]

* * *

A fortnight later, Rayner sent the following letter to the Chief Rabbi:[46]

> At a meeting of the executive committee of the Council of Reform and Liberal Rabbis yesterday, we spent some time reviewing 'the communal situation' and considering the meeting [of the Consultative Committee] scheduled for 4 March. I thought I should let you know what, in the light of that discussion, I have in mind by way of an 'agenda'.
>
> I should like to begin the meeting by saying a word of appreciation about my predecessor, Rabbi Hugo Gryn, which you might wish to endorse. Then I think we should spend a few minutes (not more than five or ten) reminding ourselves about the genesis and function of the Consultative Committee, and clarifying the question of its composition.
>
> On function, I propose to submit that the committee should continue, normally, to deal with Jewish–Christian relations only, but that it may nevertheless be useful – once in a long while, one hopes – to use the opportunity of such a gathering for the exchange of thoughts and feelings about any serious issues that may have arisen in internal Anglo-Jewish relations.
>
> I shall then say that we find ourselves in such a situation and that the present meeting is – exceptionally – to be devoted to that topic only: not with a view to reaching any decisions (we are not that kind of body, and therefore no one need feel under any pressure to agree or not to agree to anything on behalf of themselves or any organisation they may feel they must represent), but merely in order that we may reach a better understanding.
>
> I think we should then allow ourselves a strictly limited period (half an hour at the most) hearing how each 'side' sees the events (recent ones only) which have led up to the present situation, for which purpose I would ask first you, then Tony Bayfield as chairman of the Committee, to give a brief review; after which I would try to persuade the gathering to desist from any counter-questioning or counter-commenting and to move straight on to the main business, which concerns the future, not the past.

Thereafter, the discussion should be based, I suggest, on Rabbi Unterman's draft memorandum, which I will distribute to all present, and the purpose of which I would sum up as an attempt to make a fresh start in intra-communal relations, based on an undertaking by the leaders of both 'sides' to abstain from mutual denigration or provocation in the public media.

There will then follow a general discussion in the course of which it will, I hope, become apparent that all are willing to endorse Rabbi Unterman's draft, with or without minor amendments. At some stage, Rabbi Bayfield will wish to make a proposal which involves an amendment to Rabbi Unterman's last phrase.

His [Rabbi Bayfield's] view, shared by the executive of the Committee, is that what is needed is a little more than just 'monitoring', namely a small committee that will, in the course of time, explore and define in some detail (a) what are the rules we must observe so that we may on occasion publicly discuss divergent views without provoking a crisis; and (b) what possibilities there are of joint activities which would allow us to co-operate without raising the spectre of reciprocal 'recognition'.

What is envisaged is a committee of four (two from each 'side'), or at the most six, and if this is agreeable to you, you may wish to give some thought to its membership, which I hope would include yourself as well as the chairman of the Consultative Committee. Please let me know if you wish the above 'plan' for the meeting to be modified in any way.

I certainly hope that the meeting will help to bring about a new period of communal peace, not only in the sense of a 'non-aggression pact', but of shalom in a positive sense. It is good to know, as I do, that you share that hope.

Attached to Rayner's letter was a 'Draft Proposal by Rabbi Maurice Unterman':

That a 'moratorium' on statements of a recriminatory or discourteous nature should be observed by the leadership of the Orthodox and Progressive communities, and efforts made internally by each community for the exercise of a discipline of propriety, on the widest possible scale; that a spirit of fellowship between the leadership at several levels be inaugurated for the friendly discussion of such differences as may occur from time to time, whereby problems may be resolved or else left as matters upon which 'we agree to disagree' amicably; and, to avoid a further recurrence of the confrontation of misunderstanding, each community should appoint an ecclesiastical liaison to monitor jointly the progress and conduct of the improved relationship.

A copy of the 'Draft Proposal' had already reached Jakobovits directly from Unterman, who had added the comment: 'Herewith, as promised, the note I handed to Rabbi Rayner, with which, he said, "I agree 100 per cent."'[47]

On the day Rayner dispatched his suggestions to Jakobovits, Bayfield sent a memorandum to four of his colleagues. Relating that he, Gryn and Rayner had had private meetings with the Chief Rabbi over recent days, he described the mood as 'one of conciliation. We have impressed upon him the need to build good personal relationships and trust, and to tackle certain basic issues. Both of these points are accepted.

> The executive of the Council of Reform and Liberal Rabbis met last night and came to the following conclusions: that the Unterman statement should be warmly welcomed; and that the last two lines should be elaborated.
>
> We would like to see established a small ecclesiastical liaison committee of six – myself, Hugo Gryn and John Rayner on our side, the Chief Rabbi and two of his nominees on the other, to meet on a regular basis to try to build up relationships of understanding; to explore a number of important issues, such as what the Chief Rabbi's representation of us means, how rabbis from either side work together, how public statements on religious issues are best made, etc.; to act as a monitoring body; and to develop personal contact to a point where problems could be dealt with on the telephone rather than in the columns of the Jewish press.
>
> This would enable the Consultative Committee to be restored to its proper role as a forum for discussing matters regarding our relationship with the Christian world. It would also help to clarify for the Chief Rabbi with whom actually he should deal. Some of the interventions which have been going on have complicated matters, especially in a situation where the concept of a democratically elected chairman of the Council of Reform and Liberal Rabbis is a foreign one to the Orthodox leadership.

Preliminary conversations have suggested that the above is acceptable to the Chief Rabbi. John Rayner will be phoning him to confirm this before the meeting. It is very much the wish of the Council of Reform and Liberal Rabbis executive that 4 March [subsequently changed to 5 March] is not excessively recriminatory; so full of false bonhomie and papering-over of cracks that no forum for looking at real issues is created; nor a meeting which makes hurried decisions.

We suggest that the lay leadership may also like to set up a forum for establishing contact and building understanding.[48]

* * *

The minutes of the inaugural meeting of the Unterman Committee,[49] held in the absence of its namesake (who was indisposed), did not reflect comfortably the aspirations of Bayfield and his colleagues. Opening the gathering, Rayner remarked that its purpose was 'not designed to deal with the normal business of the group, but rather to consider the recent dissension in the community and, while accepting the inevitability of clashes of opinion from time to time, to try to recreate a satisfactory *modus vivendi*'.

Called upon 'to present his view of the recent occurrences', the Chief Rabbi stated that two matters of consultation had recently arisen on which his view and that of the Progressives had differed. 'This resulted in the Board of Deputies not conveying any comment to the Government departments concerned [on wider national issues], giving rise to a subsequent attempt to prevent any recurrence by the introduction of a Code of Practice.

'Another cause has been that, as a result of pressure from members of my Cabinet, who felt that there were instances wherein the participation of Orthodox rabbis was being represented as an endorsement of the non-Orthodox position, I had circulated a memorandum to my colleagues, not saying that they should not appear on joint platforms, but asking them to ensure that they did not place themselves in false positions. Our objectives should be to work together where we can agree, and to agree to differ where we cannot.'

Bayfield replied by pointing to recent changes in Clause 74 of the Deputies' constitution, 'where it was felt that there was an attempt to take away that limited recognition which had been achieved in 1971. This was exacerbated by a number of letters, both private and public, which not only repeated old canards, but portrayed a level of hostility incompatible with harmonious relationships. The real question is how to avoid such situations arising in the future.'

Chapter Four

There was a need, said Bayfield, to establish a forum 'in which the leadership of both sides can get to know each other as people and build up a measure of trust.... The Consultative Committee is perhaps not the best body for such contact: it is far too large, and a new forum for contact should be considered.'

Rayner remarked that 'the minimum objective should be to avoid mutual denigration and provocation. The ideal would be an *entente cordiale*, but at least we should try to achieve a "non-aggression pact", with the Progressives accepting pluralism *de jure* and the Orthodox accepting it *de facto*'.

That the gathering remained indecisive was evident from its closing observations. 'It was suggested [noted the minutes] that perhaps a small group should get together to present a plan to the next meeting. The chairman felt that it would be valuable for people to go away and think over what they had heard, and come back at the next meeting to try to formulate some clear ideas. A date for a further meeting was not fixed, but it was suggested that it would be as well if the Committee were to arrange to meet at regular intervals.'

The closest the outside world came to learning of these moves was evident some weeks later, when the *Jewish Chronicle* reported that 'discreet talks have been held in the past few months between Orthodox and Progressive leaders in an attempt to promote a better understanding between them and to avoid public bickering.

'Rabbi Maurice Unterman, who has been acting on behalf of the Chief Rabbi, said this week that he had had a number of "cordial" meetings with Rabbi John Rayner and Rabbi Tony Bayfield. The two sides had "crystallised" their thinking and had agreed to co-operate "in a spirit of mutual respect" in those areas of concern in which they could unite for the well-being of the community.

'Rabbi Bayfield commented: "There are, of course, differences between the two sectors of the community, but work will continue on clarifying and solving the problems which cause these differences to spill over into public acrimony. Anglo-Jewry can ill afford to spend time and resources on unedifying displays of inter-community strife, and it is our hope that such episodes are now behind us."'

The meetings had come to light, the JC reported,[50] 'as a result of comments made last week by Mr Jack Wolkind, former chief executive of Tower Hamlets'.

Unaware of the precise discussions at the March meeting, but fully aware of the circumstances for which talks had been called, Wolkind – the author of a report some years earlier on the Board of Deputies – had decided to enter the fray. Delivering a lecture on 'London and its Jewish Community', he observed:

> In a civilised society, it ought to be possible to differ without either of the differing parties abusively questioning the sincerity of the other. It is, I think, important not to overstate the frequency of this problem.
>
> I am not suggesting that we spend all our energies and time questioning the sincerity and *bona fides* of those with whom we disagree, but whenever it occurs, it is not only painful in the extreme, but also, in my view, does considerable harm to the Jewish community. Nor am I suggesting that fault lies only with one side of the religious divide.
>
> There are, of course, fundamental differences between the Orthodox and Progressive wings – even polarisation, as the learned and highly respected Chief Rabbi recently described the situation. Accepting that fundamental differences exist, do they have to be accompanied by sour, bitter and abusive comments? No right-thinking and concerned member of the community would subscribe to such a necessity and, for my part, I will not give credence to abuse by repeating or quoting from it.
>
> It is urged upon us from some quarters that, in matters of principle, there is no room for compromise. I have doubts about such a widely stated and generalised proposition. However, we are not asked to accept views and practices which are contrary to our strongly held principles; but we should, and must be asked to, respect the sincerity of those who hold those views and follow those practices; and, further, to work for the good of the community with all others, whatever are their religious convictions.
>
> I accept the view adopted by some that, while it is a serious enough situation to face what has been described as a 'war of religion', it will be even more damaging if it results in the opening of a communal divide which might affect joint action in support of causes vital to all of us.[51]

* * *

For several months thereafter, the two sides coexisted in relative calm. But temperatures rose again the following February, with the publication of another controversial editorial in the *Jewish Chronicle*.[52]

Chapter Four

What follows will be deeply offensive, but not deliberately so, to some of our readers. This is inevitable if there is to be discussion with any degree of openness about what remains the major unresolved problem – apart from peace for Israel – on the agenda of the Jewish people: the question of Jewish identity, of who is a Jew.

As the Israeli Prime Minister, Mr Shimon Peres, told this newspaper recently, this is not solely a religious matter. It concerns the unity of the Jewish people. Israel (as is already the case in the diaspora) is very close to the situation in which one 'Jewish' person will not be able to marry another. It will split the nation, Mr Peres warned.

It is already affecting Anglo-Jewry, as virtually any rabbi will confirm. There can be scarcely one who has not had cases of young men or women who, brought up in the belief that they are Jewish, and indistinguishable in their life style from any other mainstream Jew, find on the threshold of marriage that they are not recognised by the Orthodox religious authorities as Jewish in fact, and have to undergo a form of religious conversion before they can go under the chupah.

Orthodoxy condemns the Reform and Liberal movements for creating this situation, by admitting to marriage non-Jewish partners who have not been converted according to the halachah, or by granting divorces without a *get*, or for a dozen different reasons. At the same time, those individual rabbis and batei din who stand four-square with the school of Hillel will search for the least onerous and yet halachically correct way of resolving the issue of Jewish identity. But there are some, a slowly increasing number here, but potentially a majority in the State of Israel, who would veer – not only in matters of personal status – to the strict school symbolised by Shammai.

There is, undoubtedly, a new and worrisome streak of Jewish fundamentalism evident in all our religious life, one which places the emphasis on the minutiae of performance and practice and has almost no time at all for the spirit of Judaism. Its representation of the Almighty is not that of the understanding and forgiving Father, the One who knows the weakness of man but loves him because he is His creation.

The God they would have us accept is the One who wreaks terrible vengeance on the household which desecrates His name by the possession of a television set. These fundamentalists turn their eyes from the fact that Judaism teaches that God created all mankind, not just the Jews, and they use His name to sanctify all kinds of political and personal acts which fly in the face of that most overwhelming of Jewish teachings: thou shalt love thy neighbour as thyself.

Anglo-Jewry, where notional attachment to at least the central core of Orthodoxy is still the norm, remains hardly aware of the fact that the largest Jewish community today is overwhelmingly non-Orthodox. By far the largest number of synagogue-going American Jews (83 per cent) belongs to the Conservative and Reform movements. Soviet Jewry, the next largest community, can scarcely be characterised as one which is reaching out for Orthodoxy, even were this to be possible, given the conditions of Soviet life, and despite the sacrifices being made by some to follow the way of observance.

Even in communities such as our own, the mass of so-called Orthodox Jews hardly follows the religious way in their observance of the laws of kashrut, family purity or Sabbath. We are a people which, throughout its life, has always counted among its numbers more sinners than saints, but which, nevertheless, has always shrunk from conducting its own inquisition in order to root them out.

Not that it is for any mere mortal, whatever his learning, to categorise those who stand religiously outside the Orthodox camp to cut them off from this people, outrageous though at times their behaviour may be to those who follow the halachic way. But then, is the overnight conversion by a Conservative rabbi of a Scottish footballer more outrageous than the equally speedy conversion by an Orthodox rabbi of a Jewish notability's non-Jewish wife?

It is unquestionable that those who adhere to the halachah have the right and duty to demand an observance equal to their own from those who would be counted among their number. It must also be accepted that those who recognise the halachah as central to their life as Jews, but can only aspire to its observance, have the inalienable right to demand that the Gates of Heaven be kept open to them.

But must not we also accept that those who have another and non-halachic sense of their Jewishness are also entitled, by their sacrifice for and devotion to this people, to their own Jewish identity? Necessarily, if they want to join the halachic camp, they must observe its rules; but if they wish to remain outside, they surely have a right to do so without being denied their historic, cultural and even, in their own terms, religious identity.

The diaspora, if not pressed, can deal with most of the personal problems this creates by its own means. Israel can deal with them not by applying a religious means test, which is abhorrent even to many inside Orthodoxy, but by disestablishing the Orthodox rabbinate as the only arbiters of personal status and the sole authority for conducting marriages and granting divorces.

They will still retain their authority within their communities, and will even strengthen it by not having to be party to procedures which make a mockery of the halachah. At the same time, those who cannot accept the traditional religious code will not face the constant threat of being cut off from this people of which they are a vital and integral part.

Brichto was quick to respond. 'You are to be congratulated on the courageous leader,' he told the JC.[53] 'Your ultra-Orthodox readers will no doubt expect such a response from a Liberal rabbi. May I assure them that it is in the mutual interest of Orthodox and Progressives that we should find a *modus vivendi* along the lines you suggest.

It is in this hope that I record the following facts and offer some proposals for consideration by the Orthodox rabbinic authorities. First, one must appreciate the reaction of the ultra-Orthodox when confronted by the request to officiate at the marriage of persons who, unknown to themselves, are not Jewish according to halachah.

In this connection, let me confirm that all Liberal converts sign a document which confirms their knowledge that their conversion will not be accepted by the Orthodox. In the course of their instruction, they are also informed many times that the children of women converts will not be considered Jewish according to Orthodox halachah.

Appropriate advice regarding Orthodox law is given to all those who marry without a *get*, though we encourage all divorcees to obtain Orthodox *gittin*. The Beth Din of the Federation of Synagogues can attest to this.

Secondly, in the good old days of trust and tolerance, when children of a couple married in a Liberal synagogue wished to be married under Orthodox auspices, the clerk of the Beth Din would ring the appropriate marriage secretary and ask whether the Liberal marriage was 'halachic'. With the assurance that it was according to Orthodox standards, the marriage would be permitted without need for further evidence.

I point all this out to indicate that we have no desire to wreak havoc within the community. In all our practices, we seek only to make it possible for Jews to maintain their identity.

It is not our desire to capitalise on the failure – due either to halachah or to its overly strict interpretation – of the Orthodox to meet the needs of their members who come to us because they wish to remain within the Jewish community. Were we not willing to be sympathetic to their problems, the community in this country and throughout the diaspora would be even more decimated than it is now due to the inroads of assimilation.

May I propose that the Orthodox authorities, whose integrity I have always respected in the past, accept the reality of Jewish life as you spell it out and seek to come to grips with it. The Liberal Jewish movement is prepared to co-operate in any attempt to build bridges of trust, and even to make certain compromises to bridge the halachic gap between us.

For example, I am certain that, for the sake of enabling Jew to marry Jew, we would recommend that our converts undergo *mikveh* and the further acceptance of an Orthodox Beth Din, so long as they were not required to be hypocritical in the affirmation of the Orthodox *kabbalat mitzvot*. As to *gittin*, I think we would be prepared to insist on Orthodox *gittin*, were its authorities to find the means to compel recalcitrant divorcees to give or receive the *get*.

'Like so many others', Brichto concluded, 'I am terrified by the increasing polarisation within our community. For this reason, your leader could not have been better timed. I implore the Orthodox to treat it with the seriousness it deserves. Let us reason together, for only by doing so can we guarantee that our people's future will be ensured in Israel and the diaspora.'

Sending a copy of his letter to the Chief Rabbi, Brichto referred to a request he had made 'to see you for a general discussion. It was actually on the problems of polarisation that I had in mind. I am deeply worried that the goodwill between the different sections of the community, which you fostered upon your arrival, is seeping away and, to use a metaphor, could become a flood to drown our communities.

'I am especially concerned what will happen when you retire from your position. I do know that personally you use your Office for the purpose of keeping the channels of communication open on areas of mutual concern, such as public relations and education. However, the fact that these activities are never publicised, for fear of the reaction from the ultra-Orthodox, gives the community the impression that our people are totally divided.

'I feel that some initiative should be taken in the last years of your office to ensure that your period as Chief Rabbi will have made a lasting impact upon the community. I know that you are not lacking in the required courage, as your views on the use of power by the religious parties in Israel, and your statements on relations with the Palestinians,[54] have proved beyond doubt.

'There was a time when you were right to maintain that the way to improve relations between the sections was a slow educational process, and that to act with any flair would just be counter-productive. This is no longer the case. It would seem to me that unless you take advantage of your invulnerable position during your final years in office, all the good you have done will be like footprints in the sand.'[55]

Replying a week later, the Chief Rabbi wrote: 'In your JC letter, as now published, the crux of the problem between us lies in your sentence "... we would recommend that our converts undergo *mikveh* and the further acceptance of an Orthodox Beth Din, so long as they were not required to be hypocritical in the affirmation of the Orthodox *kabbalat mitzvot*".

'It is precisely because we object to such hypocritical acts as much as you do that your formula is so unacceptable to us. After all, how can an Orthodox Beth Din validate a conversion without *kabbalat mitzvot*? That itself would be hypocritical, since it would flout the essence of a conversion as we understand it.

'So long as this gulf remains, and thousands will be declared as Jews (or as divorced) by some of our people and as non-Jews (or married) by the rest, I cannot see that the growing havoc inevitably created by these divisions can be eliminated, whatever the public declarations of unity, goodwill, etc.

'Turning to your private letter, therefore, I do not really understand what action on my part could help to solve the problem, short of an agreement on procedures towards which I have been working ever since I assumed office, and quite recently again at a special consultation in Israel.

'Whether the peace of the community, and the personal relations we have established, will be retained beyond my retirement (to leave more than mere footprints in the sand) will hardly be determined by anything I say or do now. It is difficult enough to bind my contemporaries: I doubt if I can tie down my successors!

'In any event, I am not contemplating retiring just yet, and I would not want to act as if I did – at least not for another few years. All this does not, of course, prevent us from having a chat, as suggested in your letter.'[56]

Closing this round of correspondence, Brichto replied: 'I do appreciate your points about conversion, though I do know that the degree of acceptance of *kabbalat mitzvot* has been differently interpreted during our history.

'This, however, is not the essential matter. It is the maintenance of tolerance between the two communities which you and I had fostered when you became Chief Rabbi, and the positive results of which I see disappearing. Even I don't have that many years to go in my position to make sure that my own work in this area has not been to no avail.'[57]

* * *

Events in the coming year bore out, at least in Brichto's view, his affirmation that 'the positive results of tolerance between the two communities' showed every sign of disappearing. But in early 1987, Jakobovits apparently saw it differently, as he told the *Jewish Chronicle* in an interview to mark the twentieth anniversary of his Chief Rabbinate:

'All in all, I have been very fortunate. Despite our diversity, there is a greater sense of unity than ever, and I have no reason to regret the decision I took [to become Chief Rabbi], not for a single moment. I never feel that the problems and pressures have grown beyond me. I have a perhaps naive proclivity to see a silver lining in every cloud, and I've never found myself facing a problem without an absolute conviction that it would be solved.'[58]

Not many days passed, however, before the 'silver lining' was blown away. Following publication of an article by Jakobovits in *The Times*, Progressive rabbis accused him of implying that the Holocaust had been caused by the advent of Progressive Judaism.

Gryn asserted that he had 'debased the currency of the Holocaust', and Brichto questioned his position as 'Chief Rabbi of the whole community'.

Jakobovits, in turn, was said by his Office to be 'bemused' by the attacks on him, and charged the rabbis with 'a deliberate distortion and misreading' of the article, which had dealt with the effects of the Holocaust, and not its cause.[59]

There followed a long and confidential exchange between Brichto ('written more with sorrow than anger') and Jakobovits ('rough draft, uncorrected, unsent', though later sent 'after our conversation, and because you asked me to let you see it').

For his part, Brichto wrote, *inter alia*: 'I read the article again and again, and I had to accept that you were indeed making a connection between the early Reform and the Holocaust... I am relieved that you disclaim the inference that the Holocaust was in any way related to an attempt at assimilation by German Reform.'

Jakobovits, in turn, concluded his lengthy response 'in the hope that your next letter to me will withdraw the baseless charges against me and express regret for the damage done to communal harmony, not to mention the unwarranted slur against my Office and myself. A frank admission that you misread both my article and Jewish history would probably stretch my faith in *Menschlichkeit* unduly.'[60]

This was not, however, the end of the episode. Six months later, in his movement's journal, Brichto again referred to the article, and to other alleged infractions, and added: 'In my letter to *The Times*, in response, I indicated that if these were his [Jakobovits'] views, he could no longer be considered our spokesman or representative.

> This episode caused me to consider my past attitude to him. I was not sure if he had always acted under Right-wing pressure, or whether this had been his excuse and a convenient cover for his own ultra-Orthodox views, in a bid to have the non-Orthodox accept his right to remain their representative. I determined, however, that the existence of ultra-Orthodox pressure would no longer be justification for his behaviour.
>
> If Sir Immanuel is to have the privilege of universal acceptance as our spokesman and representative, he will have to earn it by a strong and conciliatory leadership. It is his problem if the ultra-Orthodox put pressure on him. We, too, have the right to pressure him. Let him choose!
>
> My anxiety was increased by his recent outrageous ruling that the children of Progressive Jewish converts should not be allowed

religious instruction at the King David School, Birmingham. We cannot tolerate this new attack. We must now demand our rights. If we are being victimised, we cannot be criticised for rejecting as our spokesman the person who is the cause. Let no one say the victims are causing disharmony by resisting gross injustices.

Furthermore, let those who strive to have the Jewish community appear as a united force to the non-Jewish world stop blaming the Progressives for that disharmony, and do something to remove the causes – the refusal of established Orthodoxy to tolerate and live with the differences which exist between Orthodox and Progressive. They must stop treating us as pariahs in order to frighten off those in their own group who might be tempted to join us.

I give warning *on my own behalf* that, as we fight for equal rights for Progressive Jews in Israel, we will also demand the rights and respect due to us in Great Britain.[61]

Alongside this 'warning' had come an attack from Brichto at the annual meeting of the ULPS, where he accused the Chief Rabbi of 'not reflecting the moderate, tolerant aspect of Orthodox Judaism that we Progressives once felt he did'.

Expressing 'deep concern at the frightening polarisation in the Jewish community', he described Jakobovits as 'extremely Right-wing. I used to think, when he said that we Progressives were not authentic Jews, that he meant we were not representative of authentic Judaism. But now I am convinced that what he really means is that we are more of a danger to Judaism than support to it. That is very worrying for our community; it seems that the Orthodox leadership wishes to write us off.'[62]

In the face of this growing antagonism, Unterman wrote to Bayfield in the latter's capacity as chairman of the Unterman Committee,[63] accusing Brichto of breaking the 'moratorium' signed the previous March.

'I have received the *ULPS News*, in which he again breaches the terms of the agreement in an offensive diatribe against the Chief Rabbi, with the difference that here he writes that he speaks on his own behalf. Since his statement is almost verbatim that which appeared in the JC, this kind of deviousness about speaking on his own behalf wears rather thin.

'Two things I have tried to do: a) to resist the growing pressure to advise for the abolition of the Consultative Committee, to which the Chief

Rabbi has given so much hospitality, in a variety of senses, and whose existence is clearly incompatible with Brichto's sentiments which he presents in the name of all Progressives; and

'b) to refrain from responding to the growing clamour to hit back in kind at the Progressives, and expose those who pretend to be apostles of harmony yet act as fomenters of discord, as though obsessed.... I am, with you, most anxious to avoid a rupture which will become increasingly more difficult to heal, and which must be laid at the door of Rabbi Brichto in the first instance.'[64]

Bayfield responded: 'I have now had two conversations with Rabbi Brichto, the second – and more extensive – only yesterday, in the company of Raymond Goldman, of the RSGB, and Rabbi Jonathan Magonet, from Leo Baeck College.

> First, a minor point: The term 'Progressive' is often used to cover both the Reform and Liberal movements. However, Rabbi Brichto is a Progressive, additionally by virtue of being chief executive of the ULPS, a sovereign institution. I can advise and suggest, but I cannot do more than that. To threaten the existence of the Consultative Committee because of a disagreement with the chief executive of one constituent of the committee seems ill-considered, and makes my position as convenor untenable.
>
> The agreement is actually of no great help, since Rabbi Brichto sincerely believes that he is not in breach of it. He would reject your phrase 'offensive diatribe'. He sees himself as responding to statements and actions emanating either from the Chief Rabbi personally or from the Orthodox community, which, he feels, either do not express the totality of Jewish perspectives on a subject or are contrary to the interests of the Progressive community.
>
> Here I do feel that he has a point. His letters and articles are, indeed, *reactive*.... The moves in Birmingham to exclude the children of Liberal converts from Jewish religious education, and to institute status checks for the children of all those parents who have non-Orthodox *ketubot*, represent actions that are clearly divisive and provocative. Rabbi Brichto is reacting and will, I believe, continue to do so.
>
> This brings me to the nub of the matter – and one I have touched upon at the Consultative Committee before but which we have shrunk back from trying to resolve. The Chief Rabbi has an increasingly high profile in the general community. He is now writing regularly for *The Independent*, I believe. He writes as

'The Chief Rabbi' and is widely accepted as the spokesman for Jewry/Judaism.

While I have a profound respect for both his scholarship and his integrity, he often adopts stances on moral and medical issues – AIDS was a recent example – which are far more conservative than the stance taken by many Progressive rabbis on the same issues. The Progressive community will want to respond, not by being offensive to the Chief Rabbi, not by impugning his integrity or his scholarship, but simply by saying that there are other views within the Jewish community, and stating them.

We are not a monolithic community; if we were, there would be no need for a Consultative Committee! Thus there must be room for the expression of more than one Jewish viewpoint. I am troubled if such responses are to be considered as breaches of our agreement.

Two points follow. First, I would be grateful if you would assure the Chief Rabbi that nobody who holds a leading position within the Progressive community wishes to offend him, to attack him personally, or to impugn or slight him in any way. I know that Rabbi Brichto would join me in these sentiments. Second, we cannot forego the right to react to what we see as attacks on us. Nor can we forego the right to respond to public statements of a Jewish view on which we have a different perspective.

You may think that it would be useful for us to have a discussion on this matter at the Consultative Committee. If so, let me know and I will extend the next meeting by half an hour to permit this. Alternatively, you may think it more useful for a smaller group of us to meet. I will be guided by you.

'Let me conclude by saying that there really is no desire in our section of the community for acrimony or for statements of a recriminatory or discourteous nature. However, I simply cannot prevent statements reactive to articles and actions or expressions of alternative Jewish perspectives. I would be very grateful for your advice as to where we go from here.'[65]

This debate, however, temporarily subsided in the shadow of another, between Brichto and Jakobovits two months later, that was to resonate for many years. Having reconsidered over an extended period the halachic issues of personal status, Brichto declared that 'it would be an act of abhorrent and unforgivable self-destruction were we not to find the means of agreeing on a unified halachah in those areas which divide Jew from Jew and lead to enmity and internecine strife.

> In view of the seriousness of the situation, the time has come to put forward a solution – which will, however, in the present climate, most likely be rejected by both the Progressives and the Orthodox. Yet I do this now because now is the time for responsible Jews to have the courage to go out on a limb. When the future of the Jewish people is at stake, organisational and personal considerations are of secondary importance....
>
> For the preservation of *Klal Yisrael*, I am prepared to entrust the halachah to the Orthodox. Why? Because there is no one else. Because the Orthodox have retained the structure of halachah for the sake of *Klal Yisrael*, I am prepared to accord them the responsibility of finding the means to enable *all* religious sections to achieve a standard practice in the important areas of Jewish status, marriage and divorce. They must appreciate, however, that we Liberals and Progressives have a great interest in the matter.
>
> Orthodox rabbis entrusted by us to administer the halachah must do so with humility, compassion, ingenuity, creativity and, above all, a love for *Klal Yisrael*. The areas requiring their immediate consideration are conversion, *get*, Jewish remarriage when a *get* is difficult to obtain, and *mamzerut*.[66]

In a lecture in London two months later,[67] Jakobovits responded to Brichto's 'offer' in the following terms:

> What has recently been described as an 'unprecedented and revolutionary offer' – namely, to place all these matters under Orthodox jurisdiction – contains among other conditions, in the rather small print or strings attached, the following: 'The Orthodox Beth Din could demand only knowledge of Orthodox practice and not its observance.'
>
> Now this is just not on. It is one thing for those who have abandoned our traditions not to believe in them, and therefore to require only a knowledge of them. But as traditional Jews, as Orthodox rabbis who are bound by conscience and by the terms of the trust reposed in us to uphold the Shulchan Aruch, we cannot make hypocrites of ourselves, telling converts that all you

have to do is to know what is expected of you, but that you do not have to observe it.

This would turn us into hypocrites, never mind the convert. Any non-Jew could know all there is to know about Judaism: there are plenty of very learned non-Jews, but that does not make them into Jews. You do not become a Jew by having knowledge of Judaism.

Therefore, any such proposal is too laughable even to be referred for serious consideration. The last thing we can do is to sell our consciences, and make a mockery of our convictions, by subscribing to the idea of separating between knowing what is right and carrying it out.

Similarly we are asked: 'The Orthodox Beth Din would have to find loop-holes to nullify the marriage when it cannot proceed to a proper dissolution by *get*.' No Beth Din can be told you must find loop-holes. If they do not exist, you cannot invent them. Once again, these are suggestions which are simply non-starters, to put it mildly....

If there is to be any rapprochement, any serious examination of where we can find common denominators, how to narrow the gap, trying to redress the enormous damage, the havoc wrought in Jewish ranks and now threatening a major schism in the very oneness of our people, then it will certainly not be done and not be advanced by public-relations exercises, by publicity forays playing to the gallery.

This can be done only by quiet, delicate, discreet exploration in the first instance. Any hope of success requires a mandate given to those who will deal with this very highly complex area – at least to the extent that, when faced afterwards with having to give an account and securing the support of the constituency on whose behalf they purport to speak, they will not be rebuffed and disowned, as has happened with the recent 'initiative'.

Therefore, the absolute need here is to approach this with the utmost sense of responsibility, and not with the desire to obtain any form of public acclaim. Obviously, the points to be considered are complicated and of the utmost gravity. They cannot be argued out in public forums which are not exactly all dedicated to the same reverence for the ideals that should unite us.

'You will not be surprised to hear' – wrote Brichto to the Chief Rabbi in response to these words – 'that I was very disappointed by your reaction to my proposals in your address given at the Royal Society of Medicine, especially as I had expressed my hopes when I met you that you would not cast aspersions on my sincerity.

'There were three points in your lecture which I thought unfair: 1. the accusation that I was playing to the gallery; 2. that my proposals were laughable (which received publicity on the front page of the JC); 3. that I had rejected "agreed" proposals. So as not to exacerbate the situation, I wrote a moderate letter to the JC after making a neutral comment on your lecture when approached by its reporter.

'You left me with a dilemma. I certainly had the right to reply to your lecture, as silence would be interpreted as acquiescence. On the other hand, I did not wish to offend, as I do sincerely want talks to be opened on the subject.

'My conclusion was that, if I were not to pursue the matter, I would be giving credence to the suggestion that my only attempt was to seek publicity. As I really believe that a compromise is possible – as proved by the support my proposals have had in the USA, and from some important individuals in the UK, though they have not gone public – I had the obligation to act on the basis of my deeply held convictions, as you have to act on your own convictions.... Be assured that, were you to agree to discussions, they would be held in the strictest confidentiality.'[68]

The Chief Rabbi, in his final response on the subject, did not mince his words. 'While I have publicly stated that I accept the good faith in which our previous negotiations and discussions have been conducted', he told Brichto, 'I am bound to say, privately at least, that I deem your entire approach in the present "initiative" disingenuous.

> It is disingenuous to suggest that the 'initiative' is a 'revolutionary and unprecedented proposal' when, in fact, you of all people know that this very proposal was made, discussed and rejected in negotiations between us years ago.
>
> It is disingenuous to tell me in your letter that my lecture left you in a dilemma lest your silence be taken as acquiescence, when in fact my lecture was given before a relatively sparse audience, while you publicised your views, and now your response, before thousands who never even saw my arguments.
>
> It is disingenuous to charge me with having 'attacked the proposals ... as laughable' when, in fact, I declared as laughable

the suggestion that Orthodox conversion requirements should be restricted to a knowledge of Judaism without reference to its practice.

And, above all, it is disingenuous for someone who does not himself accept the halachah in the traditional sense to advise Orthodox batei din how they should administer the halachah.

Since you went public, obviously with an eye 'to the gallery', or to the 'enormous groundswell of support', before exploring the feasibility of such proposals with those concerned, I cannot believe that you meant them to be taken seriously as a basis for renewed negotiations. At least, that is not the way in which I operate in matters of supreme concern to me when I know that I have to convince others in order to reach vital agreements.

I have no intention to make publicity capital out of this episode, any more than I did when the blatant rejection of basic moral imperatives in the Bible offered me ample opportunities to do so. I will continue my search for narrowing gaps and for promoting the oneness of our people in the only way I know: by honest inquiry and truthful faith to the beliefs I preach and practice. I prefer 'Halachah with honesty' to self-proclaimed 'humility'. But this is *entre nous*.[69]

For his part, Brichto concluded the exchange with this brief message: 'Thank you for your letter. We have spoken since then on the matter. I want only to confirm my sincerity in my desire to help resolve the deep divisions which result from matters of status. I only hope that you will be prepared to give the powerful leadership of which I know you are capable.' And, in a postscript, he added: 'For the record, I still must insist that the impression given to all was that you did imply that at least parts of my proposals were laughable.'[70]

* * *

As the year turned, so did the debate regarding relationships between the parties on the Consultative Committee. A 'bothered and perplexed' Bayfield had written to Unterman: 'I am aware that it is now your view that the work of the Committee should focus wholly on Jewish–Christian relations, and that a new and smaller group needs to be constituted to deal with inter-community problems.

'I agree with that entirely and, indeed, made exactly the same point – emphasising precisely the need to build up good personal relations – when

I took over as convenor of the Committee more than a year ago. However, there is a gap between what we want and what actually exists. Surely we have to have the discussion at the Consultative Committee, first because they have requested it, and secondly because only they can make the decision to form a separate new committee to deal with these matters in the future.'[71]

After a lengthy discussion at a meeting of the Committee two months later,[72] under the heading 'Relationships within the Community', the parties agreed that 'Rabbis Unterman and Bayfield would take steps to set up the sub-group suggested'. At the same meeting – attended by, among others, the newly ennobled Lord Jakobovits[73] – Bayfield presented a lengthy paper entitled 'Some Reflections on the Consultative Committee', on which, he began, 'I have been a member for some years.

> Although our ostensible task is to consider matters relating to Jewish–Christian relationships and, by extension, matters relating to the Jewish community and other religious or ethnic groups, it is clear that because this is one of the few occasions when the leadership of the United Synagogue and the leadership of the Progressive movement sit down together, there is a second agenda as well. It is this second agenda that I would like to address.
>
> I suspect that it is not simply a mark of my obtuseness that, after all these years, I am still unclear as to whether our underlying aim is the creation of some form of peaceful coexistence between Orthodoxy and non-Orthodoxy, or whether we actually seek simply to conduct the armed struggle in a more civilised and private way. I really cannot tell whether there is any consensus as to whether peaceful coexistence is either desirable or possible.
>
> It would demand risk-taking from both sides, and I am sure that there is no need for me to spell out what the risks and the difficulties are. I stress the point because it makes discussions like these so difficult, and constructive initiatives so tentative. Until both sides are honest about what they want, we will presumably continue to have these three-times-a-year meetings and they will continue to have value, but only a limited value: a rather stilted group in search of topics to discuss and ill-constituted to address the ostensible agenda....
>
> If we were at least able to agree that Maurice Unterman's moratorium on trading insults should be reaffirmed, and should

be extended to the writing of articles which are likely to be perceived of as insulting by the other side, we need to give more careful consideration to our use of language in all public spheres of speaking and writing. It is clear to me that Orthodoxy does not relish (or merit) such adjectives as 'medieval', 'antique', 'antediluvian', 'fundamentalist' and 'outmoded'. Equally, Progressive Jews are outraged by 'neo-Christian', 'Baal-worshippers', and 'assimilationist'.

It is considerably unhelpful to accuse Orthodoxy of being ayatollah-like, of being unable to change, develop and respond to new situations, and of being out of touch with the needs of the twentieth century. It is equally unhelpful to draw connections between nineteenth-century Reform, Divine punishment and the Holocaust, and to accuse Reform of lacking principles and seeking only to dilute. We get absolutely nowhere by indulging in such language.

Surely people are bored to tears with rehearsing the arguments and refuting the accusations and deliberately failing to notice that we often use the same terms to mean subtly different things. If we cannot dialogue in the press effectively (and all the evidence is that we cannot), can we at least agree to stop wasting each other's time and energy? And can we agree and take active steps vis-à-vis colleagues to watch our language, even at the risk of giving up some much-cherished and finely honed insults?

Let me move to a second and more difficult issue. The elevation of the Chief Rabbi to the peerage is a matter for pride and unqualified congratulations. It does, however – and I hope you will not think me churlish for acknowledging this – increase the likelihood of future conflict unless we are careful. The profile which the Chief Rabbi has earned, the interest that his views have provoked, the new platform provided by the House of Lords, will all serve to increase the general public attention given to his statements.

I do not want to discuss substantive issues today. I merely want to give you a number of instances. There are many Jews within the Progressive Jewish world who would argue that the teachings of Torah and of the Prophets demand much more active intervention by society in the problems of the inner cities; there are those who would argue that basic Jewish values demand more sensitive and accepting treatment of adult homosexuals; there are those who would give more prominence in discussions on abortion to the principle that 'the pain of the mother comes first'; and there are those who would argue that Judaism positively demands the use of the condom as a weapon in the fight against the plague of Aids.

Let me repeat that I do not seek to debate these issues today. Only to point out that there are sincerely held interpretations of Judaism which run counter to how British society today understands the Jewish view as it has been so eloquently and convincingly articulated by the Chief Rabbi. We are going to have to face a growing pressure from the Progressive sector to articulate such contrary views in public.

How is this to be done without it being perceived as a personal attack on the Chief Rabbi, a questioning of his 'authority', and an attempt to split the community? The very success which Lord Jakobovits has achieved in fulfilling the obligation to make Judaism a light unto the nations contains its own questions and problems which, if unaddressed, are likely to lead to substantial ill-feeling and considerable political posturing....

If we wish to maintain a situation in which the Orthodox community, on the one hand, acknowledges the existence of a non-Orthodox group but actually wishes to see it diminish, ultimately wants to see it shrivel, and regards it as heretical and therefore to be isolated and marginalised, meeting like this three times a year, then keeping our splits from the non-Jewish world and avoiding trading insults is probably the best we can hope for. If, on the other hand, the Progressive community wishes to make no compromises for the sake of *Klal Yisrael*, wishes to take every opportunity to erode the middle ground of Anglo-Jewry, and will eschew no opportunity for self-advancement – likewise.

If we seek a more fruitful mode of relationship, something I have (slightly facetiously) described as peaceful coexistence – that is, a realisation of the de facto likelihood of the continuation of both groupings for the foreseeable future and a desire to operate on as positive a basis as possible, without trespassing into issues of legitimacy and authenticity – then maybe we need to change the way we operate.

Maurice Unterman and I phone each other from time to time when one or other of us perceives that trouble is looming. In objective terms, we are not terribly effective, since we are two isolated individuals, with limited influence on our colleagues. But one positive thing has happened. We have grown to know each other, to respect each other – even to like each other.

I have taken to sending Maurice copies of lectures I have given, and he has taken to giving me helpful, fatherly advice. Whatever divides us, I suspect that we would never now insult each other or knowingly hurt each other. Maurice suggests (and I agree with him) that we cannot usefully hold together the double agenda of this group any longer.

There may or may not be a continuing need for a group to discuss Jewish–Christian relations. It is probably not suitably constituted at present. Maurice and I would argue that there is certainly a need for a small group to monitor and improve relationships between mainstream Orthodoxy and the Progressive section of the community. Such a group would consciously work at developing trust, understanding and good relations between the members of the group. It might then be able to make a real contribution to communal harmony.

'I know that other ventures in this area are in existence {Bayfield concluded], but I wonder whether we are prepared to risk something on a slightly more formal and official level. I note that the Chief Rabbi has recently assumed a prominent position in a Jerusalem-based organisation that seeks on an international level to promote Jewish unity.

'Perhaps now the time is propitious. It would, if it served no other purpose, at least clarify that we do have a commitment to achieving peaceful coexistence and are prepared to look honestly at the implications of taking such a goal seriously for our respective sections of the community.'[74]

Four months later, preparations towards 'achieving peaceful coexistence' began with a meeting, at Unterman's home in Marble Arch, to discuss the formation of an 'Inter-Communal Strife Monitoring Committee'.[75] Following these exploratory talks, Bayfield recirculated the text of the 1985 'moratorium' together with a series of questions 'which Rabbi Unterman and I feel would be helpful at our first meeting on Tuesday, 18 October [1988]':

1. Do we believe that it is possible to initiate such a moratorium on recriminatory statements and, if so, how do we define 'recriminatory'; what influence do we have over colleagues, and how can we act to promote a moratorium?

2. The statement refers to 'problems' that may either be resolved or left to amicable disagreement; is it possible to anticipate problem areas and identify them as either?
    a. matters concerning theological differences which are, at present, irreconcilable;
    b. matters which are fundamentally about the political relationship between the two communities; and
    c. matters which could be reconcilable with common sense and goodwill on both sides.

If we can identify problems which belong in these three areas, might it be possible for us to develop strategies appropriate to each?

3. How do we see the status of our group, and what recording and reporting process (if any) are we going to adopt?[76]

On the appointed date, Rabbis Bayfield, Unterman and Gryn – accompanied by three lay colleagues – met for the first meeting of the Unterman-Bayfield Group. The minutes (in large part) read as follows:

The meeting was spent sharing thoughts on realisable aims for the group. There was substantial consensus, and the following objectives were advanced:

1. *The elimination of public acrimony.* It was suggested that a code of conduct might be drawn up, focused particularly on restraint of language. It would be necessary to feed this into such places as the rabbinic training colleges.
2. *Building good relations.* Good relations between the United Synagogue and the Progressive movement cannot be established without developing proper contact between the individuals concerned and building harmony, friendship and mutual respect.
3. *Altering the climate in the community and the public perception of that climate.* This will involve working with the Jewish Chronicle. It will also involve making known the existence of our group.
4. *Identifying areas where we can co-operate and should be seen as co-operating.* Jonathan Lew circulated a note which suggested seven areas for co-operation, and these should be examined and expanded.

Education is particularly important, and we need to look at the possibility of developing 'portraits' of each other which are mutually acceptable and which can be used in education within the two movements. Thus, we will not present each other to our children in an offensive or negative manner.

5. *Retaining and developing the good things that do exist.* Anglo-Jewry has a long tradition whereby Orthodox and Progressive rabbis can appear on the same platform. This tradition must not be eroded. The Chief Rabbi and Rabbi Gryn attended a lunch organised by the Board of Deputies for Dr [Robert] Runcie [Archbishop of Canterbury]. Rabbi Gryn made *motzi* [grace before meals], and the Chief Rabbi spoke. Such harmony must be retained beyond the term of office of the present Chief Rabbi.

6. *Monitoring and resolving inter-community problems.* It is clear that there are theological differences on which we have to agree amicably to disagree. However, there is a considerable number of other problems which we may be able to assist in ameliorating or resolving.

The above represents an agenda for future discussion. The group has a clear and separate identity from the Consultative Committee (which can now deal with Jewish relations with other religious communities), though a brief report will be made to the Consultative Committee (text to be drafted by Jonathan Lew in consultation with Tony Bayfield).

Before embarking upon the discussions indicated above, it may be helpful to look realistically at our ability to influence others outside our own group and the mechanisms by which we intend to achieve our objectives.[77]

In advance of the next proposed meeting,[78] Bayfield circulated a 'proposed agenda' which stipulated, *inter alia*, that 'the name and function of the Committee ought to be formalised under the auspices, on the Orthodox side, in consultation with the Chief Rabbi, and on the Progressive side, in consultation with the appropriate authorities'. He also suggested that 'the name should be descriptive without being publicity sensitive – e.g., The Council of Concern'.

On other aspects of its work, Bayfield proposed that 'the attempted reconciliation of theological differences, or matters of doctrine or practice, should not fall within the functions of the committee'; and that 'the function of the committee should be to take such steps as they think fit to advise and inform the community upon matters which affect the relationship between the Orthodox and Progressive communities'.

* * *

The relationship between the two communities took a turn for the worse, however, following public statements by Bayfield and Rayner in June 1989, one during a 'Jewish Unity' discussion at the RSGB annual conference, the other relating to what became internationally known as 'the Paula Cohen affair'.

Addressing the Reform gathering, Bayfield began his account of intra-communal disputes with the period 'before I was thought of'. Then, turning to more recent times, he personalised his narrative: 'Let me bore you for a few moments with organisational banalities, because interesting things have a habit of happening in the most unlikely places – like 85 Hamilton Terrace, for instance.

> By the time I became chairman of the Council of Reform and Liberal Rabbis and then convenor, the Consultative Committee was meeting three times a year in the Chief Rabbi's drawing-room, and membership consisted of the leadership of the United Synagogue, RSGB, ULPS and Board of Deputies, plus a few individuals who appeared to have been there for rather a long time and to have earned membership out of force of habit.
>
> The meetings were very formal, *extraordinarily* polite and *exceedingly* stiff. They began pleasantly enough, with Lady Jakobovits serving tea and biscuits. The Chief Rabbi and the convenor sat in twin thrones of glory. And a significant part of the discussion was not devoted to Jewish–Christian matters at all, but to intra-community affairs – for those of you who prefer plain English, 'Progressive–United Synagogue *broigeses*'.
>
> Some time before I took over the convenor's role from Rabbi John Rayner, I began to express some mild dissatisfaction with the Committee. It was hard in such a formal setting and with so many people – between 20 and 25 – to build the kind of personal relationships on which any real work of co-operation must be founded.
>
> Furthermore, there was a strong element of mixed agenda which never quite seemed to work. We were going through a

bout of unedifying name-calling in the columns of the Jewish Chronicle. It was apparent that something needed to be done, if only to obviate a widespread 'plague-on-both-your-houses' reaction from the rank-and-file (if they exist) of Anglo-Jewry.

John Rayner and Maurice Unterman, emeritus rabbi of Marble Arch Synagogue and a special adviser to the Chief Rabbi, produced an agreement which was submitted to and accepted by the Consultative Committee. Maurice and I were appointed monitors of the relationship between the Orthodox and Progressive communities and asked to act as telephonic firefighters if trouble loomed.

It was a difficult assignment, not least because the Progressive community is neither monolithic nor hierarchically structured – and I certainly have no power to prevent colleagues from writing intemperate letters to The Times or the Jewish Chronicle. Nor does Maurice have the authority to tell the London Beth Din not to make unnecessary difficulties on matters of status.

But we came to speak to each other more and more regularly: I was welcomed warmly in his flat, and there were a number of occasions where one or the other of us was able to pour oil on troubled waters or prevent occurrences likely to lead to ire and threats.

When Maurice phoned me on erev Rosh Hashanah to wish me *shanah tovah*, I realised that it was possible, just as some of my colleagues have found, for Reform and Orthodox Jews to have warm personal relationships, even if both are rabbis. But the Consultative Committee was little changed. So, in February of last year, I took my courage in both hands and gave a short paper, *ex cathedra*, sharing some fairly frank thoughts.

I suggested that the Consultative Committee was neither fish nor fowl and needed to make up its mind whether it was going to really address intra-community questions or whether it was going to devote all of its time to Jewish relations with the Christian, Muslim and other religious communities. I asked whether people really wanted peaceful coexistence or whether they simply sought to conduct the armed struggle in a more civilised and private way than in the worst excesses of the letters column of the Jewish Chronicle.

I asked what purpose was served by endless articles in the JC which purported to be reasonable but which actually sought to score points off the other and served only to give the home side a couple of cheap goals to cheer about. I asked whether we could give up the writing of such articles and whether we could also give up the buzz-words which so annoy our respective camps – buzz-words like 'medieval', 'antediluvian', 'Ayatollah-like' – in 'our' discourse about 'them', and 'neo-Christian', 'illegitimate' and 'assimilationist' in theirs.

I asked how we should deal with the new, heightened profile of the Chief Rabbi, allowing the world at large to see that he does not always speak for the Jewish community as a whole or, in our view, for the whole of Jewish tradition, without at the same time turning the disagreement into a presumed attack on his authority and into personal invective.

Finally, I suggested that, if there were a real will to move from armed struggle to peaceful coexistence, a small group would be needed to tackle these issues: a group of people who could actually get to know and trust each other; who at the same time could be seen to meet and would be known to meet; and who could try to set a realistic agenda for closer co-operation, both through firefighting and pre-emptive action.

To my complete surprise, the Consultative Committee agreed – and the Liaison Group, as it has come to be known, was born. It has the blessing of the Chief Rabbi and is substantially independent of the Consultative Committee, which is now able to devote itself wholly to our relationship with other religious communities.

Maurice and I agreed that a membership of eight was the maximum for effective action. We were asked to invite whoever we liked to form the group, and our only ground rule was that neither of us would invite someone unacceptable to the other.

As a result, the United Synagogue members, in addition to Rabbi Unterman, are Jonathan Lew, the chief executive of the United Synagogue; Dr Linda Stanton, one of its leading women; and Lionel Swift, QC. On the Progressive side, we are represented by Raymond Goldman, Hugo Gryn, David Lipman (a past-chairman of the ULPS) and me.

We are moving slowly, establishing ground rules, separating the possible from the not-possible at the moment, getting to know and trust each other. Real progress, if it is to be made, will take time. We have already discovered limitations – namely, a reluctance on the part of our United Synagogue colleagues to enter into areas which they would designate 'theological' or 'rabbinic'. And they have perceived the limitations on our democratic organisations in being able to 'control', even if we wanted to.

But we meet. Not just as individuals, but as people who are part of, representative of, organisations. It was Jonathan Lew who suggested that one of our long-term objectives should be to ensure that a fairer and more balanced picture of Progressives is given in Orthodox education, and vice versa. The recent and somewhat misleading and mischievous JC headline suggesting that the Reform movement was going to attempt to subvert Orthodox communities caused a lot of pain and anguish which Raymond, Jonathan Lew and Maurice Unterman have worked on to minimise.[79]

Days earlier, delivering a Shavuot sermon at the Liberal Jewish Synagogue – with its timely link to the biblical Ruth, a convert to Judaism – Rayner spoke in an entirely contrasting vein:

Let me begin with a topical and public debate and remind you about the particular case which triggered it off: that of Paula McKenzie Wilson, born in Newcastle, who at the age of 23 went to Israel to work on a kibbutz as a volunteer, became interested in Judaism, and eventually applied for, and received, an Orthodox conversion.

But, by that time, she had formed a relationship with a fellow kibbutznik by the name of Cohen, whom, as a proselyte, she was not allowed to marry under Orthodox law. Why? Because people with a name like Cohen are presumed to be descended from the ancient Jewish priests who, in the choice of their marriage partners, were subject to certain stringencies not applicable to other Israelites; and in Orthodox Judaism these stringencies are still maintained in anticipation of the day when the Temple will be rebuilt and the *cohanim* will once more carry out their ancient priestly functions.

The young couple therefore came over to England to be married in the Reform synagogue of Paula's home town, Newcastle, then returned to Israel for another six years and had three children before deciding, two years ago, to settle permanently in Newcastle. And then their troubles began, for when they sent their children to the local Jewish school, their Jewish status was queried.

To cut a long story short, it transpired that Mrs Cohen's conversion certificate had on it the extraordinary endorsement 'not valid outside Israel', and this circumstance, together with the fact that she had contracted a marriage forbidden under Orthodox law, was used by the London Beth Din as an excuse to deny the validity of her conversion, and consequently also the Jewish status of her children.

The whole episode would be a bad joke if it were not also a tragedy. It is a tragedy, most obviously, for the Cohen family. It is also tragic that the London Beth Din should have acted in such a stupid and vindictive manner. But what is even sadder, in terms of the broader consequences, is that the Chief Rabbi, Lord Jakobovits, has seen fit publicly to defend his Beth Din, at least by implication.

I am referring to an article by him that appeared in *The Times* on 15 May. It is true that the article ended on a positive note by saying: 'Anyone prepared to follow Ruth's example of total loyalty will be accepted into the Jewish faith with open arms.' But the general tenor of the article nevertheless conveyed a negative impression of Judaism's attitude in this matter, namely that it has no real interest in receiving proselytes, that it makes extremely stringent demands on those who seek conversion, that it interprets these demands in coldly legalistic terms, and that, like some immigration officer examining the credentials of an undesirable alien, it is essentially looking for good reasons to say 'no' rather than 'yes'.

All of which, as a description of contemporary Orthodox Judaism, may be all too accurate. But Lord Jakobovits doesn't speak only for Orthodox Judaism; he purports to speak, and he is widely understood as speaking, for Judaism generally; and that is where I get worried, because I believe that he gives the British public a distorted impression of what Judaism, historically speaking, is actually like, not only on the subject we are now discussing, but on many subjects.

Rayner furthered his case by referring to several positive approaches – biblical and midrashic – to Jewish conversion, and concluded: 'It is this kind of evidence which, I believe, entitles us to say that classical Judaism, at its characteristic best, obliges us to be courteous, respectful and friendly towards non-Jews among whom we live, and warmly welcoming to any of them who pay us the compliment of wishing to identify themselves with us.'[80]

* * *

In their contrasting approaches, that of Rayner and his Liberal colleagues won out, prefaced by an increasingly angry exchange between Brichto and Jakobovits over the Paula Cohen affair. In a letter to the JC, Brichto wrote:

> Progressive as well as other non-Orthodox Jews can respect Orthodoxy when it is true to its principles, especially when the articles of their faith and practice are steeped in scholarship and knowledge of the law. Indeed, the breadth of Orthodox scholarship fills me and other Progressive Jews with deep admiration. And, however irrational and atavistic some of their laws and rituals may appear to us, we must accept that Orthodox Jews are being true to a halachah which they believe is divinely revealed.
>
> The ruling of the London Beth Din, supported by the Chief Rabbi, on the conversion of Paula Cohen and the religious status of her three children has shocked the Progressive Jewish community, not because we do not concur with it, but because it is totally unhalachic.
>
> No halachic authority, no Jewish scholar of any merit outside these shores, would agree that a conversion could be conditional. The stamping of a conversion certificate as 'invalid outside Israel' is as irrelevant and unhalachic as the certificate itself. A conversion certificate, as its name suggests, only certifies that a conversion has taken place in accordance with the rites and practices of the converting rabbis.
>
> A conversion requires no certificate. The *ketubah*, the marriage contract, is an essential part of the wedding ceremony and may have a bearing on the halachic validity of the marriage, but a conversion certificate has no significance whatever on the validity of a conversion.
>
> The use of a certificate intended to give proof that a conversion has taken place for the opposite purpose, namely to invalidate a conversion, makes a mockery of halachah, and must lead objective and fair-minded individuals to question the integrity and motivation of those who performed the conversion.

But what must shock these Jews even more is a Beth Din declaring the children of a Jewish mother retroactively as not Jewish. Even if one could argue, which one cannot, that the London Beth Din had the right to declare Paula Cohen no longer Jewish when she moved from Israel to Newcastle, how can they rule that the three children born to a Jewish mother in Israel are no longer Jewish?

In this situation, it is naive for the victims and their sympathisers to ask the Beth Din and the Chief Rabbi for compassion. Such a plea presumes that the dayanim are being too strict in their adherence to the halachah and are being asked to show flexibility. But the very opposite is true. They are flouting the halachah in order to punish Mrs Cohen for her misdemeanour in marrying a Cohen in a Reform synagogue. In doing this, they are giving warning signals to anyone who questions their authority or goes to the Progressive movement for an alternative ruling.

Of course, it was halachically impermissible for Paula, a convert, to marry a Cohen, but, once done, the marriage is nevertheless valid, and the children suffer no stigma except that they do not inherit the priesthood. They certainly do not cease to be Jewish.

The time has come for the Jewish community to recognise that the London Beth Din, the Court of the Chief Rabbi, is using its authority unhalachically as a deterrent against those who have the temerity to break any halachic rule. Unless there is a reversal of its ruling in the Cohen case, it must be condemned for exploiting its authority for political rather than holy purposes.

The failure to reverse its decision will make it increasingly difficult for Progressive Jews to retain their respect for Anglo-Jewish Orthodoxy, and the desire and the will to seek an accommodation with it to achieve a stronger and more united Jewish community.[81]

After the case became a national issue, with the Lord Chancellor, Lord Mackay of Clashfern, suggesting that 'a legal action against the Orthodox Jewish authorities in Britain might help a Newcastle family caught in a religious quarrel over the definition of a Jew',[82] Brichto wrote to the Chief Rabbi: 'I was most disturbed to see in The Times the publicity given to the possibility of legal action against the Beth Din on the basis of natural justice.

'I do hope that you will resolve this issue. As an halachic authority, you must know that there can be no basis for the retroactive denial of the Jewish status of the children. Even the threat of legal action reported in The Times besmirches our reputation.

'Can you not do something before it receives more publicity? Were it to become a full-blown public issue, I might have no alternative but to defend the Judaism which I know both you and I believe in, whatever differences we have.'[83]

The Chief Rabbi replied: 'I am not aware that "natural justice" – in the sense of which this is legally used – was a Jewish invention, nor can I see its remotest relevance to the case at hand. You must know as well as I do how this has been manipulated and deliberately used in an attempt to defame Jewish law and its administrators publicly.

'The truth is that when [Israeli] Chief Rabbi Goren found that the conversion had been obtained under false pretences, he invalidated it – not retroactively, but as a fraudulent act from the beginning. To avoid enlarging the chillul hashem [desecration of God's name], we did not want to tell the entire story in public, or to quote the actual words he used.

'Whether you agree or disagree with our conversion practices, you surely would not wish us to be a party to deceit and bad faith, especially not under the threat of a public campaign of vilification and disinformation. On this, too, we surely ought to agree.'[84]

Dissatisfied with this reply, Brichto concluded his own response: 'There will be a greater chillul hashem if your Office and the Beth Din appear to be acting in an arbitrary fashion. Unless you prove that the London Beth Din ... is acting according to halachah, the Judaism you and I represent will be besmirched.'[85]

He added, in a further letter to the Chief Rabbi a fortnight later: 'For [your Office] to say that the Beth Din is merely confirming the action of Rabbi Goren is no more acceptable than for a British mullah to say that, in calling for the death of Salman Rushdie (l'havdil)[86], he is merely confirming the edict of Ayatollah Khomeini.'

Tempers rose further when the Chief Rabbi counterattacked with the declaration: 'All I can say is that the comparison of Chief Rabbi Goren (no friend of mine) with Ayatollah Khomeini is contemptible. I wonder whether you really expected the Orthodox rabbinate to capitulate to Reform threats, and to act against their conscience and against the halachah as they understand it.'[87]

Brichto retorted: 'I did say, in making the analogy, l'havdil. You know quite well that I was not comparing the two individuals.... I am very sorry that you are not prepared to take some action which would prevent what is already an unsavoury situation from developing into an ugly demonstration of Jewish intolerance and internecine strife.'[88]

In his final contribution to this exchange, Jakobovits replied: 'L'havdil hardly answers my charge of a contemptible comparison. Now comes the front-page clamour for disunity by the apostle of unity. I really think we should call it a day if hypocrisy is not to become a basic feature of communal and personal relations.'[89]

* * *

'The front-page clamour for disunity' was emblazoned across the columns of The Times on Saturday, 16 December, 1989, under the byline of its religious affairs editor, Clifford Longley. 'Leaders of the liberal Jewish community in Britain,' he wrote, 'have decided to stop treating the Office of Chief Rabbi as the titular head of all Britain's 300,000 Jews.

'After the retirement of Lord Jakobovits as Chief Rabbi next spring, the Union of Liberal and Progressive Synagogues says it will regard his successor as the leader only of Orthodox Jews. They will describe him as "Chief Rabbi of the United Hebrew Congregations", the main Orthodox organisation.

'Mr Harold Sanderson and Mrs Rosita Rosenberg, chairman and director of the ULPS, said in a statement that "our relationship to the Office of Chief Rabbi is not dependent on the person who fills it", which was why they had decided to make their position clear before Lord Jakobovits' successor was known.

'Before making their decision, the ULPS wrote to the council of the United Synagogue, the governing body of the United Hebrew Congregations, asking whether there was any intention to consult Progressive Jewish bodies and were told there was not.'[90]

In its entirety, the ULPS statement spelled out the Liberals' stand:

> In view of the procedure now being implemented to appoint a successor to the present Chief Rabbi, we feel it important to clarify our own relationship to the Office of the Chief Rabbi.
>
> The Chief Rabbi of the United Hebrew Congregations of the British Commonwealth is elected by a committee appointed by the officers and council of the United Synagogue. All members of the committee are members of constituents of the United Synagogue and associated synagogues. No other synagogue body is formally consulted in the election of the Chief Rabbi.

Accordingly, it is appropriate for us to say on behalf of the Union of Liberal and Progressive Synagogues that the Chief Rabbi to be elected has no authority over our own rabbis or lay people, nor does he represent us or speak on our behalf. Our community appoints its own rabbinic and lay representatives and spokespersons.

This statement does not seek to detract from the status of the Chief Rabbi of the United Hebrew Congregations or his authority over his constituents, but only to reaffirm that the Jewish community is not monolithic, but pluralistic in nature. In Judaism, as in other faiths, there is much diversity of belief and practice, even though the common ground far exceeds the differences.

We make this statement before the forthcoming appointment to make it clear that our relationship to the Office of the Chief Rabbi is not dependent on the person who fills it. We will respect the view of the new appointee and seek to co-operate with him in our mutual efforts towards the strengthening of the Jewish community. We hope that he, too, will respect the differences between his views and ours, and that those differences will not be allowed to diminish co-operative endeavour in areas of common interests and objectives.[91]

Two days later, *The Times* reported that 'the Board of Deputies of British Jews yesterday condemned a statement by the Union of Liberal and Progressive Synagogues, that they were to reject the Chief Rabbi's authority to represent them, as damaging to the Jewish community. "These comments are purely destructive", Dr Lionel Kopelowitz, the Board's president, said. They caused division where there was no division at all. The Chief Rabbi's traditional role as titular head had "worked to the benefit of the entire community".'[92]

In an address that Sunday to members of the Board, Kopelowitz revealed that 'last night several Deputies were in touch with me by telephone, and indeed one Deputy was so concerned that he asked to see me personally. I thought it would be helpful, therefore, if I made the position abundantly clear.'

Explaining that the Chief Rabbi was appointed 'by the representatives of those synagogal bodies who contribute to the maintenance of the Office of the Chief Rabbi and who recognise his religious authority', Kopelowitz pointed out that there were others – Orthodox and non-Orthodox – that did not. 'However,' he added, 'the Chief Rabbi has a second role, a representational role which is not defined.

'He is recognised, both within and without the Jewish community, as the public religious representative of the entire British Jewish community. This is a role which has worked to our advantage. I am firmly of the view that it is not in the communal interest for any group to take up a hard position at this stage, before a new Chief Rabbi has been appointed, to say whether they would or would not accept him in a representative capacity. The statement in yesterday's *Times* was ill-conceived and badly timed.'[93]

Hours before publication of the *Times* report, Brichto had written to Geoffrey Paul, editor of the *Jewish Chronicle* – which that day had carried no account of the statement – to explain that he had tried to delay its appearance. 'I spoke to Clifford Longley as quickly as I could. When we finally made contact, he told me that it was too late – the story had been submitted. As you say, this will be worse for us than for you. It was not what I had intended, but that's life.... Never mind, we will both survive!'[94]

The JC survived by briefly reporting the controversy in a back-page account the following Friday, accompanied by a leading article five times its length:[95]

> There is nothing new in the statement from the Union of Liberal and Progressive Synagogues disavowing the authority of the Chief Rabbi – any Chief Rabbi – over its members. Indeed, it is difficult to imagine a situation in which the incumbent would be regarded as a spiritual guide to it, or its members as a natural flock for him. The same would apply to almost all the Reform movement.
>
> The strictly Orthodox Right has always gone its own way, even to the extent of having its own burial and kashrut authorities, and a Beth Din which regards itself as second to none. The Federation of Synagogues, which would appear to be the natural ally of the United Synagogue, has separate kashrut and a Beth Din. The Sephardim, still lacking a Haham, have devised a dual religious leadership which, essentially, acts in concert with the Chief Rabbi (but, again, maintains its own kashrut authority and can, on occasion, assemble its own Beth Din). Masorti has placed itself outside the United Synagogue mainstream by its rejection of the classic Orthodox understanding of Revelation.
>
> Thus, it is essentially that collectivity known as the United Synagogue, and those many mainstream traditional congregations in the regions and a number overseas, which regard the Chief Rabbi as their guide and mentor. It is from their strength, which is predominant in Anglo-Jewish life, that he draws his.

Lord Jakobovits has put his own special stamp on the Chief Rabbinate to the extent that the global perception of him is that of sole spiritual leader of the Anglo-Jewish community.

His is not necessarily the role model which should dictate the choice of his successor. Indeed, the changing needs of the United Synagogue family may well demand someone with a narrower and more focused vision of the next decade in Anglo-Jewish religious life. It is no secret from any regular worshipper at United Synagogue services that the 'shtiebelisation' of the major North-West London community has attracted many potential US members to such new congregations as Ner Yisrael, Yakar and the minyan headed by Dayan Chanoch Ehrentreu, the head of the Beth Din.

The role of 'cathedral synagogues' is diminishing, and there is a thirst among many of the younger synagogue-goers for a learning environment rather than one in which they are audience for rabbi and chazan. On the other hand, there is a growth of new communities on the periphery, where young families are anxious about their children's Jewish identity and where education, formal and informal, is a prime interest.

The challenge to the United Synagogue in the next decade will be to devise a philosophy of traditional Judaism that will appeal both to the questing believer and to the many potential members who choose a synagogue not out of conviction, but because of its physical proximity or the range of services it provides. It will be the task of the Chief Rabbi to spearhead this essentially educational task, one which calls for a many-pronged approach.

There is a crying need for a restatement of the philosophy of what we call United Synagogue Judaism. The intense interest in the fate of mainstream religious thinking was amply demonstrated by the massive attendance at the 'Traditional Alternatives' conference in London earlier this year. However, the US, both in its lay leadership and its rabbinate, failed miserably, with one or two honourable exceptions, to pick up the ball and run with it.

There is a perception of a rabbinate always looking over its shoulder lest it fall foul of the Right. The US takes pride in a Beth Din which, whatever the truth, is perceived as being unbending in its approach to the interpretation of Jewish religious law. It has taken on a life of its own, outside its traditional role as 'Court of the Chief Rabbi'. What is to be the relationship between the two? This question should be addressed before the mantle of the Chief Rabbinate is placed upon other shoulders. That consideration could well dictate the character of the successful candidate.

So, too, could his approach to working with other segments of the community which do not share his religious outlook, but which share a common interest in defending Anglo-Jewry against its enemies, and in uniting its strength in support of Israel and local causes. There probably does not exist one man who embodies all those merits which the position demands. But the minimum that can be asked is that his deep religious conviction should be allied with a vision of a revitalised United Synagogue community, and an ability to translate that vision into a sense of purpose for a community which so often seems to be without one.

This editorial prompted a forceful, if delayed, response from Rosita Rosenberg, telling the JC's editor that it had 'certainly clarified the exact nature of the Office of the Chief Rabbi for a large number of your readers.

'Although the leader was motivated by the statement issued the previous week by the ULPS, I am surprised that you chose not to carry the statement itself, but confined your reportage to the comments made by Dr Kopelowitz, president of the Board of Deputies, and my response to it....

'Far from stirring storms, it was our intention, by issuing the statement at this stage in the selection process, to avoid confrontation. We sought merely to clarify our own relationship to the Office of Chief Rabbi and to point out that only the United Synagogue and its associated congregations were involved in the choice.

'We stated that we did not seek to detract from the status of the Chief Rabbi of the United Hebrew Congregations or his authority over his constituents.... The wisdom of expressing just where we stand was amply borne out when we read the reported words of Rabbi Jonathan Sacks.

'If Rabbi Sacks, a leading candidate for Chief Rabbi, known as a moderate, can reject the possibility of a pluralistic religious Jewish society (one which exists satisfactorily in the USA in the absence of a Chief Rabbi)[96], how can anyone claim that there is a likelihood that the new holder of the post could or would wish to speak satisfactorily for Progressive Jews?'[97]

Meanwhile, the Progressives had also taken issue with Kopelowitz, and in a letter to him ULPS president Harold Sanderson spelled out his disappointment. 'We think it was unwise of you,' he wrote, 'to comment on an unverified newspaper report, and we question the validity of the "second role" you ascribe to the Chief Rabbi of the United Hebrew Congregations.

'He has never been recognised by either wing of the Progressive movement as the *religious* representative of the whole of the British Jewish community or the Commonwealth. It may have slipped your memory that the chairman of the Council of Reform and Liberal Rabbis has been our representative in this area for two decades.... It is our opinion that it is not our statement which has caused division, but your comments which have helped to mislead the Jewish community.'[98]

Undeterred, Kopelowitz replied in equal measure: 'I am firmly of the view that the statement I made at the Board accurately reflects the position of the Chief Rabbi, both as the Religious Authority of those congregations who recognise that Authority, and also as the public religious representative of the totality of British Jewry. I can see no reason whatever why a statement made by the Union of Liberal and Progressive Synagogues, on a matter which is of concern within the Jewish community, should have appeared in *The Times*.

'I have now had an opportunity of discussing this matter with your president, Lord Goodman, who has indicated to me that he saw the statement in draft, when it was shown to him by Rabbi Dr Sidney Brichto. Lord Goodman has assured me that he agreed to it "with great reluctance".

'Having carefully considered the matter in all its aspects, I am firmly of the view that it is not in the communal interest that the matter should be pursued any further. Any statement by me, at the next meeting of the Board, would in no way be helpful. I am sure, that on reflection, you will share this view.'[99]

Differences also arose among the leaders of the Reform and Liberal communities. Clarifying their position, the RSGB issued their own statement:

> The authority of the Chief Rabbi of the United Hebrew Congregations of the British Commonwealth, to give him his full title, extends to those Orthodox congregations – forming a substantial majority in the community – who are 'United' for the purpose of appointing a chief rabbi as their principal rabbinic authority.
>
> There are differences in ideological interpretation and religious practice within Judaism, and Reform synagogues are guided in religious matters by their own Assembly of Rabbis. Similarly,

there are smaller Orthodox groupings who appoint their own independent rabbinic authorities.

There are many areas of common interest and concern to all Jews in which the Chief Rabbi is seen as a leading spokesman for British Jewry. Rather like the Archbishop of Canterbury, the Chief Rabbi, when making statements, speaks with the standing that derives from his Office.

No one perceives the authority of the Archbishop as extending to the Free Churches or to other sectors of the Church. Similarly, to our knowledge, the Chief Rabbi has never claimed to speak for all Jews. There are many contemporary issues where opinions differ within the Jewish community, on which it is accepted that there is room for open and courteous debate.

Despite doctrinal differences with the Reform and Liberal movements, Lord Jakobovits has sought in a number of ways to foster greater unity or, as he has put it, 'to build bridges' in the community; for this he has sometimes been criticised. We trust that, whoever is appointed the next Chief Rabbi, he will have the courage to advance the work started by Lord Jakobovits and will help to bring greater harmony and sense of common purpose to the whole of British Jewry.[100]

Taking issue with this approach, John Rayner wrote to RSGB chairman Marcus Bower: 'As chairman of the Council of Reform and Liberal Rabbis – which is by its very nature both an expression of, and a means of promoting, the essential unity of the two Progressive Jewish movements in this country – I am inevitably distressed by the lack of unity manifested by the divergent statements they have recently made about the Chief Rabbinate....

'Should it not be possible, and would it not be highly desirable, for the two movements to follow up their separate statements with a joint one which would make it clear that they are essentially in agreement about the role of the Chief Rabbi, and so help to undo the impression of serious disharmony between them which has so unfortunately been conveyed to the general Jewish (and non-Jewish) public? If so, would you be willing to take an initiative to that end?'[101]

The best Bower could produce was a letter to the JC reaffirming that 'there are many areas of common interest and concern to all Jews in which the Chief Rabbi, by virtue of his office and of his own personal standing, is seen as holding a unique position within British Jewry.

Statements made by him are rightly treated with respect both inside and outside the community, but he has never claimed to speak for all Jews.'[102]

* * *

A month after the *Times*' report, Brichto wrote to the Chief Rabbi referring both to the ULPS statement and to Jakobovits' letter in which he had asserted: 'I really think we should call it a day if hypocrisy is not to become a basic feature of communal and personal relations.'

> I was deeply saddened by your letter [Brichto responded].[103] Your accusation against me of hypocrisy is unfounded. The ULPS statement was made after lengthy consideration and unanimously agreed by all the honorary officers, council members and rabbis.... It promises your successor our full co-operation and is worded in a very positive and, indeed, totally non-confrontational way.
>
> I have always admired your conviction and dedication to promoting Judaism. Your desire to represent all of Anglo-Jewry, however, has been in conflict with your deep, and not surprising, loyalty to the small but increasing band of the very Orthodox whom you believe will provide the sole future for Judaism. I think this has been the reason for the increased differences between us over the past few years.
>
> While I differ from you on many issues, my respect for your sincerity and good intentions makes me hope that you will think again about closing the doors to dialogue between us. I would very much regret this.

Writing to Sir Sigmund Sternberg a month later, the Chief Rabbi was in no mood to mince his words: 'Let me be quite frank,' he wrote. 'Ever since Sidney Brichto's outburst – on the front page of *The Times*, no less! – informing the world that they would not recognise the next Chief Rabbi (as if they ever did in the past), I have had a feeling that his present efforts at reconciliation through dialogue are an exercise in hypocrisy and futility. I have told him so quite bluntly.

'I know that his absolutely unwarranted intervention has deeply embarrassed the entire Reform movement, and he himself has admitted that he should not have acted in this way. But he has offered no apology to me or to the Orthodox community. The dust cannot settle before then. Hence the disinclination of our team to be involved in a dialogue at this moment. I am sure you will understand.'[104]

The episode concluded with the following letter from Brichto to Sternberg:

> I have now had the opportunity to consider Lord Jakobovits' letter to you of 15 February. You will see from copies of the enclosed correspondence that I have attempted to work a reconciliation without success. I therefore doubt that you could do anything to improve our relationship.
>
> For the record, I must point out that there was no outburst from me in *The Times*. The statement on the Chief Rabbinate was signed by the ULPS chairman and director, and the decision to make it was a unanimous decision of the ULPS council.
>
> The rabbis, officers and council members would be very offended at the suggestion that their decision was my 'unwarranted intervention'. The ULPS is a very independent body, as proven by the fact that it decided to make the statement without the joint sponsorship of the Reform....
>
> The Chief Rabbi is also wrong to say that I admitted that I 'should not have acted in this way'. I have not done so, nor would I apologise for an action taken by my own organisation. You may or may not send a copy of this letter to Lord Jakobovits, but I would ask you at least to correct this impression....
>
> On the deeper issues, I fail to understand why, if our statement was saying the obvious, he was so upset, unless he feels that such a truth should be kept within the family. Why is he so frightened that the non-Jewish world should know that Judaism is not monolithic? Does he think that the Gentiles will think less of us?
>
> Equally, the honest statement of the facts should not create disunity in the Jewish community. The *Jewish Chronicle* editorial found nothing divisive in the ULPS statement.
>
> Why should I not express a different view from his in the national press? Is only the Orthodox Chief Rabbi to be allowed to rush into print on any occasion he wishes, without regard to the views of others, especially on issues of a non-religious nature?

I am deeply saddened by the whole matter. I respect and admire Lord Jakobovits and have enjoyed an excellent relationship with him for years, and there is ample public record of this. It is unfortunate that it has soured. But, Siggi, I must tell you that if the price of this friendship is the limitation of my freedom of speech, I cannot accept it. Nor do I think would he were he in my situation.[105]

CHAPTER FIVE

1990–2000

Kinship and Courtesy

In a letter to Clifford Longley, of *The Times*, soon after the ULPS statement dissociating itself from the Chief Rabbinate's authority, Brichto declared: 'I am delighted with the forthcoming appointment of Rabbi Jonathan Sacks. He will have my full co-operation, and I look forward to a non-confrontational relationship during the period of his office.'[1] Responding to a congratulatory note the following week, Sacks wrote to Brichto:

'As you know (or, it occurs to me, perhaps you don't), as soon as I read your article, "Halachah with Humility", I called it publicly "the most courageous statement by a non-Orthodox Jew this century." I felt it was a genuine way forward. Others turned out not to share my view. It will be a while – eighteen months – before I take up office. But I believe we can still explore that way forward together. For if we do not move forward, I fear greatly for our community and for *Am Yisrael*.'[2]

Sacks had received his 'call' from the United Synagogue's president, Sidney Frosh – head of the selection committee – and had indicated that he would assume office in September of the following year, after a period of study in Israel. Jakobovits, meanwhile, had agreed to remain in office.

> Outwardly calm [the *Jewish Chronicle* reported], but clearly stirred by the prospect of what lies ahead, Rabbi Jonathan Sacks watched the trees outside his office window bend before the gale-force wind, and reflected on his meteoric rise to Anglo-Jewry's top appointment.
>
> He was, he admitted, delighted at the thought of becoming Britain's next Chief Rabbi, and frankly overwhelmed by the

torrent of congratulatory messages that this week have kept the telephone at his North-West London home ringing from dawn until late at night.

At 41, Rabbi Sacks has been picked for the position less than twelve years since he was inducted as a rabbi by the man he is to replace. 'I feel honoured and privileged,' he said. 'And my family and I are also very excited,' he added with a smile.

Although he will not take over at the Chief Rabbi's Office until September next year – and although his appointment has still to be formally ratified by the full Chief Rabbinate Council – Rabbi Sacks is already contemplating the task. He will step down as principal of Jews' College and as rabbi at Marble Arch Synagogue 'in the near future'.

Then he will spend a full year of study in Israel 'with some of the great Torah sages. I want to come to the position having immersed myself in the atmosphere of Torah learning and Eretz Yisrael', said Rabbi Sacks, whose relative lack of yeshivah experience has been highlighted in some reports of his appointment.

His Chief Rabbinate, he added, 'will aim to heal some of the rifts that divide the community. It will encourage debate, and it will not shy away from communicating Jewish values to the wider community. I am determined, as far as possible, to emphasise what unites Jews and to encourage an atmosphere of mutual respect. But there can be no compromise in matters of halachah – there are no short cuts.

'The Jewish people have suffered too tragically and too often from internal divisions. I hope that divisive words will be at a minimum from all sectors of the community.'

Rabbi Sacks said he intended to run 'a very open Chief Rabbinate. I want to encourage communal debate. The sages had great faith in the concept of "argument for the sake of heaven". By that they meant that not even the greatest sage in history could get it completely right all the time. But if he listened to constructive criticism, he was more likely to do so.'[3]

In the run-up to Sacks' installation, the activities of the Consultative Committee – as Jakobovits had indicated – were stalled, but statements from some of its members, and from others of prominence, continued to flow. In a paper entitled 'Must Jews Have a Chief Rabbi?', Louis Jacobs described the post as 'a modern innovation, totally without support in any of the classical sources of Judaism....

> The idea of a Chief Rabbi, with authority over other rabbis, is contrary to the thrust of tradition and is unknown in Jewish history until recent times. The Right-wing Orthodox refused to recognise the authority of the Chief Rabbinate on the grounds that it is contrary to the Jewish norm.
> Jewish teaching nowhere states that a community must have a Chief Rabbi and, indeed, the tendency is against such an institution. However, a contract once made must be honoured like any other contract freely entered into by both parties.
> Those not party to the contract – some of the Orthodox, the Reform, Liberals and other Progressives – have no obligation to recognise the Office, though, of course, they may chose voluntarily to do so. Whether those who do so choose are well-advised in demoting their own rabbis by accepting the Chief Rabbi as the 'titular head' of British Jewry is another matter.
> That there is nothing in Judaism which requires the Office, and that religious Jews can manage very well without a Chief Rabbi, can be seen from the great American Jewish community, in which Jews of every persuasion look upon the British pattern with an amused tolerance, and would not dream of surrendering the stern independence of their rabbis and congregations. Judaism does not demand it. Why should they?[4]

Unsurprisingly, Brichto took a similar line, asserting that recent controversies involving Jakobovits – 'added to previous divisions over some of his statements and writings – must make many consider whether the Office of the Chief Rabbinate is of benefit to Anglo-Jewry. The conclusion must be that it has been, and is, a mixed blessing....

> One can argue the importance of an Office which gives the non-Jewish community the idea that Jewry is a cohesive and united community. It is also very useful for us to be represented on State occasions by an individual as the Archbishop of Canterbury and the Moderator represent Anglican and non-conforming Christianity.
> It would be a fair approximation to say that 75 per cent of Anglo-Jewry are either secularists, Progressive or non-believing and non-practising members of Orthodox synagogues, and as

such are miles apart from the Chief Rabbi's theological beliefs and convictions. This means that a community which is basically tied together not by religious but by ethnic bonds has as its only spokesman a person who, while he may express the views of Orthodox Judaism, does not reflect the feelings of most Jews.

The Chief Rabbinate, as a manifestation of Jewish unity, has one other great disadvantage. When the incumbent expresses a very controversial viewpoint which catches the headlines, other Jewish leaders feel compelled to take issue in the strongest possible terms, which they would not do if the view had been expressed by an 'ordinary' rabbi.

In spite of these negative aspects of the Office, one can still appreciate the importance for our community to have a spokesman who can express the anxiety or pleasure of the community on important issues.

The holder of this Office, however, should be required to reflect the views of the community, even when they do not agree with his own. When his views are either his or those of the Orthodox community alone, he should be expected to say so. If this restriction on the Office is impractical, it would make more sense to accept that it represents, and speaks only for, the Orthodox.

Other communities should be invited to appoint their own spokesmen. This would make the reality of Jewish life in Britain apparent — namely, that we are as capable of differences within our own religious faith as are Christians, Moslems and others within theirs. Indeed, the non- Jewish community could be more interested in what a religious body had to say on a specific issue than to hear an amorphous but superficial view which is assumed to reflect the views of all Jews.[5]

Despite their acrimonious exchange of recent months, Brichto sent the Chief Rabbi a typewritten copy of his article, with the message: 'I wish you well in your retirement. We never did get together as we promised to do. Once the pressure is off in the autumn might be a good time for a chat.'[6]

Jakobovits replied: 'Your comments on current squabbles are much appreciated. Sometimes one needs arguments to find out who one's friends really are. Your idea of "converting" the Chief Rabbinate has, of course, been aired before. I somehow cannot see that either side is quite ready yet. But, in any case, I must leave the decisions to a new generation — and I won't be sorry that the onus is no longer mine.

'Thank you indeed for your good wishes on my retirement. It is not likely to keep me idle, and some renewed get-togethers with you will be as welcome as before.'[7]

Days later, discussing in Reform's quarterly magazine, *Manna*, the Chief Rabbi's role as spokesman for the community, the journalist Chaim Bermant[8] wrote of Jakobovits: 'It is not easy to place him in the theological firmament, for he is such a mass of contradiction.

'He is, in many respects, an outstanding example of Modoxy [Bermant's term for Modern Orthodoxy], yet, if one turns to domestic issues, there is nothing modish about his Orthodoxy. He has surrounded himself with men who, on most issues, would not feel out of place in Bnei Braq. The dominant sound of his ministry is the sound of clocks being turned back.'

Bermant cited as an example the substitution in his local synagogue of a six-foot-high curtain [*mechitzah*] for a nine-inch one separating the women from the men. 'One does not suggest that this was due to orders from on high, but it does arise from the prevailing atmosphere induced by the Chief Rabbi and his colleagues. And yet, when they rebuilt the Edinburgh synagogue and placed the ladies on the same level as the men, with only a gangway to divide them and no curtains whatever, it was sanctioned as kosher by the Chief Rabbi.

'So where does that leave us? A trifle perplexed, I would say. Were the Chief Rabbi an out-and-out reactionary – as he is on some issues – it might have led to large-scale defections from the United Synagogue and to a dramatic growth in the Masorti movement. But British Jews are extremely conservative, and it takes a major crisis to make them think deeply about their religious affiliations....

'The dominance of the Chief Rabbinate is such as to make it difficult for rabbis to flourish in its shadow. There is, however, Dr Jonathan Sacks, who has used his position as principal of Jews' College to emerge from the shadows. He has all the necessary credentials of a Modox rabbi, but though he is an elegant speaker and accomplished broadcaster, he has said little to suggest the direction of his own ideas.

'Modernism is no virtue in itself; it has more than a few defects. But one searches for an Orthodoxy which is compassionate, forward-looking and not wholly irrational. And Sacks may yet provide it.'

Perhaps most relevant of the prevailing remarks was an editorial in the same issue of *Manna*, which commented:

> Over recent years, Anglo-Jewry has got stuck in an uncomfortable no-man's land. British Orthodoxy has fought shy of taking its

objections to the extreme conclusion, but has been equally reluctant to speak too much of common ground lest this be seen as conferring a tacit blessing or legitimation.

It has therefore pursued a policy of marginalisation. The Reform and Liberal movements have been seen as groupings of Jews, which probably provide a useful place to hold those who might otherwise be lost through assimilation. But their Judaism has been peremptorily dismissed, and the Progressive community has been actively sanitised, placed neither in nor out, but in no man's land....

More recently we have seen, with the blessing of the Chief Rabbi and his Consultative Committee, the establishment of a Liaison Group between the United Synagogue and the Reform and Liberal movements, so that the Consultative Committee can devote itself to that which its title implies, and its 'moratorium' can be implemented in a more effective manner.

There are clearly limitations to what the Liaison Group is likely to achieve. It cannot mend or bridge the profound theological differences between the two communities. It is unlikely to have much impact on the workings of the London Beth Din.

But it does bring together key people on either side of the divide and can offer a framework for trust and friendship on which a better future could be built.... It suggests that some within the United Synagogue have conquered their fear of being seen to legitimise Progressive Judaism by talking amicably to its leaders.

Perhaps the very development of Reform in Britain in the 1980s has laid this ghost by underlining the fact that Progressive Judaism neither seeks nor needs legitimation from anyone. Above all, it suggests that, for some at least, working to maximise the common ground is the strategy which has the best interests of Jewry and Judaism at its heart.[9]

* * *

Interviewed four years earlier, Jakobovits had pulled no punches in describing his relationship with the Progressives. 'While they will argue that they do not seek any recognition or legitimisation by the Orthodox,' he had declared, 'they will in the same breath say that they are part of the mainstream of Judaism and represent merely another legitimate branch of the tree of Judaism – and want the Orthodox majority here to subscribe to that notion. This is something we cannot accept, something we cannot deliver.

> You cannot have two branches of the same tree, one of which carries fruits that proclaim the sanctity of the Sabbath, of the dietary and marriage laws, and another which denies the validity of these laws. This is not a common tree.
>
> So long as this is a preponderantly traditional community – some 75 to 80 per cent still identify happily with the Orthodox community, despite all the attractions and distractions – we cannot acknowledge that we are all equals, that it is merely a matter of choosing between different forms of Judaism.
>
> The Progressives quite plausibly tell me that, in that case, I cannot represent them as Chief Rabbi. My answer is that I have two functions: I am not only "chief" in the sense of being religious spokesman for the entire community, but I am also "rabbi". As a rabbi, I head an Orthodox establishment and I have my beliefs which I cannot sacrifice for the sake of good neighbourly relations.
>
> I believe the religious stability of the community will determine the future of the community more than our unity. Unity is a precious thing, an important thing. But even more important than a façade of unity where none exists is that we should convey to our children, and our children's children, loyalties and allegiances, beliefs and practices, which are the sole raison d'être of Jewish existence. I cannot compromise on that.
>
> We had reached a gentleman's agreement with the Progressives which has worked splendidly over these nearly eighteen years that I have been in office, whereby it was understood that, while I would make statements on behalf of the Jewish community where they represented a consensus of opinion, if these statements were on Judaism I would not look for a consensus.
>
> On Judaism, I am the spokesman not for the majority (even if I speak of Sabbath observance, I recognise that I do not speak for the majority), but I speak for authentic Judaism as I see it. It has always been understood that this would not compromise my ability to be a spokesman in the tradition of the Chief Rabbinate of this country.
>
> I believe that four-fifths of Anglo-Jewry and the vast majority of non-Jews will continue to recognise my Office. This will be so

irrespective of challenges that are made by the minority, that I do not speak for them when I pronounce on matters of Jewish belief, Jewish practice and Jewish ethics which they themselves know are the authentic Jewish law as halachically interpreted.

I think that if we were to continue with this mutual understanding, we should concentrate, as I have pleaded throughout my incumbency, on our constructive work, putting our own houses in order, strengthening our education and our synagogues, without abusing one another, without throwing mud at one another.[10]

A year after his retirement, Jakobovits returned to the thrust of his Chief Rabbinate, its successes and failures, and his vision for the future:

Among the objectives I announced on assuming office were the preservation of 'the Orthodox traditions of my position and the predominantly traditional character of our community', and the befriending of dissenters, 'to work with them in Jewish and general causes unaffected by our religious differences'.

My chances at first seemed rather slim. I arrived at a time of acute crisis, when the embers of the 'Jacobs Affair' were still glowing dangerously. Friends in America had warned me that there was no Office left to take over, that major congregations were on the brink of seceding, and that the whole atmosphere was choking with dissension and bitterness.

But, as I met people on my visits up and down the country, I won increasing support across the community. By eliminating the strife of the past, I made possible the constructive work ahead. Some of my early antagonists became good friends....

Turbulent as the times were externally, on the domestic front they were more tranquil than under any of my four predecessors over the past 150 years. Chief Rabbis Nathan and Hermann Adler witnessed major challenges to communal unity, with the breakaway to the Right by the Federation and the Machzike Hadass, and by the Reform to the Left.

Little is comparable to the fury with which Dr Hertz attacked 'the New Paths' of the Liberals. He was on several occasions locked in bitter conflicts with his lay leaders, first over the Balfour Declaration, and later over the British White Paper on Palestine.

His successor, Israel Brodie, faced a major rebellion which threatened the Chief Rabbinate itself, as well as the cohesion of the community. I was fortunate to enjoy closer personal bonds of friendship with all lay leaders than did any previous Chief Rabbi. And the community enjoyed greater stability than even I myself had anticipated....

Of course, I realise all too painfully that I had my great disappointments and setbacks. But my own assessment of crisis and failure does not necessarily correspond to public or press perceptions. Futile was my effort to secure some real Jewish unity when I convened, and engaged in, intensive parleys with Progressive leaders, seeking an agreement on marriage, divorce and conversion to which all sections could subscribe.

Such an agreement would have removed the calamitous rift whereby members of one community could not marry those of another, and whereby persons deemed non-Jewish by some were accepted as Jews by others. This sad rupture distressed me endlessly.

Another objective which eluded me was to help eliminate, or reduce, the polarisation of our people into ever-more extremist groups, widening the gap between the religious and the secular, the Orthodox and the 'ultra-Orthodox', and even the political divide. The trend is global, though less pronounced in Britain, with its more mellow tradition, than in Israel and America. But for me, committed as I am by nurture and conviction to *Torah im derech eretz*, in a setting of tolerance and moderation without sacrifice of principle, the process was and remains profoundly disturbing....

I do not relish public controversies, but I must be at peace with my conscience, and as a spiritual leader I cannot suppress it. On communal and public policies, I have always tried to be guided by my sainted father's motto: 'One enemy is too many, a hundred friends are too few.'

My efforts to cultivate friendships have, I believe, proved rewarding to the community and to the Jewish people, no less than to me. I have never yielded to the temptation to resort to mere gimmicks. In public utterances, I avoided expressing views with which all would agree – the convinced need no persuasion from anyone! After all, the task of a rabbi is to speak for Judaism and not necessarily for Jews.

What of the future? My successor faces both an easier and a harder task than I did. The community is less factious, better educated and no longer as much in despair as I found it. On the other hand, it is in greater economic distress and beset by more external uncertainties, all placing more question-marks over communal stability such as has distinguished Anglo-Jewry for over a century.

According to Jewish teaching, each generation calls for leaders 'of these days', attuned to contemporary needs. Hertz, Brodie, Jakobovits, Sacks – each faced different challenges, and has had to respond in the light of their times. Yet, transcending all these variations, there remained inviolate the determination to preserve the continuity of what is the world's oldest Chief Rabbinate.

With the community's unfailing support for my worthy successor, I have every confidence in the progression of achievement as the ship of Anglo-Jewry, with its noble traditions, sails hopefully in calm waters towards a place of honour in the record of Jewish history.[11]

* * *

Under Sacks' early stewardship, the Consultative Committee and Liaison Group made tentative progress. The new incumbent had familiarised himself with the tasks ahead, formulated during early discussions – on consecutive weeks – with Jakobovits and Bayfield. In the first of the meetings,[12] Jakobovits noted of himself that he

1. 'retains a high stake in the success of the Office of Chief Rabbi, yet emphasised that he does not expect the Office to be built in his image.'

2. The Reform movement

Lord Jakobovits says that the Reform movement during his reign continually felt inferior. To that end, he wanted to grant them some type of recognition and created a Consultative Committee, which was hosted by the Chief Rabbi at Hamilton Terrace, but convened and conducted by the Reform movement.

Lord Jakobovits suggested that one resists at all costs a Progressive representation on the presidium of the CCJ. The reasons for this are that it will be the first inroad into fully fledged recognition for the Progressive community. However, one way in which he presented his opposition to the Progressives was to inform them that this type of representation would tell the outside world that the divisions between the Reform and the Orthodox within Judaism are as great as those between Catholics and Protestants within Christianity.

Lord Jakobovits strongly advised the Chief Rabbi to create personal relations, particularly with Hugo Gryn.

Lord Jakobovits feels that the Chief Rabbi can take shelter under an 'academic umbrella' for six months, but following this initial honeymoon period he will have to take a stand.

3. The United Synagogue

Lord Jakobovits' great fear is that the middle ground of the United Synagogue will be eroded, and then the organised community will be finished.

Even though the United Synagogue must loosen up control of its constituents, the Chief Rabbi must not be perceived as actively moving it towards disintegration. Lord Jakobovits constantly reiterated that without a strong United Synagogue, all of its structures – the Chief Rabbinate, the Beth Din, and the Orthodox hegemony of the community – will collapse.

4. Consultations

Lord Jakobovits warns the Chief Rabbi not to build rival consultative groups outside of the United Synagogue. This will become dangerous and divisive. If one establishes a 'rival government', one will affront those elected, and the Chief Rabbi will loosen his own position within the community.

5. Media

Lord Jakobovits advised the Chief Rabbi never to respond through the press to any personal attacks in writing.

A memorandum of Sacks' meeting with Bayfield the following week[13] noted that 'Tony gave the sense of one who is a pursuant of peace, but is being pressurised by his colleagues. There are clearly those in the Progressive world who would like to see progress on certain key issues, such as personal status. At the same time, there is a desire to work together in possible areas such as the process of educational planning.

'The short-term possibility of achievement, as far as Tony is concerned, is at least public acknowledgement of the private meetings. Tony feels that the mechanism for a Liaison Committee needs to be looked at again. It is possible that its members need to be given tasks to work on, rather than just be talking-shops. He feels that the Consultative Committee is not a committee with direction or a sense of purpose.'

* * *

Before Sacks assumed office, a 'Mission Statement'[14] was prepared, opening with a declaration that 'the task of the Chief Rabbinate is to provide Anglo-Jewry with a sense of direction: to liberate and mobilise energies toward the achievement of collective goals. In so doing, it will seek to project four loves.'

The first was *ahavat Yisrael*, a love of the people of Israel. 'Each Jew, regardless of where he or she stands, is holy, a fragment of the *Shechinah* [Divine Presence].... We will fight against all expressions of intra-Jewish conflict and animosity. We will listen to all voices, for the Divine Presence rests not in one section of the Jewish people, but in the conversation of the whole people with itself, its heritage and its destiny.

'We believe in the unity of Israel, not in the sense of uniformity (for there are many ways of serving God), nor in the sense of the acceptance of all interpretations of Jewish identity (for that is a road to fragmentation, not convergence), but in the sense that we are all travelling along the same road, even though at different points and at different speeds. We identify with the Jewish past. We share a commitment to the Jewish future. We feel a sense of kinship with other Jews. And we must make the Jewish future collectively.'

The other three 'loves' were *ahavat Eretz Yisrael*, a love of the land of Israel as the centre of the Jewish world; *ahavat Torah*, a love of Torah as the historic vocation of the Jewish people; and *ahavat Hashem*, the love of God.

The statement concluded: 'At all times, the Chief Rabbinate must stand for

- a willingness to listen;
- respect for the variety of Jewish life, and the integrity of those who take different views from our own;
- the compassion of the halachah;
- the dignity and courtesy of a Judaism whose 'ways are ways of pleasantness, and all its paths are peace';
- the conviction and courage born of a clear spiritual and ethical vision'.

A second paper – 'The Chief Rabbinate: A Scenario for the Future',[15] written by Sacks in the first person – declared that 'until now, the Chief Rabbinate has been primarily conceived as a reactive and representative institution. As such, it has historically exercised great influence. The question is: is this an appropriate model for the current state and needs of Anglo-Jewry? The answer, I believe, is "No"....

'How, in short, are we to motivate, inspire and empower? The Chief Rabbinate is almost certainly the only institution through which one could achieve these ends. It is almost universally recognised within and outside the community. It has the power to transcend narrow institutional boundaries. It can and should be above "Jewish politics" of various kinds. With varying degrees of authority, it can speak to Orthodox and non-Orthodox, religious and secular Jews. It can, by strategically placed initiatives and interventions, affect the tone and mood of the community.

'My vision of a Chief Rabbinate for the 1990s is not one of authority and centralised power, but rather of an institution that inspires and motivates others – across the whole spectrum of Anglo-Jewry – to leadership, creativity and achievement.... The aim is, within a five-year period, to change the mood of Anglo-Jewry, and the key individuals within it, toward a sense of the vast unexplored possibilities of innovation and excellence.

'The Chief Rabbinate must be seen to be communicating a message of confidence in the abilities of individuals and groups to achieve for themselves – and it must be seen to be leading, by example, from the front.'

* * *

Presiding over the first meeting of the Consultative Committee since Sacks assumed office, Reform's Rabbi Colin Eimer 'expressed the committee's gratitude that it is to continue to have the privilege of meeting in the Chief Rabbi's home'. He then proceeded with a résumé of the group's history:

'... In time, as an atmosphere of trust was built up, the group occasionally digressed into matters concerning internal communal conflict, with both sides agreeing to try to exert a measure of restraint on the more militant opinion within their ranks – in particular, as regards the language in which disagreement was expressed in the media.

'Ultimately, this aspect of the work gave birth to the Liaison Group where, at the suggestion of the former Chief Rabbi, Rabbi Maurice Unterman and Rabbi Tony Bayfield convened a small group of rabbis and laymen, both to try to prevent fires starting or, where they did, to try and ensure that they were extinguished as quickly and with as little communal damage as possible. This group continues to meet three or four times a year and will come back to the Consultative Committee only if it is unable to resolve a difficulty – and so far that has not arisen.'

During the ensuing discussion, Bayfield observed that 'the origins of a custom are not necessarily indicative of its current function. In this case, what has been achieved is that leaders of Anglo-Jewry sit together – and that, in itself, is of inestimable value.

'Our function is to influence the climate in Anglo-Jewry for the better, by meeting and getting to know each other. From this, there has developed a situation of respect, trust and personal affection between our members. This does not mean the fudging of issues, or trying to peddle the trite view that "all views are equally right".

'It does mean that there can be responsible theological debate and a civilised exchange of opinions without the need for internecine strife. It is false to see public discussion in terms of one sector of the community receiving legitimation from another: each sector's legitimation is derived from the support it receives from its own membership.'

In response, Sacks remarked 'how much I welcome the opportunity for such deliberations, which carry in them a spark of the *Shechinah*'. Stressing 'the importance of people talking to each other as an antidote to *sinat chinam* [causeless hatred]', he added: 'For a people with a long history, we seem incapable of functioning cohesively; but if we do not start to do so, history will not forgive us.

'None of us should be guilty of contributing to "an argument that is not for the sake of Heaven". If our arguments *are* for "the sake of Heaven", then relating to each other does not demand unanimity.

'If God lives within the community, then each of us has a part to play, and each can have something to learn from the positive tensions that will exist in the community. It is to that end that my ministry will be dedicated.'[16]

Support for this approach was voiced at a meeting of the Liaison Group later in the year when, discussing the need for national representation, its members agreed that 'in all cases it is necessary to seek out people on either side able to attract broad support in their sector of the community, who will be able locally to suggest ways of avoiding communal *machloket* [dispute] and, where it occurs, are able to negotiate and be seen as "honest brokers."'[17]

A gathering of the Consultative Committee the following month, held once again at the Chief Rabbi's residence, devoted itself 'to reviewing the effect of its work during the first year with a new Chief Rabbi.'[18] Sacks acknowledged 'a debt of gratitude to the forces of moderation' and mentioned Bayfield's help in trying to divert tensions into a constructive direction.

Between everyone, they had succeeded in 'keeping the show on the road', and he had set himself the task of improving communal relationships. His initiative of a 'Walkabout', directed to all members and sectors of the community, was 'a positive public manifestation of that intent'.

The Chief Rabbi said he 'recognised the desire in some quarters for more openness and less secrecy in intra-communal matters, such as the Consultative Committee itself. He had set a date for a meeting with the leadership of the Council of Reform and Liberal Rabbis to discuss the exclusion of the Jewish Gay and Lesbian Helpline from his Walkabout.

'Certainly, I have no desire to persecute homosexuals, and I respect the fact that the helpline is a welfare organisation. Regrettably, those involved were more concerned to exploit the political value of the occasion than to advance its welfare purpose. In this situation, a "yes" to their participation would have alienated much lay and rabbinic support.

'In many ways, I have gone out on a limb to promote greater communal harmony, and have been frequently criticised by those nearest to me on whom I rely for much of my support.' He was, he added, 'the most liberal Chief Rabbi you will ever have'.

Gryn remarked that 'the moderates are moderate because their conviction is that moderation is the correct path. There is a need to promote the concepts of *kahal* and *Klal Yisrael*, to seek commonality rather than confrontation.'

Bayfield argued that 'if discipline is being maintained among the rabbis of the United Synagogue, every effort must be made to persuade Reform and Liberal rabbis not to step out of line. But the covert nature of much of the cross-sectarian contact gives rise to a good deal of scepticism in non-Orthodox rabbinical ranks, and feeds opportunities to the press for misrepresentation and the exertion of pressure.'

Meetings of the committees over the succeeding year were of minor consequence, but early in 1994, following a series of disputes across the communal divide – particularly relating to Masorti[19] – Rayner wrote to Sacks in anticipation of talks between the two, planned for the coming days.

'Even though I don't yet know what you wish to discuss,' he told the Chief Rabbi, 'perhaps I may put to you a thought that has been going through my mind for many years, but has become crystallised and reinforced by recent happenings.

'It is that the position of a Chief Rabbi who is regarded by himself, by most Jews, and by the general public as the spiritual leader of the whole of our pluralistic Anglo-Jewish community is sustainable only on condition that, during his tenure of office, and as a self-restraint imposed by its nature, he refrains from publicly denying the legitimacy of pluralism, or impugning non-Orthodox kinds of Judaism – leaving it to other Orthodox rabbis to do these things, if they must.

'You may feel that such self-restraint would be intolerable, but in that case one would have to conclude that the Chief Rabbinate is not sustainable, and that some other, more democratic form of spiritual leadership needs to be devised.'[20]

Days later, Rayner wrote to four Liberal and Reform colleagues whom he was meeting for a lunchtime discussion, in advance of a gathering of the Consultative Committee the following month. 'I look forward to seeing you at the Sternberg Centre on Monday and am jotting down a few thoughts which might help to focus our discussion.'

1. The Committee is scheduled to meet on 8 March. We must decide what we want to suggest by way of agenda.
2. I hope it will be agreed that one item, if not the only one, should be the future of the Committee – at least a preliminary discussion about that.
3. The reason is that some of us have come to feel increasingly uncomfortable with the Committee in its present form.
4. On the one hand, it seems to serve little purpose. We receive reports; we listen politely to the CR's [Chief Rabbi's] self-justifications; and we register complaints about non-consultation without achieving any remedies.
5. On the other hand, we aid and abet the perpetuation of a manifest falsehood (hereinafter to be referred to as The Myth): that we are a monistic community with the CR at its apex.
6. It was in order to explode The Myth that, in 1967, we talked about the idea of the chairman of the CRLR becoming a second Jewish president of the CCJ.
7. What was important about that idea was not the CCJ, but the fact that it would have given public recognition to the fact that we are a pluralistic community.
8. The idea, unsurprisingly, was opposed by those who had a vested interest in maintaining The Myth, including the CR and the Board of Deputies.

9. More surprisingly, our own leadership (Leslie Edgar and Lionel Cohen, as, more recently, Sigi Sternberg) advised us not to press it.
10. Instead, Jakobovits offered us a 'compromise' (hereinafter to be referred to as The Sop) in the form of the Consultative Committee.
11. The whole purpose of The Sop was to maintain The Myth, and to keep us quiet about it.
12. We bought The Sop. But some of us were always against it, and most of us, I suspect, have come to feel increasingly uncomfortable with it of late.
13. Here are some of the factors that may have contributed to the feeling of discomfort and that might constitute reasons for discontinuing The Sop that sustains The Myth.
    a. It never was just – and 'justice delayed is justice denied' (Avot 5:18).
    b. It always was – as it was intended to be – detrimental to our interest.
    c. Our constituency has grown dramatically since 1967 (consider, for example, the number of Progressive rabbis then and now).
    d. The CR has publicly denied the legitimacy of non-Orthodox Judaism.
    e. The CR has publicly rejected pluralism: how, then, can he be regarded as the head of a pluralistic community?
    f. The CR has failed to stop his Beth Din from sending out letters telling people that if they marry in non-Orthodox synagogues, their marriages will be invalid. Indeed, he is known to endorse that policy.
    g. The CR has taken public stands on issues such as homosexuality and women's rights from which we must dissociate ourselves.
    h. The CR has refused to sit with us on public platforms.
    i. The CR has consistently failed to deliver meaningful consultation over allegedly communal projects such as the Community Walk and Jewish Continuity.
    j. The CR has deliberately excluded our synagogues and our rabbis from eligibility for his allegedly communal 'Awards for Excellence'.

k. The CR represents a form of Orthodoxy which rejects modern scholarship, and is closer to Lubavitch Judaism than that of any of his predecessors, and there is reason to fear that he will allow Lubavitch Judaism increasingly to infiltrate into the community.

14. All this amounts to a strong case for discontinuing The Sop in its present form. Against that case only two points can be made, but it must be admitted that they are very powerful:
   a. We have always wanted to act, and be seen to act, in a spirit of klal Yisrael; always anxious to maintain communal harmony; always ready to initiate, as well as respond to, any and every opportunity for communication, consultation and co-operation across the communal divisions, even to our own disadvantage. Therefore we would not wish to do anything that might look like breaking off relations.
   b. The Committee has served, and can continue to serve, as a trouble-shooting agency. (When there are no troubles to shoot, the Committee may have little to do, yet that may be to some extent a sign of its success rather than its failure.)[21]

The outcome of this agenda, and of the meeting that followed, was never released.

* * *

A year later – on 8 March, 1995, at 85 Hamilton Terrace – only one subject was on the agenda of the Consultative Committee. In the presence of Sacks and fourteen other members, representing religious and lay organisations across the board (though not Masorti), Rayner – as convenor – asked: 'How can we avoid future disharmony, and what can be done to achieve greater harmony both in façade and in reality?'

Opening the discussion, the Chief Rabbi stressed the importance of the Consultative Committee as 'a forum for friendship'. With regard to the controversy over Masorti, he said, members of the Committee had 'helped to stabilise a potentially damaging situation, and the friction has not been with those groups fully represented on it'.

Chief Rabbis in the past had operated 'within the dignified part of the constitution, acting as spiritual leader of the United Hebrew Congregations and playing a representative role. Neither of these traditional functions has been the source of the present controversy.'

Sacks pointed out, however, that he had come into office 'at a time of great difficulty for the United Synagogue and the Board of Deputies', and had 'needed to bring a third dimension to the Office – that of executive action.

'It might be better,' he admitted, 'if in future other agencies play a major part in the Decade of Renewal [the platform on which he had launched his Chief Rabbinate]. In the meantime, a period of stability, healing and contemplation is required.

'We need to be guided by knowledge of what causes each other pain. Orthodoxy experiences great pain when the fundamentals of its beliefs are attacked in intemperate language.' While Masorti's representative on the Consultative Committee had not engaged in such attacks, said Sacks, others had, and it was necessary 'to discuss further what gives each other pain'.

Gryn then asked: 'How can we avoid parading our controversies in public? If we feel the need to go public on an issue, we should at least let each other know beforehand. One of the things that causes me pain is media pleasure in our disunity.'

Summing up the lengthy discussion, in which many others participated, Sacks underlined 'the importance of the friendships that exist within the Consultative Committee in stabilising the situation.

'I have a profound desire to avoid coming this near to disaster ever again. It is important to develop the protocols and etiquette of intra-communal relations. There is a need to develop early-warning mechanisms and, while advocating our own positions, we should not negate the positions adopted by others.'[22]

* * *

A further two years on, pointing to an article published weeks earlier,[23] Jakobovits addressed the subject of unity – 'Anglo-Jewry's "obsessions" and "illusions"' – in the columns of the *Jewish Chronicle*.

'The bold article,' he wrote, 'contained many valuable insights, but it also included two assertions that I find unacceptable: "The Jewish people are more divided today than possibly at any time since the destruction of the Second Temple"; and: "The unity of the Jewish people is the central value around which other values must revolve."

I dispute both assertions, for historical as well as contemporary reasons. The current dissension is hardly comparable, in intensity or substance, to the far more radical divisions of earlier times.... The disputes today are more sterile. I can never forget the penetrating remark by my late revered teacher, Rabbi Dr Isidore Epstein, then principal of Jews' College, who once told me that, bitter as the earlier sectarian divisions were, they yet yielded enormously creative by-products.

Out of the arguments between the Sadducees and the Pharisees emerged much of the edifice of the Talmud. And from the fierce controversy between the Karaites and Rabbanites grew the vast enrichment of Judaism through Jewish philosophy, lexicography, poetry and Bible exegesis. All these developed mainly in response to the need for defending the rabbinical tradition against the assaults of its Karaite critics.

Today, said Rabbi Epstein, nothing positive grew out of the Reform challenge – with, perhaps, the early exception of Rabbi Samson Raphael Hirsch, Rabbi David Hoffmann and Rabbi Ezriel Hildesheimer. The new quarrels produced little but mud-slinging and mutual denunciation.

Nor can I agree that the unity theme will determine the future strength of the Orthodox community – or, indeed, of any part of the Jewish people. Our capacity to survive as Jews will not depend on whether we sit round the same table, or publicly debate our differences, or pursue a search for common ideals where none exist.

While I was Chief Rabbi, I cared greatly about communal harmony and tolerance – as, I am sure, does my successor now. In all areas on which religious differences did not impinge, I encouraged working together, and I formed a Consultative Committee which met regularly at my home, under a Reform or Liberal chairman, to discuss such common concerns as Jewish–Christian relations, Israel, Soviet Jewry, anti-Semitism, and threats to amicable relationships within the community.

Happily, during my incumbency, we never experienced the vitriol such as occurred at the time of the 'Jacobs affair', which spilt over into the national press. Nor did we witness public denunciations of the 'new paths' of the Liberals and the Reformers comparable to the vehemence of the widely circulated attacks under that title by the late Chief Rabbi Joseph Herman Hertz.

Promoting goodwill within the community – however desirable – was never my top priority. I had no illusions that, simply by talking with the dissidents, we would heal the rift of their defection; or save a single Jew from the prospect of marrying out; or make our youth more observant, our university students more committed to Jewish values, and our professionals more Jewish in the practice of their vocation. For these objectives, we need not tolerance, but learning and commitment.

I was, and remain, convinced that the key to the religious stability and growth of Anglo-Jewry lies in intensive Jewish education, not in debating chambers and declarations of goodwill. Indeed, we are now beginning to reap the benefits of greatly expanded and intensified Jewish day-schools, into which such enormous efforts have been invested over the past twenty years.

For me, communal unity was important – not as an intrinsic ideal, however, but to remove the distraction from constructive enterprise. If, week after week, the community's attention is drawn to recrimination and hate-mongering, this is bound to displace interest in building up powerful communal instruments for reclaiming Jews from the wastelands of ignorance.

Columns devoted to recording strife are necessarily denied to subjects of intrinsic value – from articles on Jewish thought or relevance to the modern world, to reports on outstanding Jewish contributions to scholarship, art, science and moral pioneering.

The obsession with communal unity is a peculiarly Anglo-Jewish trait. It does not feature in such a form among American or European Jews – and certainly not in Israel. It is time we shifted our concern from form to substance: how to live as fuller and better Jews, rather than how to gloss over differences and proclaim a unity which turns out to be a mirage.[24]

* * *

True to their word, following their exchanges in mid-1991, that same autumn had turned out to be 'a good time for a chat' between Jakobovits and Brichto. Despite their wide differences, there were points of mutuality in their upbringings, shared values in their philosophies, and common features in their relationships that drew them together even during the most hostile of circumstances.

In a memoir composed later,[25] Jakobovits wrote of his father, Julius, a dayan in Germany before holding a similar post in the London Beth Din:

> My father represented the Hungarian pattern of rabbinical Judaism rather than that projected by the Lithuanian or Polish yeshivot. These differences were very real in the rabbinical world, though not so obvious outside.
>
> He did not, however, subscribe to the complete ban imposed on contact with the Reform movement. While totally rejecting its ideology, of course, he was able to establish cordial personal relationships with some of the Reform or Liberal religious leaders with whom he came in contact at various stages of his career.
>
> One Berlin colleague whom my father esteemed highly was Dr Leo Baeck, the religious leader of the Progressive community. Despite their great differences in belief and practice, he respected Baeck as a spiritual guide of rare stature and integrity....
>
> My father's unification of the Königsberg community was a case in point. He had originally been called to the city as rabbi of the separatist Orthodox congregation in succession to Dr Ezra Munk (a relative of the family into which I was to marry), who later maintained the independent Orthodox line as the distinguished rabbi of the Berlin Adath community. But he soon succeeded in merging the two Königsberg Orthodox congregations – the one inside and the other outside the general communal structure – into a single Orthodox grouping within the wider community, which included a major Reform component....
>
> From my earliest years, working with communal and religious leaders who were not necessarily Orthodox in thought or practice was perfectly natural, a philosophy that was to leave a permanent mark on my attitudes and convictions in later communal life. In this, as in so many other respects, my father's impact on me was dominant from my childhood to the present day.

Born in Philadelphia into a strictly Orthodox family, Sidney Brichto underwent fluctuations of conscience and character before being persuaded by his rabbinical brother Chanan to enter the Reform ministry. 'Chanan', he wrote later, 'was my mentor in life. He questioned everything, and taught me to do the same.

'He was a cynic but, like Diogenes the founder of that movement, a seeker after truth, even when it was soul-destroying. He became a rabbi and, by doing this, he both cast in his lot with the angels and joined generations of Jews who have, by their actions and prayers, affirmed their faith in the ultimate victory of truth over falsehood, and of good over evil.

> I would attribute my decision to become a rabbi to my desire to remain a Jewish Jew. Had I gone for another profession, I could imagine myself drifting away from Judaism as a result of other interests and pressures. A rabbi can be a bad person: after all, he is only human. There is nothing to prevent him from being a philanderer, so long as he does not get caught, or from playing golf on Yom Kippur, though he won't be able to tell anyone if he scores a hole in one.
>
> But, at the very least, observant or non-observant, moral or immoral, one thing is for certain: a rabbi cannot escape his Jewishness. However much I rebelled against Orthodoxy, I loved my Jewish background, and becoming a rabbi was a decision to put my Jewish identity into an irreversible situation.
>
> Had I not done this, I could see myself as a two-day-a-year Jew, boasting to my rabbi that my zeida [grandfather] was a rabbi and that my ancestors were great scholars. He would reply politely, as I do now, 'Really, how interesting', but thinking, 'How often have I heard this before?'
>
> In view of this, it is ironic that in order to rationalise and justify this decision, I had to resolve two issues: on the one hand, zeida and abba [father] would be shattered by my decision. By becoming a Reform rabbi, I would be confirming my heresy, and not only that, I was going to be teaching it to others. I would be a sinner and one who caused others to sin.
>
> My father would prefer a non-practising Orthodox son who was a doctor to a son who was a rabbi practising the wrong Judaism. By becoming a Reform rabbi, I would be causing him and zeida public embarrassment. On the other hand, was my faith strong enough even to be a Reform rabbi? Would not my questioning spirit prevent me from giving my congregation the security they required to maintain their belief in Judaism?
>
> I resolved the first issue by selfishly declaring that it was my life and not theirs, and that whether they knew it or not, I was

affirming the Jewish background my zeida and abba had given me by choosing the rabbinate.

I rationalised the second on the basis that, in Judaism, action not faith was the essence, and that our religion was more concerned with what God demanded of humanity than the nature of His reality. As a rabbi, I would follow in the tradition of those Chasidic rabbis who had, because of the human suffering, constantly questioned God's justice.

Zeida accepted my decision more easily than my father. I don't know what happened, but I soon discovered that he had persuaded himself that both Chanan and I were infiltrators in the Reform movement, that we had become rabbis only in order to bring Jews closer to true Judaism, and not to the Reform heresy.

His love for us both was too deep to allow him to believe that we could betray him. So it was that I was to become one of zeida's two spies in the camp. Strangely enough, while this had never been my intention when I chose the rabbinate, the effect was, in fact, to bring my zeida's world closer to that of the Jews I led, and made them join me in the journey around my zeida.[26]

* * *

For many years, the former Chief Rabbi and former executive vice-president of the Liberal movement remained in touch. In April 1997, responding to a request from Jakobovits to seek out some papers, Brichto wrote back: 'How fortunate it is that, when I left the ULPS headquarters, I took with me the file on our discussions.... I decided to have a look through the history of our own relationship. Therefore, I was in a position to get my hands on the correspondence and statements that you required from me.'[27]

Jakobovits replied: 'I am most grateful to you for so kindly and promptly sending me the material from your files on our discussions in 1969 and 1970. While much water has flown down the Thames since then, I think that some of our deliberations, and perhaps even suggestions, are still as relevant now as they were then.

> Somehow I was wondering whether, in addition to two points made in my memoir, there had not also been a suggestion for the acceptance in some form of the Progressive congregations in return.

I know I was thinking at the time of the pre-war German model in which my father and Leo Baeck were rabbinical colleagues serving the same community, and in which all Beth Din matters were left to be administered by the Orthodox Beth Din serving the entire community.

I know this model was certainly discussed between us. But I think there might also be some reference in our correspondence or proposals at the time.

Meanwhile, my renewed appreciation. I will now consider whether and in what form I could best use the experience of that time to promote some progress now.[28]

'Thank you for your note,' Brichto responded. 'I am sure there was some suggestion of the possibility of Reform and Liberal allowing all Beth Din matters to be administered by the Orthodox Beth Din serving the entire community. This is actually what I was proposing in "Halachah with Humility".

'I was only expecting that, to achieve Progressive co-operation, it would be necessary for the Orthodox Beth Din to be as lenient as possible in its approach. Realistically, it could mean that wherever was possible for the Orthodox Beth Din to administer cases of Jewish status, the Progressives would insist upon it.

'But were there cases beyond its capacity for leniency, such as a *mamzer* (where the marriage of the parents could not be nullified), or in the case of an *agunah* – two issues of principle in which we could not allow individual suffering – the Progressives might have to enable these individuals to enjoy a Jewish wedding.

'I appreciate that the matter is so terribly complicated, but the attempt to resolve these issues would in itself reveal goodwill and a common purpose, two factors so sadly lacking among our present religious leadership.'[29]

'It seems,' wrote Jakobovits in return, 'that you could in fact find no direct reference to the German Gemeinde model in your records of our discussions and correspondence nearly thirty years ago.

'Your analysis of the current situation and its challenges is broadly correct, I believe, though solutions will be harder to find – especially in the present climate. But I still think the idea is worth pursuing further, yet am not sure who are to be the dramatis personae in the next act.'[30]

'I would imagine,' answered Brichto, 'that ultimately the key actors would need to be the active leaders of the religious communities, but I see no reason why some of us could not meet – without the pressures of office, time and publicity – to see what we could come up with. If, between us, we saw something remotely feasible, we could submit it to the community as a Blue (discussion) Paper for consideration.'[31]

'I agree with you,' concluded Jakobovits, 'that "ultimately the key actors would need to be the active leaders of the religious communities" if a broader agreement is to be explored. The idea of some new understanding does bear further exploration. For my part, I shall keep my eyes and ears open for any opportunity to encourage the search.'[32]

It was not to be. Lord Jakobovits of Regent's Park passed away in London two years later, and was laid to rest the following day on the Mount of Olives in Jerusalem. Sidney Brichto survived him by nearly a decade, and was buried at the Edgwarebury Cemetery in Greater London.

* * *

Jakobovits' last words in print took the form of a Rosh Hashanah article entitled 'Creation and the crisis of faith', published just fifty days before he died.[33] In it he wrote: 'Greater than man's ingenuity in releasing the most powerful forces of nature, and in conquering the ultimate forces latent in our universe, is his ability to remain master over the forces he has released, and to control the energies at his command.

'The real test is not in the six days of creation, but in the seventh day – in suspending creation and in curbing that which has been created. On this will depend human survival, and to this end should Jewish insights be applied on Rosh Hashanah, the universal "birthday" of the Creation….

'Far more remarkable than what has been discovered is what has not been discovered. Essentially, the world is no different from what we have known it to be for thousands of years – and, strange as this may sound, it is a momentous discovery. The stability of human intelligence and the confines of human understanding ought to humble us, and at the same time raise us infinitely above all other creatures – for we are a form of life as radically different from anything else in the vastness of space as can be found or imagined.

'The biblical readings on these Days of Awe depict not the drama of physical creation, but the promise of historical fulfilment, through the people charged to become partners in the consummation of the human purpose. The focus is on destiny rather than origin; on where we are heading rather than on whence we came.'

Notes

PREFACE

1. *Jewish Chronicle*, 19 March, 1993, 1.
2. The freehold house was sold by the United Synagogue to a private buyer in July 2015 for a sum 'significantly more than the property's estimated value of £10 million [and was later rebuilt]. Net proceeds from the sale will be reinvested into United Synagogue capital projects – for example, supporting congregations with significant membership growth', *ibid*, 7 August, 2015, 16.
3. See Chapter One, 6-11.
4. Rabbi Dr Immanuel Jakobovits: '*Your Call and My Response*: Memorandum to the Members of the Chief Rabbinate Committee', attached to a personal letter from Jakobovits to Sir Isaac Wolfson, Bt., chairman, Chief Rabbinate Council, London, 9 August, 1966: 'In this decision [to accept the Chief Rabbinate], I have been influenced, in large measure, by the great friendliness, the sincere yearning for leadership, and the enthusiastic reaction to my policy proposals which I encountered in the numerous discussions with the leaders of the community during my recent encouraging visit to London. I am now convinced that, with dynamic, imaginative and tolerant leadership on my part, I can reasonably count on the unflinching support of the overwhelming majority of Anglo-Jewry, and on the respect and goodwill of the rest.' Jakobovits Papers.
5. Simon Rocker, 'Collapse in "Orthodox middle" shul numbers', *Jewish Chronicle*, 7 July, 2017, 1, 4-5. Donatella Casale Mashiah and Jonathan Boyd, *Synagogue Membership in the United Kingdom in 2016* (London: Institute for Jewish Policy Research, on behalf of the Board of Deputies of British Jews, July 2017). The 46-page report includes the following executive summary:
    - In 2016, 79,597 Jewish households across the United Kingdom held synagogue membership.
    - There were 454 synagogues in operation across the United Kingdom in 2016, the highest number in recorded history.
    - Household synagogue membership figures have declined by 20% since 1990, the equivalent of 20,166 households, and by 4% since 2010, the equivalent of 3,366 households.

- An estimated 56.3% of all households across the UK with at least one Jew living within them held synagogue membership in 2016, although the proportions in Scotland, Wales and Northern Ireland were significantly lower.
- The vast majority (96%) of synagogue members in the UK live in England, and Jews living in England are much more likely to belong to a synagogue than those living in other parts of the UK.
- The largest denominational group in 2016 was 'Central Orthodox' (comprising synagogues affiliated to the United Synagogue or the Federation of Synagogues, as well as independent modern Orthodox synagogues around the country), which held 53% of all household synagogue memberships.
- The remaining synagogue memberships are held by other denominations: Reform (19%); Strictly Orthodox (13%); Liberal (8%); Masorti (3%); and Sephardi (3%).
- The most significant changes in synagogue membership since 1990 can be seen in Central Orthodoxy, which has experienced a 37% decline over the period, and in Strict Orthodoxy, which has experienced a 139% increase.
- These trends have continued since the last synagogue membership report was published in 2010. The Central Orthodox share has declined by 8% over the past six years, while the Strictly Orthodox share has grown by 18%.
- Three quarters of all synagogues in the UK are situated in Greater London (64%) and the adjacent areas of South Hertfordshire and South-West Essex (10%). 11% of all synagogues in the UK are in Greater Manchester; 15% are located across other parts of the country.
- Half of all synagogue members in the UK belong to synagogues located in just five areas: Barnet, Westminster, Hertsmere, Redbridge and Stamford Hill.

6 Jonathan Boyd, 'Belonging to a shul matters: The view from the data', *Jewish Chronicle*, 7 July, 2017, 41.
7 Stanley Kalms (chairman), *United Synagogue Review: A Time for Change* (London: Stanley Kalms Foundation, September 1992, Ellul 5752). Sub-titled 'A Report on the Role of the United Synagogue in the Years Ahead', the 300-page review – drawing on the insights of (among others) lay and rabbinical leaders, academics, social scientists, educationists, lawyers, administrators, financiers and publicists – provides an informed and unprecedented insight into the state of Anglo-Jewry's 'centrist-Orthodox' communities.
8 Ibid, 1.
9 Ibid, 230.
10 Ibid, 255.

CHAPTER ONE

1   Joseph Herman Hertz (1872–1946) was born in Slovakia, emigrated with his family to the United States in 1884, and served in synagogues in America and South Africa before being elected British Chief Rabbi in 1913. His American wife Rose (née Freed) predeceased him in 1930.
2   *Public General Statutes passed in the Fourth Session of the Sixteenth Parliament of the United Kingdom of Great Britain and Ireland.* 19 & 20 Victoria, 1856, Chapter CXIX (London: George Edward Eyre and William Spottiswoode, 1856), 793-806.
3   Neville Laski (1890–1969), a barrister, was president of the Board of Deputies 1933-39; presiding elder of the Spanish and Portuguese Jews' Congregation, 1961-67; and vice-president of the Anglo-Jewish Association.
4   Sir Robert Waley Cohen (1877–1952), a leading industrialist, served as a vice-president of the United Synagogue 1918–1942, and president 1942–1952.
5   Hertz to Laski, January 1935, in Bernard Homa, *Orthodoxy in Anglo-Jewry, 1880–1940* (London: Jewish Historical Society of England, 1969), 34-35. The Chief Rabbi's ruling applied specifically to the Liberal Jewish Synagogue, St John's Wood. Two years later, he granted similar certification to the Liverpool Liberal Jewish Synagogue, but a fiercer battle followed after his death in relation to other Liberal congregations (see Meir Persoff, *Faith Against Reason: Religious Reform and the British Chief Rabbinate 1840–1990*, London: Vallentine Mitchell, 2008, 272-282).
6   On Abramsky and his appointment to the London Beth Din, see *ibid*, 237-239; and Aaron Sorasky, 'The Life and Times of Rabbenu Yechezkel Abramsky,' in *Emunah: Pathways in Contemporary Jewish Thought*, No. 2, January 1990 (Kollel Tal Torah, Tel Ganim, Israel).
7   See *Faith Against Reason*, 252-257; and Jonathan A. Romain, 'The Establishment of the Reform Beth Din in 1948: A Barometer of Religious Trends in Anglo-Jewry,' paper presented to the Jewish Historical Society of England, 20 May, 1993, in *Jewish Historical Studies*, Volume XXXIII, 1992–1994 (Jewish Historical Society of England, London, 1995), 249-263. For a detailed study of the subject, see Romain, *The Reform Beth Din: The Formation and Development of the Rabbinical Court of the Reform Synagogues of Great Britain, 1935–1965* (unpublished PhD thesis, University of Leicester, 1990).
8   Dayan Mark Gollop to the Rev Vivian Simmons, 30 October, 1930, Reinhart Papers, MS 171, Hartley Library, University of Southampton.
9   Immanuel Jakobovits, *Rabbinical Tasks in the Present Era*, Amsterdam, 5 November, 1957 (Conference of European Rabbis, London, 1958), 1, 7-8.

10 Immanuel Jakobovits, 'The Rabbinical Conference: Plea for Unity,' letter to the *Jewish Chronicle*, 15 November, 1957, 18.
11 On Brodie, see *Faith Against Reason*, 260; and Meir Persoff, *Hats in the Ring: Choosing Britain's Chief Rabbis from Adler to Sacks* (Boston: Academic Studies Press, 2013), chapters 4 and 5.
12 Romain, *The Reform Beth Din*, 210.
13 Ibid, 210-212, citing minutes of the West London Synagogue council, 18 October, 1962, and of the Assembly of Ministers, 31 October, 1962.
14 Born in Philadelphia in 1936, Brichto moved to Britain in the 1960s and became the first executive director of the Union of Liberal and Progressive Synagogues.
15 A so-called levirate marriage (*yibum*) involves the obligation on a man to marry his widowed sister-in-law, if she is childless, and thus to produce children 'to build up the house' of his deceased brother (Deuteronomy 25:5-6). If he refuses to marry her, the ceremony of *chalitzah* takes place and she is free to marry someone else (ibid, 7-10). An *agunah* is a 'chained wife' or 'tied woman' whose husband has disappeared with no evidence of his death, or whose husband has deserted her and refuses to give her a *get*, leaving her unable to remarry.
16 Sidney Brichto, 'Validity of Liberal Marriages,' *Jewish Chronicle*, 3 December, 1965, 8.
17 Ibid, 17 December, 1965, 1. The gathering was attended by this writer in both a private capacity and as a JC reporter.
18 Ibid, 24 December, 1965, 12.
19 Ibid, 11 May, 1962, 10. This statement was made to the paper by the joint treasurers of the College, Laurence Jacobs and Felix Levy.
20 Ibid, 22 December, 1961, 10. Letter from Jacobs dated 14 November, 1961, and read to the Jews' College council at a meeting in London on 18 December, 1961.
21 Ibid, 2 February, 1962, 8.
22 Liverpool-born Dr Chaim Pearl (1919–1995) succeeded Jacobs at the New West End in 1960, but his leftist tendencies beckoned him to the Conservative Synagogue in Riverdale, New York, where he ministered for twenty years before retiring to Jerusalem.
23 Brodie's refusal was contained in an exchange with Alfred H. Silverman, secretary of the United Synagogue, who had written to him (17 January, 1964) regarding the vacancy. *Statement by the President of the United Synagogue*, special meeting of the United Synagogue council, 23 April, 1964, 2-3.
24 Israel Brodie, Opening Address, Second Conference of European Rabbis, Westcliff, 22 March, 1960, in *Jewish Chronicle*, 25 March, 1960, 8.

25 Joseph Ber Soloveitchik (1903–1993), a scion of the Lithuanian Soloveitchik dynasty, talmudist and philosopher, was rosh yeshiva of the Rabbi Elchanan Theological Seminary at Yeshiva University, New York City.
26 Leo Jung (1892–1987), Professor of Ethics at Yeshiva University and Stern College for Women, and member of the supreme council of Agudath Israel.
27 *Statement by the Very Rev the Chief Rabbi, Dr Israel Brodie*, meeting of rabbis and ministers of the Anglo-Jewish community, Adolph Tuck Hall, London, 5 May, 1964 (United Synagogue, London, 1964). A detailed account of the meeting and its background is in *Faith Against Reason*, 302-312.
28 Brodie to Jakobovits, Office of the Chief Rabbi, 85 Hamilton Terrace, St John's Wood, London N.W.8, 30 April, 1964–5724, Jakobovits Papers. The typed letter concluded with a handwritten postscript: 'Our affectionate greetings to you, Mrs Jakobovits, and the children.'
29 '… of all people' because Saul Lieberman (1898–1983) served as Professor of Talmud at the (Conservative) Jewish Theological Seminary of America, New York, for over four decades, and later as dean and rector of the rabbinical school. For many years he was also president of the American Academy for Jewish Research.
30 Emanuel Rackman (1910–2008) was at the time rabbi of Congregation Shaarey Tefila in New York City and, in 1967, became rabbi of Fifth Avenue Synagogue in succession to Jakobovits. He was elected president of the New York Board of Rabbis in 1955, and also served as president of the Rabbinical Council of America.
31 Jakobovits to Brodie, 'with fondest regards,' 6 May, 1964, Jakobovits Papers.
32 Jakobovits to Soloveitchik, and subsequently to Brodie, 26 May, 1964, *ibid*.

CHAPTER TWO

1 *Jewish Chronicle*, 12 June, 1964, 1, 14.
2 *Ibid*, 28 May, 1965, 15.
3 *Ibid*, 27 August, 1965, 13.
4 On the interregnum and Chief Rabbinate-in-Commission, see *Hats in the Ring*, op. cit., Chapter 6, notes 45 and 67, 289-290.
5 Yaacov (Jacob) Herzog (1921–1972) was an Israeli attorney and doctor of international law, diplomat, ordained rabbi, and translator and commentator of the Mishnah. A former adviser to Israeli Prime Minister David Ben-Gurion, he had served as Minister Plenipotentiary in Washington and Ambassador to Canada.
6 Jakobovits to Wolfson, 14 April, 1965, Jakobovits Papers.

7   'Report of the delegation sent to wait upon Rabbi Jacob Herzog in Jerusalem, 24 May, 1965,' LMA/ACC/2712/15/01/128.
8   *Jewish Chronicle*, 10 September, 1965, 1, 15. A full account of this episode is in *Hats in the Ring*, 160–179, 187–191.
9   Rabbi Dr Ignaz Maybaum, *The Office of a Chief Rabbi*, London: Reform Synagogues of Great Britain, 1964, 13.
10 Rabbi Sidney Brichto, 'What is wrong with the Chief Rabbinate?', London: *Liberal Jewish Monthly*, May 1965, 101–104.
11 Rabbi Dr Chaim Pearl, 'About "Chief Rabbis,"' New York: *The Jewish Spectator*, January 1967, 21–23.
12 *Jewish Chronicle*, 28 January, 1966, 1, 12.
13 Ibid, 22 July 1966, 1.
14 Ibid, 22 July 1966, 11.
15 Slowe to Brichto, 11 November, 1966, Brichto Papers.
16 Correspondence between representatives of all parties, November 1965–September 1966, ibid.
17 Slowe to Brichto, 18 April, 1966, ibid.
18 Brichto to Gaon, 19 August, 1966, ibid.
19 Gaon to Brichto, Office of the Haham of the Spanish & Portuguese Jews, 22 August, 1966–7 Ellul, 5726, ibid. Brichto's suggestions likewise came to nothing.
20 *Jewish Chronicle*, 21 October, 1966, 11.
21 Jakobovits to Wolfson, 9 August, 1966, Jakobovits Papers; LMA/ACC/2712/15/1/159.
22 'The attached terms and conditions' were contained in the final sections of a memorandum – *Your Call and My Response*' – sent to the Chief Rabbinate Committee by Jakobovits following his week-long visit to London the previous July, covering, among other topics, the Chief Rabbi's emoluments, his public-relations team, and his assumption of office (Jakobovits Papers). *Prelude to Service*, 5, London: Office of the Chief Rabbi, Adar II 5727–April 1967.
23 *Jewish Chronicle*, 16 September, 1966, 1.
24 These included members of the Beth Din; the Haham and other prominent rabbis; the United Synagogue honorary officers; and – at their request – the chairmen of the Reform and Liberal movements.
25 *Prelude to Service*, 4-5, London: Office of the Chief Rabbi, Adar II 5727–April 1967.
26 *Pointer*, Vol. II, No. 2, winter 1966, 2, London: Union of Liberal and Progressive Synagogues.
27 Ibid, Vol. II, No. 3, spring 1967, 4.
28 Ibid, 5.

29 Jakobovits to Brichto, 28 February, 1967, Fifth Avenue Synagogue, New York, Brichto Papers. Perhaps mistaking the reference to 'each other's platforms' as a call for early action, Brichto wrote back asking whether 'it would be premature [for you] to accept an invitation to speak to a Liberal conference.' Jakobovits replied that he 'looked forward to continuing our "dialogue" in person once I am settled in London,' but added: 'At this early stage in our search for a *détente*, I am most anxious to avoid anything which may be construed as provocation by those who still have to be conditioned to the new climate we need,' Brichto to Jakobovits, 6 March, 1967, Jakobovits to Brichto, 9 March, 1967, ibid. (see illustration between Chapters III and IV).

30 Rayner to Slowe, 6 February, 1967, ibid.

31 'The major tasks ahead,' *Jewish Chronicle*, 16 December, 1966, 6.

32 Ibid, 13 January, 1967, 6. The letter was signed by Lord Cohen, Rabbi Sidney Brichto, Rabbi Dr P. Selvin Goldberg, Sir Louis Gluckstein, Sir S. E. Karminski, Judge Alan King-Hamilton, Rabbi Jakob Kokotek, Rabbi Michael Leigh, Rabbi John D. Rayner, S. G. Schwab, Malcolm Slowe, and Rabbi Dr Werner Van der Zyl. Composition of this response to the Chief Rabbi's approaches occupied the King-Hamilton committee for several months. In the event, the *Jewish Chronicle* letter replaced a welcome to Jakobovits intended for publication in *The Times* and opposed by Karminski, Brichto Papers (see illustration between Chapters III and IV).

33 For Jakobovits' installation address, see *Hats in the Ring*, 207-215.

34 'Reform and the Chief Rabbi,' *Living Judaism*, summer 1967, 114-118, London: Reform Synagogues of Great Britain.

35 *Prelude to Service*, 5-6, London: Office of the Chief Rabbi, Adar II 5727–April 1967.

36 Brichto to Jakobovits, 14 July, 1967, Union of Liberal and Progressive Synagogues, St John's Wood, London NW8, Brichto and Jakobovits Papers.

37 Rayner to Jakobovits, 18 September, 1967, Anson Road, NW2, LMA/ACC/2805/7/6/007.

38 Rogosnitzky to Jakobovits, 15 January, 1968, Winchester Avenue, Penylan, Cardiff, Jakobovits Papers.

39 Jakobovits to Rogosnitzky, 23 January, 1968, ibid.

40 *Jewish Chronicle*, 3 December, 1965, 8.

41 Ibid, 29 December, 1967, 15.

42 Rose to Brichto, 7 July, 1969, Office of the Chief Rabbi, Brichto Papers.

43 Ibid.

44 Brichto to Jakobovits, 9 July, 1969, ibid.

45 14 December, 1987, in a lecture to the Jewish Marriage Council, London.

46 See Chapter Three, pages 59 seq.
47 Jerusalem Talmud, Chagigah 3:6.
48 Rabbi John Rayner, 'Anglo-Jewish Unity,' sermon delivered at the Liberal Jewish Synagogue, St John's Wood, London, 18 May, 1968, Jakobovits and Brichto Papers; and LMA/ACC/2805/07/06/001, which includes a copy of the text subsequently annotated by Jakobovits. Sending the sermon to Brichto, together with the resultant correspondence, Rayner wrote: 'You may be interested in seeing the enclosed for the light it throws on Dr Jakobovits' state of mind.'
49 Jakobovits to Rayner, 21 June, 1968, Office of the Chief Rabbi, Adler House, Tavistock Square, WC1, Jakobovits and Brichto Papers; and LMA/ACC/2805/07/06/001 (to which all subsequent responses apply). Points 1, 2, 5, 7, 10, 11, 13, 14, 15, 17, 18, 19 and 21 are covered here.
50 Rayner to Jakobovits, 24 June, 1968, Anson Road, London NW2. Rayner concluded his response: 'I am sorry to have wearied you with such a long letter, but I hope that it has clarified some matters and that we shall no longer talk at cross-purposes.'
51 Jakobovits to Rayner, 28 June, 1968.
52 Rayner to Jakobovits, 17 July, 1968.
53 Jakobovits to Rayner, 31 July, 1968.
54 Rayner had given as examples Israel Mattuck's *Jewish Ethics*, Leo Baeck's *The Essence of Judaism*, and H. Schauss's *The Jewish Festivals*.
55 Rayner to Jakobovits, 2 August, 1968.
56 Jakobovits to Rayner, 5 August, 1968.
57 Rayner to Jakobovits, 23 August, 1968.

CHAPTER THREE

1 Immanuel Jakobovits, *Moving Ahead: A Review and a Preview*, A New Year Message from the Chief Rabbi to the Leadership of Anglo-Jewry, London: Office of the Chief Rabbi, Ellul 5728–September 1968, 15-18.
2 Brichto to Teff, 23 November, 1966, Brichto Papers.
3 Harold S. Langdon, 'The Place of Reform in Anglo-Jewry Today,' in *A Genuine Search*, edited by Dow Marmur (London: Reform Synagogues of Great Britain, 1979), 245-252. An Orthodox viewpoint is provided by Abba Bornstein and Bernard Homa, *Tell It In Gath: British Jewry & Clause 43, The Inside Story* (London: privately published, 1972).
4 The Board of Deputies, known originally as the London Committee of Deputies of British Jews, was established in 1760. Over time, it became recognised by governmental authorities as the representative body of Anglo-Jewry and was referred to in Acts of Parliament relating to marriage. Clause

43 (originally Clause 6) of the Board's constitution stated: 'The guidance of the Board on religious matters (inclusive of matters relating to marriages, and matters involving questions affecting the religious customs and usages of the Jews) shall remain as heretofore with the Ecclesiastical Authorities, to whom all such matters shall be referred; but since Congregations and Institutions not under the jurisdiction of the Ecclesiastical Authorities may be represented at the Board, nothing in this Clause contained, or any decision given under it, shall be taken to represent the opinion of any Congregation not acknowledging the jurisdiction of the Ecclesiastical Authorities, or shall abridge the rights of action of, or affect in any way, such Congregation.'

5 Fidler to members of the Board of Deputies, 15 October, 1971, *Tell It In Gath*, 36-38.
6 Fidler to the Very Rev. The Chief Rabbi Dr Immanuel Jakobovits, and Dr Solomon Gaon, the Haham, Ecclesiastical Authorities of the Board of Deputies, 27 September, 1971, *ibid*, 35-36.
7 Homa to Fidler, 25 October, 1971, Princes Park Avenue, N.W.11, *ibid*, 40-41.
8 Jakobovits to Homa, 28 October, 1971, Office of the Chief Rabbi, Adler House, London, *ibid*, 46-49. A copy of this letter was sent to, among others, the Haham. It was followed by a flow of correspondence between Jakobovits and Homa, and a 'Statement by the Chief Rabbi and the Haham to Members of the Board of Deputies Representing Orthodox Synagogues', briefly repeating the points made in Jakobovits' initial letter to Homa.
9 Minutes of a meeting of the Chief Rabbinate Council, 19 December, 1971, Woburn House, Upper Woburn Place, WC1, Jakobovits Papers.
10 Harold Langdon, *op. cit.*, 252.
11 Immanuel Jakobovits, 'Division and Diversion,' *Jewish Chronicle*, 26 February, 1971, 23.
12 Moshe Davis, education officer of the Jewish National Fund and director of the Chief Rabbi's Jewish Educational Development Trust, was in October 1972 appointed executive director of the Chief Rabbi's Office in succession to Maurice Rose, who had resigned in 1968 to become academic registrar and lecturer at Jews' College, before settling in Israel. Minutes of the Chief Rabbinate Council, 17 November, 1968, and 29 October, 1972, Jakobovits Papers.
13 Davis to Goldman, 24 July, 1973, Office of the Chief Rabbi, Adler House, Tavistock Square, WC1, Jakobovits Papers.
14 Goldman to Davis, 1 August, 1973 (ref.: RMG/JPW/A192), Seymour Pace, W.1, *ibid*.
15 Minutes of a meeting of the Chief Rabbinate Council, 19 December, 1971, Woburn House, Upper Woburn Place, WC1, Jakobovits Papers.

16 For further background, see Lawrence Rigal and Rosita Rosenberg, Liberal Judaism: The First Hundred Years (London: Liberal Judaism, 2004), 169; Anne J. Kershen and Jonathan A. Romain, Tradition and Change: A History of Reform Judaism in Britain, 1840–1995 (London: Vallentine Mitchell, 1995), 279-280.
17 Brichto to Cohen, 23 November, 1966, Brichto Papers.
18 Cohen to Brichto, Porchester Terrace, W2, 24 November, 1966, ibid.
19 Brichto to Cohen, 25 November, 1966, ibid.
20 Cohen to Brichto, 25 November, 1966, ibid.
21 Minutes of a meeting of the Chief Rabbinate Council, 18 November, 1973, Woburn House, Upper Woburn Place, WC1, Jakobovits Papers.
22 Proposals 1a, 2, 3viii, and 6, 23 October, 1973, USL/A1053/MS 302/24/2
23 'Orthodox in link-up with Progressives,' Jewish Chronicle, 1 March, 1974, 1. Press release, Office of the Chief Rabbi, Adler House, London, 6 March, 1974, LMA/ACC2805/07/16/001.
24 'Co-operation,' leading article, Jewish Chronicle, 1 March, 1974, 26.
25 'Steps towards a "dialogue,"' ibid, 15 March, 1974, 6. Goldman was not named in the report.
26 Minutes of the Consultative Committee on Jewish-Christian Relations, Office of the Chief Rabbi, Adler House, WC1, 2 May, 1974, Jakobovits Papers.
27 Minutes of a meeting of the Chief Rabbinate Council, 16 June, 1974, Woburn House, Upper Woburn Place, WC1, ibid. Jakobovits told the Council that it was 'also intended [though in the event not fully implemented] to invite an appointee of the president of the Board of Deputies, of the acting Rav Rashi of the Federation of Synagogues, and of other interested organisations in London and the provinces – all serving, however, in an ad personam capacity'.
28 Brichto to Jakobovits, 20 July, 1970, ibid; LMA/ACC2805/07/06/003.
29 Jakobovits to Brichto, 23 July, 1970, ibid.
30 For amplification of the issue, raised by Marmur in the RSGB newsletter, and subsequently examined by its Assembly of Rabbis, see Tradition and Change, op. cit., 236-238.
31 'Let's talk', Jewish Chronicle, 7 February, 1975, 6.
32 'Split over talks on conversion,' ibid, 28 February, 1975, 6.
33 As reported in the Jewish Chronicle ('Liberal "No" to conversion compromise'), 28 March, 1975, 7. See also Liberal Judaism: The First Hundred Years, op. cit., 187.
34 'Door still open on conversion,' Jewish Chronicle, 11 April, 1975, 5.
35 'Move to open dialogue on conversion,' ibid, 9 May, 1975, 5.
36 Minutes of a meeting held at the home of the Chief Rabbi (85 Hamilton Terrace, NW8) on Monday, 14 July [1975], LMA/ACC/2805/07/06/003.
37 Children born of an adulterous or incestuous relationship (see Deuteronomy 23:3).

38 Minutes of a meeting held at the home of the Chief Rabbi on Tuesday, 9 September [1975], LMA/ACC/2805/07/06/003.
39 *Centre*, magazine of the North-Western Reform Synagogue, Golders Green, London, April 1976.
40 Moshe Davis to Dow Marmur, Office of the Chief Rabbi, 2 June, 1976, acknowledging a letter from Marmur to Jakobovits, 20 April, 1976, LMA/ACC/2805/7/6/001. The 'aims and suggestions' related *inter alia* to Marmur's remark to the Consultative Committee that 'an agreement on *gerut* would considerably help me in relations with my movement'.
41 RSGB Assembly of Rabbis, 10 March, 1976.
42 *Tradition and Change, op. cit.*, 237.
43 RSGB Assembly of Rabbis, 2 March, 1977.
44 RSGB Assembly of Rabbis, January 1978.
45 *Tradition and Change, op. cit.*, 238.
46 Dow Marmur (editor), *A Genuine Search: God, Torah, Israel — A Reform Perspective* (London: Reform Synagogues of Great Britain, 1979), 29-39.
47 The letter at this point referred to the situation in Israel, where 'the preservation of halachic norms in the area of personal status, as traditionally defined and administered, has never been seriously challenged by responsible leaders, despite much popular agitation against it at times.'
48 See note 40 above.
49 Jakobovits to a meeting of the Jewish Marriage Council, London, 14 December, 1987.
50 'David Nathan talks with Chief Rabbi Jakobovits', *Jewish Chronicle*, 6 January, 1978, 17.
51 *Ibid*, 2 March, 1979, 7.
52 *Ibid*, 11 May, 1979, 40.
53 Brichto to Jakobovits, 15 May, 1979, LMA/ACC/2805/07/06/004.
54 Jakobovits to Brichto, 16 May, 1979, *ibid*.
55 'Chief Rabbi refuses to put ban on Reform Jews', *Jewish Chronicle*, 6 April, 1979, 1.
56 The statement was later reproduced as a full-page advertisement in the *Jewish Chronicle*, 20 April, 1979, together with 'congratulations' from Emeth (Emunah, Mitzvah, Torah), a Leeds-based organisation, LMA/ACC/2805/07/06/004.
57 Jakobovits to the *Jewish Chronicle*, sent 3 April, 1979, published 6 April, 1979, 1, *ibid*.
58 Translated and condensed here from the rabbinic Hebrew.
59 Jakobovits to signatories of the UOHC pronouncement: Rabbis H.B. Padwa, J.H. Dunner, S. Baumgarten, E. Halpern, H.I. Feldman, P. Roberts, S. Friedman, A.D. Dunner (members of the Union Beth Din); B. Rogosnitzky, B. Rakow,

M.M. Schneebalg, M. Aschkenazi, S. Rubin, L. Gurwicz, Y. Segal, N. Ordman, S. Zahn, B.Z. Rakow, E. Schlesinger, A. Sternbuch, LMA/ACC/2805/07/06/004.
60 Benjamin Chain, former chairman of Cambridge University Jewish Society, Emmanuel College, Cambridge, *Jewish Chronicle*, 4 May, 1979, 20; LMA/ACC/2805/07/06/004.
61 1838-1933.
62 'Two kinds of truth,' sermon delivered at the Liberal Jewish Synagogue, St John's Wood, London, on Shabbat, 2 June, 1979, 7 Sivan, 5739, LMA/ACC/2085/07/06/007.
63 'Attacks on Reform harm Orthodox,' *Jewish Chronicle*, 25 May, 1979, 6.
64 Marmur to Jakobovits, 31 May, 1979, USL/MS302/A1053/24/1 (draft); USL/MS302/A1053/31; LMA/ACC/2805/07/06/007.
65 Jakobovits to Marmur, 4 June, 1979, ibid.
66 Marmur to Jakobovits, 7 June, 1979, ibid.

CHAPTER FOUR

1 Dayan Dr I. Lerner, 'The attitude to halachah of the Progressive movements: Can they be considered a *kehillah kedoshah?*', *L'Eylah*, Vol. 1, No. 10, autumn 5741 [1980] (London: Office of the Chief Rabbi), 7-11.
2 Thirteen Godly attributes (Exodus 34:6-7).
3 *L'Eylah*, Vol. 2, No. 2, autumn 5742 [1981] (London: Office of the Chief Rabbi), 38-39. At the time, Bayfield was rabbi of the North-West Surrey Synagogue.
4 Referring to Reform policy on the *get*, Anne J. Kershen and Jonathan A, Romain write (*Tradition and Change*, op. cit., 238-239): 'When it was reintroduced in 1946, there were several departures from the traditional regulations.... It was now agreed that the writing, witnessing and delivery of *gittin* would follow rabbinic tradition as part of the general move towards harmonisation of procedures.... Those who hoped that these changes might make the Reform document acceptable to Orthodox authorities were to be disappointed. Others regarded it as a development that was necessary for purely internal reasons and Reform's integrity as movement combining tradition with modernity.' They later write (341): '... the refusal of one partner to award a *get* to the other can be overridden by the Reform Beth Din if it considers the grounds to be spurious.' The Progressive view is summarised by Rosita Rosenberg in *Liberal Judaism: The First Hundred Years* (op. cit., 216): "The basic objection by the Liberal movement to the *get* is on grounds of inequality of the sexes, since an Orthodox *get* can be initiated only by the man. Every attempt, however, is made to assist those remarrying to avoid putting themselves in a position that would make any future children

'mamzerim' by Orthodox law. Accordingly, Liberal rabbis will not conduct a wedding for a Jewish man who is not prepared to offer his ex-wife a *get*, and will assist a couple in obtaining an Orthodox *get*, usually through the Federation of Synagogues. In more recent years, the ULPS has instigated an optional reciprocal *get*.'

5   'Orthodox–Reform storm,' *Jewish Chronicle*, 19 November, 1982, 1.
6   'Reform hits back at dayanim,' ibid, 26 November, 1982, 18.
7   Ibid.
8   'Dayan Swift lays down the law,' ibid, 3 December, 1982, 1.
9   Ibid, 31 December, 1982, 28.
10 Ibid, 14 January, 1983, 18.
11 'Illegitimate', leading article, ibid, 3 December, 1982, 22.
12 Ibid, 10 December, 1982, 18.
13 'Progressives make an offer: will Orthodoxy refuse?', ibid.
14 'Public calamity, private amity', ibid, 28 January, 1983, 18.
15 'Minutes of a meeting of the Chief Rabbinate Council, 19 December, 1982, Woburn House, London', Jakobovits Papers.
16 'Notes on a meeting of the Consultative Committee on Jewish–Christian Relations held at the home of the Chief Rabbi, 8 February, 1983', USL/MS302/A1053/24/4.
17 Chief Rabbi Sir Immanuel Jakobovits, 'The quiet revolution", *Jewish Chronicle*, 9 November, 1984, 24-25.
18 'Sir Immanuel Jakobovits, Chief Rabbi, edited summary of lecture delivered at Yakar, 30 December, 1984,' *L'Eylah*, spring 5745-1985 (London: Office of the Chief Rabbi), 28-29.
19 John D. Rayner, 'The Council of Reform and Liberal Rabbis: Retrospect and Prospect,' chairman's report and remarks at the annual general meeting of the Council, Manor House Centre for Judaism, 12 November, 1984, Leo Baeck College Library, London, #323.
20 *Jewish Chronicle*, 19 November, 1982.
21 Ibid, 7 January, 1983.
22 Ibid, 14 January, 1983.
23 Ibid, 21 January, 1983.
24 Rayner to Jakobovits, Council of Reform and Liberal Rabbis, Manor House Centre for Judaism, London, 13 November, 1984, Jakobovits Papers (the source of the remaining sequence of letters in this section).
25 Jakobovits to Rayner, 19 November, 1984.
26 Rayner to Jakobovits, Liberal Jewish Synagogue, St John's Wood, 27 November, 1984.

27 Recording this donation, Kershen and Romain write in *Tradition and Change* (op. cit.), 290, and footnote, 355: 'The continuing financial problems ... meant that the offer of a gift ... was most welcome, even though the condition attached – that the Manor House be renamed the Sternberg Centre for Judaism – aroused some controversy.' RSGB council minutes, 2 December, 1984, RSGB archive, Sternberg Centre for Judaism [now at USL].
28 Jakobovits to Sternberg, 3 December, 1984, Jakobovits Papers.
29 Sternberg to the Chief Rabbi, 14 December, 1984, *ibid*.
30 Jakobovits to Sternberg, 17 December, 1984, *ibid*.
31 Under the heading 'Non-Orthodox platforms', Jakobovits had circulated his United Synagogue ministerial colleagues 'not to allow their presence, or their names, to be used for promoting or sanctioning any activities which could be construed as according legitimacy to non-traditional Judaism'. Office of the Chief Rabbi, Adler House [undated].
32 'Draft', Rabbi A.M. Bayfield to Rabbi Sir Immanuel Jakobovits, Manor House Centre for Judaism, 2 January, 1985.
33 Sir Immanuel Jakobovits, Chief Rabbi, 4 January, 1985.
34 Bayfield to Jakobovits, 7 January, 1985.
35 Jakobovits to Bayfield, 10 January, 1985.
36 Rabbi Hugo Gryn to Rabbi Sir Immanuel Jakobovits, West London Synagogue of British Jews, 15 January, 1985.
37 Bayfield to Jakobovits, Council of Reform and Liberal Rabbis, 15 January, 1985.
38 'Report of the Committee of Enquiry into the Education of Handicapped Children and Young People (Mrs H. M. Warnock, chairman), presented to Parliament by the Secretary of State for Education and Science, the Secretary of State for Scotland and the Secretary of State for Wales by Command of Her Majesty, May 1978.'
39 Maurice Unterman (born Porzow, Poland, 1917; died London, 2000) was the scion of a highly respected rabbinical family, and held ministerial and communal posts in Cardiff, Hove and London, before moving to the newly opened Marble Arch Synagogue in 1961. In his obituary (24 November, 2000, 25), the *Jewish Chronicle* wrote: 'His 21 years at Marble Arch were fruitful and showed his talent and desire for co-operation with all sections of Anglo-Jewry. His unofficial contacts with Liberal and Reform rabbis and lay leaders over areas of common concern won him respect and admiration.... He was motivated by Judaism's moral teachings in all aspects of his life, and known for his gentleness and consideration for others.' The then Chief Rabbi, Jonathan Sacks, added: 'Rabbi Maurice Unterman was a spiritual leader of unique presence, small in stature but vast in spirit, a man who brought impeccable dignity to his public persona and unfailing sensitivity to

his equally important pastoral work in private. He was a bridge between the pre-war world of Lithuanian piety and the quite different environment of Anglo-Jewry, and became a living synthesis of what was best in both.'
40 'More kosher than others,' The Economist, 16 February, 1985.
41 'Avoiding the collision,' Jewish Chronicle, 8 February, 1985, 18-19.
42 'Preserving unity', ibid, 16.
43 Rabbi Tony Bayfield, 'Proposals from the Progressives', ibid, 15 February, 1985, 18.
44 For the background to this amendment, see Faith Against Reason, op. cit., 355-356.
45 Rabbi Sidney Brichto, 'Mutual respect', Jewish Chronicle, 15 February, 1985, 18.
46 Rayner to Jakobovits, Liberal Jewish Synagogue, 27 February, 1985, Jakobovits Papers.
47 Unterman to Jakobovits, 18 February, 1985, ibid.
48 'Memorandum re meeting of Consultative Committee', Bayfield to Raymond Goldman, Maurice Michaels, Sir Sigmund Sternberg, Rabbi Hugo Gryn, 27 February, 1985, Jakobovits Papers; USL/MS302/A1053/24/2.
49 Despite its new appellation, the committee was still referred to in the minutes by its overarching title. 'Memorandum (Private & Confidential) of the Consultative Committee on Jewish–Christian Relations, Monday, 5 March, 1985, at 85 Hamilton Terrace, London NW8. Present: In the chair, Rabbi John Rayner; Sir Immanuel Jakobovits, the Chief Rabbi; Rabbi Tony Bayfield, Rabbi Sidney Brichto, Rabbi Jeffrey Cohen, Rabbi Dr Albert Friedlander, Rabbi Hugo Gryn, Rabbi Cyril Harris, Rabbi Norman Solomon. Messrs Shimon Cohen, Raymond Goldman, Harold Langdon, Victor Lucas, Maurice Michaels, Hayim Pinner, Mrs Rosita Rosenberg, Mr Malcolm Slowe, Sir Sigmund Sternberg, Mr Clive Winston. Apologies were received from Rabbi Maurice Unterman, who was indisposed.' USL/MS302/A1053/24/4.
50 "Bid to end squabbling", Jewish Chronicle, 21 June, 1985, 5.
51 Jack Wolkind, London and its Jewish Community, the West Central Lecture 1985, University College, London, 13 June, 1985 (London: West Central Counselling and Community Research, 1985), 15-16.
52 'One people', leading article, Jewish Chronicle, 14 February, 1986, 20.
53 'Preservation of Jewish unity', ibid, 21 February, 1986, 20.
54 A striking example appeared some years later, in an interview featured on the front page of the London Evening Standard in May 1991, when Jakobovits was reported to have described the plight of Palestinian refugees as 'a stain on humanity'. Immediately after, two communal fund-raising events were cancelled, a trustee of the Jakobovits Foundation resigned in protest, and Jakobovits postponed a visit to Israel after threats by the extremist Kach

party to mount public protests. Lionel Kopelowitz, president of the Board of Deputies, described the comments as 'unhelpful at a time when there is a need for total solidarity with Israel. On these matters, the Chief Rabbi speaks for himself, not as a representative of Anglo-Jewry. But inevitably, the world will regard his statement as authoritative and representative.' Former Israeli Chief Rabbi Shlomo Goren said Lord Jakobovits had 'negated himself to serve as a rabbi, by choosing to side with the PLO'. After the interview appeared, Jakobovits described it as a 'complete falsification' of his views, and said that he was 'angry and scandalised' by it. 'When I give an interview, I rely on the integrity and honesty of the press. In this case, there was neither.'

55 Brichto to Jakobovits, 18 February, 1986, Brichto Papers.
56 Jakobovits to Brichto, 26 February, 1986, ibid.
57 Brichto to Jakobovits, 3 March, 1986, ibid. The message ended: 'I would welcome a chat and look forward to hearing from you when this would be convenient.'
58 'The Mystique of Survival', Sir Immanuel Jakobovits talks to David Nathan, *Jewish Chronicle*, 17 April, 1987, 22-23.
59 'Chief Rabbi criticised', ibid, 15 May, 1987, 44.
60 Brichto to Jakobovits, 15 May, 1987; Jakobovits to Brichto, 18 May, 1987, Brichto Papers.
61 Rabbi Dr Sidney Brichto, 'Demanding our rights and respect', *ULPS News*, September 1987; USL/MS302/A1053/24/2.
62 'Brichto: Chief is very Right-wing', *Jewish Chronicle*, 10 July, 1987, 5.
63 Following the unanimous adoption of the moratorium the previous March, Unterman and Bayfield were appointed 'monitors of relationship between the Orthodox and Progressives'.
64 Unterman to Bayfield, Wellington Road, NW8, 7 September, 1987, USL/MS302/A1053/24/2.
65 Bayfield to Unterman, Sternberg Centre for Judaism, 10 September, 1987, ibid.
66 Sidney Brichto, 'Halachah with Humility,' *Jewish Chronicle*, 2 October, 1987, 29. For a fuller account, see *Faith Against Reason*, op. cit., 369-372.
67 Chief Rabbi Immanuel Jakobovits, *Preserving the Oneness of the Jewish People: Orthodox–Progressive divisions and discussions on marriage, divorce and conversion: can a permanent schism be averted?* Lecture to the Jewish Marriage Council, Royal Society of Medicine, 14 December, 1987 (Office of the Chief Rabbi, London, 1988), 16, 19.
68 Brichto to Jakobovits, 25 January, 1988, Brichto Papers.
69 Jakobovits to 'Dear Dr Brichto', Office of the Chief Rabbi, 1 February, 1998, ibid.
70 Brichto to Jakobovits, 5 February, 1988, ibid.

71 Bayfield to Unterman, 24 November, 1987, USL/MS302/A1053/24/2.
72 Notes of a meeting of the Consultative Committee on Jewish–Christian Relations, 85 Hamilton Terrace, NW8, 16 February, 1988, USL/MS302/A1053/24/4.
73 Jakobovits received his peerage in the 1988 New Year Honours (having been knighted in the 1981 Queen's Birthday Honours) – 'a unique tribute', the *Jewish Chronicle* remarked, 'to his spiritual leadership of the overwhelming majority of Anglo-Jewry…. He is not the first Jewish refugee from Nazism to become a peer, but he is the first for whom a Jewish inheritance has been the vehicle that carries him into the House of Lords.' See Meir Persoff: *Immanuel Jakobovits: a Prophet in Israel* (London: Vallentine Mitchell, 2002), 278-302.
74 Rabbi Tony Bayfield, 'Some Reflections on the Consultative Committee', presented to a meeting of the Consultative Committee on Jewish–Christian Relations, 85 Hamilton Terrace, NW8, 16 February, 1988, USL/MS302/A1053/24/2. The minutes noted that Bayfield's paper 'was received with approbation'.
75 Tony Bayfield to Raymond Goldman, 'Memorandum re new Inter-Communal Strife Monitoring Committee', 22 June, 1988, USL/MS302/A1053/25. The meeting was held on 5 July, 1988.
76 'Unterman/Bayfield Group', Bayfield to committee members, 12 October, 1988, ibid. Jonathan Lew, representing the United Synagogue, added a clause defining 'Statements' and 'Leadership' to include a number of individual areas, ibid.
77 Tony Bayfield, 'Unterman-Bayfield Group: Note of First Meeting', 18 October, 1988', ibid.
78 Dates were set for two further meetings: Tuesday, 3 January, 1989, 4.15–5.45 p.m. at the home of Lionel Swift, QC; and Thursday, 2 March, 1989, 4.45–6.15 p.m., venue to be decided. In the event, the 'agenda and proposals' were formulated for a meeting held on 15 February, 1989, ibid.
79 Tony Bayfield, 'Jewish Unity Discussion', RSGB conference, Harrogate, 23 June, 1989, ibid.
80 John D. Rayner, 'Outreach Again', Liberal Jewish Synagogue, St John's Wood, 10 June, 1989 (7 Sivan, 5749), Leo Baeck College Library, London, #956.
81 Rabbi Dr Sidney Brichto, 'A "political" ruling'', *Jewish Chronicle*, 16 June, 1989, 26.
82 Clifford Longley, 'Legal side to Jewish dispute', *The Times*, 23 October, 1989.
83 Brichto to Jakobovits, 27 October, 1989, Brichto Papers.
84 Jakobovits to Brichto, 30 October, 1989, ibid.
85 Brichto to Jakobovits, 8 November, 1989, ibid.
86 l'*havdil* – 'as distinct from'.
87 Jakobovits to Brichto, 11 December, 1989, Brichto Papers.
88 Brichto to Jakobovits, 13 December, 1989, ibid.

89 Jakobovits to Brichto, 19 December, 1989, ibid.
90 Clifford Longley, 'Liberal Jews will not back Chief Rabbi', *The Times*, 16 December, 1989, 1.
91 Harold Sanderson and Rosita Rosenberg, 'Statement on the Appointment of the Chief Rabbi of the United Hebrew Congregation', Union of Liberal and Progressive Synagogues, 14 December, 1989, Brichto Papers. Sanderson was the chairman, and Rosenberg the director, of the ULPS.
92 'Chief Rabbi defended', *The Times*, 18 December, 1989.
93 Lionel Kopelowitz, 17 December, 1989, Brichto Papers.
94 Brichto to Paul, 15 December, 1989, Brichto Papers. 'I appreciate the fact', Brichto had added, 'that you wished to give us fuller coverage next week. It is only a pity that I was not told that it was *not* going to appear in the *Jewish Chronicle* this week.'
95 'Not our Chief' row, *Jewish Chronicle*, 22 December, 1989, 40. 'Choosing a Chief', leading article, ibid, 20.
96 In a lecture delivered by Sacks days earlier, sponsored by the British Friends of Bar-Ilan University, Sacks had declared: 'Pluralism is not an answer. Pluralism supposes that, somehow, all the different and conflicting things that Jews believe today can be accommodated within one universe. They can't. If pluralism means that we should grant equal legitimacy to every interpretation of Judaism, it is not there to be granted. Orthodox rabbis cannot be called on to legitimate non-halachic forms of Judaism.' Ibid, 29 December, 1989, 5.
97 'Whose Chief?', ibid, 12 January, 1990, 22.
98 Sanderson to Kopelowitz, 27 December, 1989, Brichto Papers.
99 Kopelowitz to Sanderson, Board of Deputies of British Jews, 4 January, 1990, ibid. Kopelowitz concluded: 'I am, of course, copying this letter to Lord Goodman.'
100 Raymond M. Goldman, executive director, Reform Synagogues of Great Britain, 19 December, 1989, ibid.
101 Rayner to Bower, 10 January, 1990, Council of Reform and Liberal Rabbis, ibid.
102 *Jewish Chronicle*, 5 January, 1990, 21.
103 Brichto to Jakobovits, 17 January, 1990, Brichto Papers.
104 Jakobovits to Sternberg, Office of the Chief Rabbi, 15 February, 1990, ibid.
105 Brichto to Sternberg, 23 March, 1990, ibid.

CHAPTER FIVE

1 Brichto to Longley, 26 February, 1990, Brichto Papers.
2 Sacks to Brichto, 4 March, 1990, ibid. (See illustration between Chapters III and IV). In the event, neither Sacks nor Brichto was able to 'move forward'.

3   'Sacks to stress unity', *ibid*, 6. On Sacks' communal activities, writings and statements before his appointment, see Meir Persoff, *Another Way, Another Time: Religious Inclusivism and the Sacks Chief Rabbinate* (Boston, Academic Studies Press, 2010), 21-32, 45-54.
4   Louis Jacobs, 'Must Jews Have a Chief Rabbi?', January 1990, Brichto Papers.
5   Sidney Brichto, 'Office of the Chief Rabbi – A Mixed Blessing', 10 June, 1991, *ibid*; an edited version appeared in the *Jewish Chronicle*, 14 June, 1991, 20.
6   Brichto to Jakobovits, 12 June, 1991, Brichto Papers.
7   Jakobovits to Brichto, Office of the Chief Rabbi, 17 June, 1991, *ibid*.
8   Chaim Bermant, 'Can Sacks Save Orthodoxy?', *Manna*, summer 1989, 2-3. Of its contributor, the magazine wrote: 'Chaim Bermant was born in Poland, brought up in Glasgow, and now lives in Hampstead Garden Suburb. Perhaps best known as the *Jewish Chronicle*'s most provocative columnist, he is the author of numerous books and is the Chief Rabbi's official biographer.'
9   Leading article, 'Stepping out from No Man's Land', *ibid*, 1.
10 'Avoiding the collision', *Jewish Chronicle*, 8 February, 1985, 18-19.
11 Lord Jakobovits, 'Trouble and tradition', *ibid*, 25 September, 1992, 24, 26.
12 Jonathan Kestenbaum [chief executive] to the Chief Rabbi, 'Meeting with Lord Jakobovits, 8 October, 1991', memorandum dated 28 October, 1991, LMA/ACC/2805/08/01/001.
13 Kestenbaum to the Chief Rabbi, 'Meeting with Tony Bayfield, 15 October, 1991', memorandum dated 28 October, 1991, *ibid*.
14 'Mission Statement', Office of the Chief Rabbi', LMA/ACC/2805/08/03/004/001.
15 'The Chief Rabbinate: A Scenario for the Future', 12 November, 1991, *ibid*.
16 'Notes of a meeting of the Consultative Committee on Jewish–Christian Relationships, 85 Hamilton Terrace, 16 January, 1992,' USL/MS302/A1053/24/4; LMA/ACC/2805/8/3/28/001.
17 'Note of a meeting of the Liaison Group, St John's Wood Synagogue, 23 June, 1992'. Present were Rabbis Bayfield, Gryn, Middleburgh and Unterman, with Messrs Goldman and Lew, and Lionel Swift, QC, in the chair, USL/MS302/A1053/25.
18 'Notes of a meeting of the Consultative Committee, 85 Hamilton Terrace, 6 July, 1992', USL/MS302/A1053/24/4; LMA/ACC/2805/8/3/28/001.
19 Writing in the strictly Orthodox *Jewish Tribune*, Sacks had denounced Masorti's recruitment campaigns as 'dishonest, disreputable and unforgivable,' and its adherents as 'intellectual thieves.' His article was widely reported in the national press, notably *The Times* ('Chief Rabbi attacks "disreputable" group') and the *Evening Standard*, which described it as 'a declaration of open war.' While the Chief Rabbi had a policy of 'avoiding criticism of other organisations,' his

Office explained, he was prompted to speak out by 'an exceptionally mischievous campaign' by Masorti. See *Another Way, Another Time*, op. cit., 69 seq.

20 Rayner to Sacks, 29 January, 1994, LMA/ACC/2805/8/3/28/001. No record is known of the planned meeting.

21 'Memo: Future of the Consultative Committee', 22 February, 1994, sent to Tony Bayfield, Raymond Goldman, Rosita Rosenberg, Jackie Tabick, USL/MS302/A1053/24/3.

22 'Minutes of meeting of the Consultative Committee', 85 Hamilton Terrace, 8 March, 1995, LMA/ACC/2805/8//3/28/001.

23 Moshe Abelesz and Jonathan Rynhold, 'Orthodoxy "losing sight" of key values', *Jewish Chronicle*, 20 December, 1996, 19.

24 Lord Jakobovits, 'Putting Stability Before "Mirage" of Unity', ibid, 10 January, 1997, 23.

25 Meir Persoff, *Immanuel Jakobovits, a Prophet in Israel* (London: Vallentine Mitchell, 2002), 4, 6, 11. See also note 27 below.

26 Sidney Brichto, *Ritual Slaughter: Growing Up Jewish in America* (London: Sinclair-Stevenson, in association with the European Jewish Publication Society, 2001), 147-148, 152-153. Of Brichto, the book-jacket notes: 'Ordained as a rabbi in New York City, he came to London to do postgraduate work. He stayed to become leader of the Liberal Jewish movement at the age of 28. In addition to his writings and translation of the Old and New Testaments, he is a consultant to several communal organisations. He is regarded as one of the most controversial and outspoken critics on matters of religious belief and practice.'

27 Brichto to Lord Jakobovits of Regent's Park, 25 April, 1997, Brichto Papers. The documents sought by Jakobovits were to form part of an autobiography which he was planning to write and which, though never completed, featured as 'Flashbacks' in *Immanuel Jakobovits: a Prophet in Israel*, op. cit., 3-14, 44-57, 85-91, 112-120.

28 Jakobovits to Brichto, 30 April, 1997, the source also of the following correspondence.

29 Brichto to Jakobovits, 30 April, 1997.

30 Jakobovits to Brichto, 1 May, 1997.

31 Brichto to Jakobovits, 7 May, 1997.

32 Jakobovits to Brichto, 13 May, 1997.

33 'Creation and the crisis of faith: Lord Jakobovits on Rosh Hashanah's link with the mysteries of science', *Jewish Chronicle*, 10 September, 1999, 41.

Bibliography

A Special Correspondent, 'The British Chief Rabbinate,' in *The Jewish Monthly*, No. 2, May 1947, London: Anglo-Jewish Association.

A Time For Change: A Report on the Role of the United Synagogue in the Years Ahead, London: Stanley Kalms Foundation, 1992.

Abramsky, Yechezkel, *Address at the Installation of Rabbi I. Jakobovits*, London: United Synagogue, 1947.

Act for confirming a Scheme of the Charity Commissioners for the Jewish United Synagogues [33 & 34 Vict., Ch. cxvi], 14 July, 1870.

Adler, Hermann, *The Old Paths*, London: Wertheimer, Lea & Co., 1902.

Adler, Marcus N., *The Adler Family*, London: Office of the Jewish Chronicle, 1909; reprinted, expanded and translated into Hebrew, Bnei Brak: Yitzhak Kaufmann, 1993.

Alderman, Geoffrey, 'British Jewry: The Disintegration of a Community,' in *Continuity, Commitment, and Survival*, Westport: Praeger, 2003.

Alderman, Geoffrey, 'Foreword,' in Meir Persoff, *Another Way, Another Time: Religious Inclusivism and the Sacks Chief Rabbinate*, Boston: Academic Studies Press, 2010.

Alderman, Geoffrey, 'The British Chief Rabbinate: A Most Peculiar Practice,' in *European Judaism*, 23:2, 1990.

Alderman, Geoffrey, 'The Disunited Synagogue: Public Quarrels, Fragmentation and Disarray,' in *Judaism Today*, No. 4, London: Assembly of Masorti Synagogues, spring 1996.

Alderman, Geoffrey, *Anglo-Jewry: A Suitable Case For Treatment*, Egham: Royal Holloway & Bedford New College, 1990.

Alderman, Geoffrey, *British Jewry Since Emancipation*, Buckingham: University of Buckingham Press, 2014.

Alderman, Geoffrey, *Controversy and Crisis: Studies in the History of the Jews in Modern Britain*, Boston: Academic Studies Press, 2008.

Alderman, Geoffrey, *London Jewry and London Politics, 1889–1986*, London: Routledge, 1989.

Alderman, Geoffrey, *Modern British Jewry*, Oxford: Clarendon Press, 1992; revised, 1998.

Alderman, Geoffrey, *The Federation of Synagogues, 1887–1987*, London: Federation of Synagogues, 1987.

Apple, Raymond, 'Hermann Adler: Chief Rabbi,' in *Noblesse Oblige: Essays in Honour of David Kessler, OBE*, ed., Alan D. Crown, London and Portland, OR: Vallentine Mitchell, 1998.

Baggini, Julian, 'My Philosophy: Jonathan Sacks,' *The Philosophers' Magazine*, London: Philosophy Press, No. 44, March 2009.

Barnett, Arthur, *The Western Synagogue Through Two Centuries, 1761–1961*, Vallentine Mitchell, London, 1961.

Bermant, Chaim, 'The Rabbi's Rabbi,' in *Jewish Chronicle*, 5 November, 1999.

Bermant, Chaim, *Lord Jakobovits: The Authorized Biography of the Chief Rabbi*, London: Weidenfeld and Nicolson, 1990.

Bermant, Chaim, *Troubled Eden: An Anatomy of British Jewry*, New York: Basic Books, 1970.

Blackburn, David, et al., *A Community of Communities: Report of the Commission on Representation of the Interests of the British Jewish Community*, London: Institute for Jewish Policy Research, 2000.

Blank, Joseph E., *The Minutes of the Federation of Synagogues: A Twenty-Five Years' Review*, London: E. W. Rabbinowicz, 5673-1912.

Bornstein, Abba, and Homa, Bernard, *Tell It In Gath: British Jewry and Clause 43, The Inside Story*, London: privately published, 1972.

Boyd, Jonathan, 'Belonging to a shul matters: The view from the data', *Jewish Chronicle*, 7 July, 2017.

Brichto, Sidney, 'Halachah with Humility,' in *Jewish Chronicle*, 2 October, 1987.

Brichto, Sidney, 'What is wrong with the Chief Rabbinate?', in *Liberal Jewish Monthly*, London: Union of Liberal and Progressive Judaism, May 1965.

Brichto, Sidney, *Ritual Slaughter: Growing Up Jewish in America*, London: Sinclair-Stevenson, in association with the European Jewish Publication Society, 2001.

Brodie, Israel, 'Opening Address, First Conference of European Rabbis,' in *The Strength of My Heart*, London: G. J. George & Co., 1969.

Brodie, Israel, *Induction Address, Installation of Dr Immanuel Jakobovits*, St John's Wood Synagogue, London: United Synagogue, 1967.

Brodie, Israel, *Installation Sermon as Chief Rabbi of the United Hebrew Congregations of the British Commonwealth of Nations*, London: United Synagogue, 1948.

Brodie, Israel, *Statement by the Very Rev the Chief Rabbi, Dr Israel Brodie*, London: United Synagogue, 1964.

Brook, Stephen, *The Club: The Jews of Modern Britain*, London: Constable, 1989.

Bye Laws of the Constituent Synagogues, London: United Synagogue, 1881.

Bye-Laws of the Constituent Synagogues, London: United Synagogue, 1936.

Cesarani, David, *The Jewish Chronicle and Anglo-Jewry, 1841–1991*, Cambridge: Cambridge University Press, 1994.

Cohen, Arthur, 'The Structure of Anglo-Jewry Today,' in *Three Centuries of Anglo-Jewish History*, ed., V. D. Lipman, Cambridge: W. Heffer & Sons, for the Jewish Historical Society of England, 1961.

Cohen, Jeffrey M. (ed.), *Dear Chief Rabbi: From the Correspondence of Chief Rabbi Immanuel Jakobovits on Matters of Jewish Law, Ethics and Contemporary Issues, 1980–1990*, New Jersey: Ktav, 1995.

Cohen, Jeffrey M., *Issues of the Day: A Modern-Orthodox View*, Stanmore: Gnesia Publications, 1999.

Cohen, Norman, 'Non-Religious Factors in the Emergence of the Chief Rabbinate,' in *Transactions of the Jewish Historical Society of England*, Vol. XXI, London, 1968.

Cohen, Norman, 'The Religious Crisis in Anglo-Jewry,' in *Tradition*, Vol. 8, No. 2, ed., Walter S. Wurzburger, New York: Rabbinical Council of America, 1966.

Cohen, Norman. 'Trends in Anglo-Jewish Religious Life,' in *Jewish Life in Modern Britain*, ed., Julius Gould and Shaul Esh, London: Routledge & Kegan Paul, 1964.

Cosgrove, Elliot Joe, *Teyku: The Insoluble Contradictions in the Life and Thought of Louis Jacobs*, PhD dissertation, University of Chicago, 2008.

Cowen, Anne (ed.), *New London Synagogue: The First Twenty Years*, London: New London Synagogue, 1984.

Curtis, Michael, 'The Beth Din of the Reform Synagogues of Great Britain,' in Dow Marmur (ed.), *Reform Judaism: Essays on Reform Judaism in Britain*, London: Reform Synagogues of Great Britain, 1973.

Domb, Cyril, 'Dayan Yechezkel Abramsky: A Centenary Tribute,' in *L'Eylah*, No. 23, Pesach 5747, London: Office of the Chief Rabbi and Jews' College, April 1987.

Elton, Benjamin J., 'Did the Chief Rabbinate move to the right? A case study – the mixed choirs controversies, 1880–1986,' in *Jewish Historical Studies*, Vol. 39, London: Jewish Historical Society of England, 2004.

Elton, Benjamin J., *Britain's Chief Rabbis and the Religious Character of Anglo-Jewry, 1880–1970*, Manchester: Manchester University Press, 2010.

Elton, Benjamin J., *Britain's Chief Rabbis: The Jewish response to modernity and the remoulding of tradition*, unpublished PhD thesis, University of London, 2007.

Endelman, Todd M., *The Jews of Britain 1656 to 2000*, Berkeley/Los Angeles/London: University of California Press, 2002.

Finestein, Israel, 'The Jews and English Marriage Law,' in the *Jewish Journal of Sociology* 8, 1964; reprinted in Israel Finestein, *Jewish Society in Victorian England*, London: Vallentine Mitchell, 1993.

Finestein, Israel, *A Short History of Anglo-Jewry*, London: Lincolns-Prager, for the World Jewish Congress British Section, 1957.

Frankel, William, *Tea With Einstein And Other Memories*, London: Halban, in association with the European Jewish Publication Society, 2006.

Freedman, Maurice (ed.), *A Minority in Britain: Social Studies of the Anglo-Jewish Community*, London: Vallentine Mitchell, 1955.

Freud-Kandel, Miri J., *Orthodox Judaism in Britain Since 1913*, London and Portland, OR: Vallentine Mitchell, 2006.

Frosh, Sidney, 'Clause 74 And All That,' in *Hamesilah* [*The Path*], Pesach 5745, London: United Synagogue, 1985.

Goldberg, David J., and Kessler, Edward (eds.), *Aspects of Liberal Judaism*, London: Vallentine Mitchell, 2004.

Goldschmidt-Lehmann, Ruth P., 'Nathan Marcus Adler: A Bibliography,' in *Studies in Judaica, Karaitica and Islamica: Presented to Leon Nemoy on his Eightieth Birthday*, Ramat Gan: Bar-Ilan University Press, 1982.

Gollancz, Hermann, *Sermons and Addresses Setting Forth the Teachings and Spirit of Judaism* (Third Series), London: Oxford University Press, 1924.

Gould, Julius, and Esh, Shaul (eds.), *Jewish Life in Modern Britain*, London: Routledge & Kegan Paul, 1964.

Grunfeld, I., 'Problems of Modern Jewish Marriage and Family Life,' in *Addresses Given at the Tenth Conference of Anglo-Jewish Preachers*, London: Standing Committee, 1953.

Harris, Cyril, *For Heaven's Sake*, London and Portland, OR: Vallentine Mitchell, 2000.

Hart, Rona, and Kafka, Edward, *Trends in British Synagogue Membership 1990–2005/06*, London: Board of Deputies of British Jews, 2006.

Henriques, Robert, *Sir Robert Waley Cohen, 1877–1952*, London: Secker & Warburg, 1966.

Hertz, J. H., 'Recall to the Synagogue' – I and II, in *Early and Late: Addresses, Messages, and Papers*, Hindhead: Soncino Press, 1943.

Hertz, J. H., 'The New Paths: Whither Do They Lead?,' in *Affirmations of Judaism*, London: Oxford University Press, 1927; reprinted, London: Edward Goldstone, 1946.

Hertz, J. H., *Early and Late: Addresses, Messages, and Papers*, Hindhead: Soncino Press, 1943.

Homa, Bernard, *A Fortress in Anglo-Jewry: The Story of the Machzike Hadath*, London: Shapiro, Vallentine & Co., 5713-1953.

Homa, Bernard, *Footprints on the Sands of Time*, Charfield: Beaver Press, 1990.

Homa, Bernard, *Orthodoxy in Anglo-Jewry 1880–1940*, London: Jewish Historical Society of England, 1969.

Ish-Horowicz, M., 'The Case of Mrs Paula Cohen and her Children,' in *The Jewish Law Annual*, No. 11, 1994.

Jacobs, Louis, 'A Retrospect of the "Jacobs Affair,"' in *We Have Reason to Believe*, fifth expanded edition, London and Portland, OR: Vallentine Mitchell, 2004.

Jacobs, Louis, 'For the Sake of Heaven,' in *Jewish Chronicle*, 19 December, 1986.

Jacobs, Louis, 'Four Rabbinic Positions in Anglo-Jewry,' in *The Jewish Year Book 2000*, ed., Stephen W. Massil, London: Vallentine Mitchell, in association with the Jewish Chronicle, 2000.

Jacobs, Louis, 'Reflections on a Controversy,' in *Quest 1*, ed., Jonathan Stone, London: Paul Hamlyn, 1965.

Jacobs, Louis, *A Tree of Life: Diversity, Flexibility, and Creativity in Jewish Law*, Oxford: Oxford University Press for the Littman Library of Jewish Civilization, 1984.

Jacobs, Louis, *Beyond Reasonable Doubt*, London: Littman Library of Jewish Civilization, 1999.

Jacobs, Louis, *Helping With Inquiries: An Autobiography*, London: Vallentine Mitchell, 1989.

Jacobs, Louis, *Induction Sermon, New West End Synagogue*, London: Henry G. Morris & Co., for the New West End Synagogue, 1954.

Jacobs, Louis, *Principles of the Jewish Faith: An Analytical Study*, London: Vallentine Mitchell, 1964.

Jacobs, Louis, *We Have Reason to Believe*, London: Vallentine Mitchell, 1957; second edition, 1962; third edition, 1965; fourth revised edition, 1995; fifth edition, with a new Introduction by William Frankel, and a new Retrospect by the author, 2004.

Jacobs, Louis, *What We Stand For*, London: Blackfriars Press for New London Synagogue, 1964.

Jakobovits, Immanuel, 'Avoiding the Collision,' in *Jewish Chronicle*, 8 February, 1985.

Jakobovits, Immanuel, 'Division and Diversion,' in *Jewish Chronicle*, 26 February, 1971.

Jakobovits, Immanuel, 'Fragments From An Unpublished Autobiography,' in Meir Persoff, *Immanuel Jakobovits: a Prophet in Israel*, London: Vallentine Mitchell, 2002.

Jakobovits, Immanuel, 'Modern Trends in Orthodoxy,' in *Encounter: Essays on Torah and Modern Life*, eds., H. Chaim Schimmel and Aryeh Carmell, London: Association of Orthodox Jewish Scientists; Jerusalem and New York: Feldheim, 1989.

Jakobovits, Immanuel, 'SOS: The Way We Live Now,' in *Jewish Chronicle*, 10 October, 1986.

Jakobovits, Immanuel, 'The Changing Face of British Jewry: The Quiet Revolution,' in *Jewish Chronicle*, 9 November, 1984.

Jakobovits, Immanuel, 'The Evolution of the British Rabbinate Since 1845: Its Past Impact and Future Challenges,' in *The Timely and The Timeless*, London: Vallentine Mitchell, 1977.

Jakobovits, Immanuel, 'Trouble and Tradition,' in *Jewish Chronicle*, 25 September, 1992.

Jakobovits, Immanuel, 'Who is a Jew? New Questions, New Passions,' in *Jewish Chronicle*, 7 December, 1984.

Jakobovits, Immanuel, *Address Delivered at the Installation of Rabbi Dr Jonathan Sacks as Chief Rabbi of the United Hebrew Congregations of the Commonwealth*, 1 September, 1991, London: Office of the Chief Rabbi, 1991.

Jakobovits, Immanuel, *Driving Forward*, United Synagogue, London, 26 Ellul 5730–27 September, 1970, London: Office of the Chief Rabbi, 1970.

Jakobovits, Immanuel, *If Only My People: Zionism in My Life*, London: Weidenfeld and Nicolson, 1984.

Jakobovits, Immanuel, *Installation Address as Chief Rabbi of the United Hebrew Congregations of the British Commonwealth of Nations*, London: Office of the Chief Rabbi, 1967.

Jakobovits, Immanuel, *Journal of a Rabbi*, New York: Living Books, 1966.

Jakobovits, Immanuel, *Looking Ahead*, London: United Synagogue, 1967, second edition, 1968.

Jakobovits, Immanuel, *Milestones and Millstones: Centenary of the United Synagogue*, 15 Tammuz, 5730–19 July, 1970, London: Office of the Chief Rabbi, 1970.

Jakobovits, Immanuel, *Moving Ahead: A Review and a Preview – A New Year Message from the Chief Rabbi to the Leadership of Anglo-Jewry*, London: Office of the Chief Rabbi, Ellul 5728–September 1968.

Jakobovits, Immanuel, *New Priorities on the Orthodox Agenda*, London: Office of the Chief Rabbi, 1989.

Jakobovits, Immanuel, *Prelude to Service*, London: Office of the Chief Rabbi, 1967.

Jakobovits, Immanuel, *Preserving The Oneness Of The Jewish People: Orthodox–Progressive divisions and discussions on marriage, divorce and conversion: can a permanent schism be averted?* London: Office of the Chief Rabbi, 1988.

Jakobovits, Immanuel, *Rabbinical Tasks in the Present Era*, London: Conference of European Rabbis, 1958.

Jakobovits, Immanuel, *The Timely and The Timeless*, London: Vallentine Mitchell, 1977.

Jubilee of the Reform Congregation: Supplement to the Jewish Chronicle, 29 January, 1892.

Kalms, Stanley (chairman), *A Time for Change: United Synagogue Review*, London: Stanley Kalms Foundation, 1992.

Kalms, Stanley, 'On the Right Track: The Chief Rabbi's First Ten Years,' *Jewish Chronicle*, 31 August, 2001.

Katz, Steven T. (ed.), *Interpreters of Judaism in the Late Twentieth Century*, Washington: B'nai B'rith, 1993.

Kershen, Anne J. (ed.), *RSGB/ULPS: 150 Years of Progressive Judaism in Britain, 1840–1990*, London: London Museum of Jewish Life, 1990.

Kershen, Anne J., and Romain, Jonathan A., *Tradition and Change: A History of Reform Judaism in Britain, 1840–1995*, London: Vallentine Mitchell, 1995.

Kosmin, Barry A., 'Localism and Pluralism in British Jewry, 1900–80,' in *Transactions of the Jewish Historical Society of England*, Vol. XXVIII, London, 1982.

Kosmin, Barry A., 'The case for the local perspective in the study of contemporary British Jewry,' in *Jewish Life in Britain, 1962–1977*, ed., Julius Gould and Shaul Esh, London: Routledge & Kegan Paul, 1964.

Kosmin, Barry A., and de Lange, Deborah, *Synagogue Affiliation in the United Kingdom, 1977*, London: Research Unit, Board of Deputies, 1978.

Langdon, Harold S., 'The Place of Reform in Anglo-Jewry Today,' in *A Genuine Search*, ed., Dow Marmur, London: Reform Synagogues of Great Britain, 1979.

Lappin, Elena, 'Whose Chief Rabbi?', in *The Jewish Quarterly*, Vol. 44, No. 2 (166), summer 1997.

Leigh, Michael, 'Reform Judaism in Britain, 1840–1970,' in *Reform Judaism*, ed., Dow Marmur, London: Reform Synagogues of Great Britain, 1973.

Lerner, Isaac, 'The Attitude to Halachah of the Progressive Movements: Can they be considered a *kehillah kedoshah?*', in *L'Eylah*, Vol. I, No. 10, autumn 5741, ed., A. Melinek, London: Office of the Chief Rabbi, 1981.

Levin, Salmond S. (ed.), *A Century of Anglo-Jewish Life, 1870–1970*, London: United Synagogue, 1971.

Levy, Elkan, *The New West End Synagogue, 1879–2004*, London: privately published, 2004.

Levy, Isaac, *Historic Judaism Versus Liberal Judaism*, London: United Synagogue, 1949.

Liberles, Robert, 'The Origins of the Jewish Reform Movement in England,' in *AJSreview*, Vol. I, Cambridge, Mass.: Association for Jewish Studies, 1976.

Lipman, Sonia L., 'Judith Montefiore – First Lady of Anglo-Jewry,' in *Transactions of the Jewish Historical Society of England*, Vol. XXI, London, 1968.

Lipman, Sonia L., and Lipman, Vivian D., *Jewish Life in Britain, 1962–1977*, New York: H. G. Saur, 1981.

Lipman, V. D., *A History of the Jews in Britain Since 1858*, New York: Holmes & Meier, 1990.

Lipman, V. D., *Social History of the Jews in England, 1850–1950*, London: Watts & Co., 1954.

Lipman, V. D., *Three Centuries of Anglo-Jewish History*, London: W. Heffer & Sons for the Jewish Historical Society of England, 1961.

Livingstone, I., *The Union of Anglo-Jewish Preachers: A Retrospect*, London: Union of Anglo-Jewish Preachers, 1949.

Long-term Planning for British Jewry: Final Report and Recommendations, London: Institute for Jewish Policy Research, Report No. 5, 2003.

Margoliouth, Moses, *The History of the Jews in Great Britain*, London: Richard Bentley, 1851.

Marmur, Dow (ed.), *A Genuine Search: God, Torah, Israel – A Reform Perspective*, London: Reform Synagogues of Great Britain, 1979.

Marmur, Dow (ed.), *Reform Judaism*, London: Reform Synagogues of Great Britain, 1973.

Mashiah, Donatella Casale and Jonathan Boyd, *Synagogue Membership in the United Kingdom in 2016*, London: Institute for Jewish Policy Research, on behalf of the Board of Deputies of British Jews, 2017.

Maybaum, Ignaz, 'The Jacobs Affair,' in *Quest* 1, ed., Jonathan Stone, London: Paul Hamlyn, 1965.

Maybaum, Ignaz, *The Office of a Chief Rabbi* (Judaism Today – A Series Edited by Rabbi Dr Ignaz Maybaum), London: Reform Synagogues of Great Britain, 1964.

Meyer, Michael A., *Response to Modernity: A History of the Reform Movement in Judaism*, New York and Oxford: Oxford University Press, 1988.

Nathan, David, 'David Nathan Talks With Chief Rabbi Jakobovits,' in *Jewish Chronicle*, 6 January, 1978.

Nathan, David, 'The Mystique of Survival: Interview with Chief Rabbi Sir Immanuel Jakobovits,' in *Jewish Chronicle*, 17 April, 1987.

Newman, Aubrey, 'The Chief Rabbinate and the Provinces, 1840–1914,' in *Tradition and Transition: Essays Presented to Chief Rabbi Sir Immanuel Jakobovits to Celebrate Twenty Years in Office*, ed., Jonathan Sacks, London: Jews' College Publications, 1986.

Newman, Aubrey, 'The Chief Rabbinate,' in *Provincial Jewry in Victorian Britain*, London: Jewish Historical Society of England, 1975.

Newman, Aubrey, *The Board of Deputies of British Jews, 1760–1985*, London: Vallentine Mitchell, 1987.

Newman, Aubrey, *The United Synagogue, 1870–1970*, London: Routledge & Kegan Paul, 1976.

Pearl, Chaim, 'About "Chief Rabbis,"' in *Jewish Spectator*, New York, January 1967.

Persoff, Meir, 'Anti-Jacobs society to disband,' in *Jewish Chronicle*, 19 March, 1971.

Persoff, Meir, 'Stubborn resistance to change,' interview with Chief Rabbi Dr Immanuel Jakobovits, in *Jewish Chronicle*, 27 June, 1969.

Persoff, Meir, 'Wolfson overrules Chief Rabbi,' in *Jewish Chronicle*, 14 August, 1970.

Persoff, Meir, *Another Way, Another Time: Religious Inclusivism and the Sacks Chief Rabbinate*, Boston: Academic Studies Press, 2010.

Persoff, Meir, *Conflict and Conciliation: Religious Pluralism and the British Chief Rabbinate, 1840–1940*, unpublished MA dissertation, University of London, 1994.

Persoff, Meir, *Faith Against Reason: Religious Reform and the British Chief Rabbinate, 1840–1990*, London and Portland, OR: Vallentine Mitchell, 2008.

Persoff, Meir, *Hats in the Ring: Choosing Britain's Chief Rabbis from Adler to Sacks*, Boston: Academic Studies Press, 2013.

Persoff, Meir, *Immanuel Jakobovits: a Prophet in Israel*, London and Portland, OR: Vallentine Mitchell, 2002.

Prais, S. J., 'Synagogue Statistics and the Jewish Population of Great Britain, 1900–1970,' in *Jewish Journal of Sociology*, Vol. XIV, No. 2, London, December 1972.

Prais, S. J., and Schmool, Marlena, 'Statistics of Jewish Marriages in Great Britain, 1901–1965,' in *Jewish Journal of Sociology*, Vol. IX, No. 1, London, 1967.

Prais, S. J., and Schmool, Marlena, 'Synagogue Marriages in Great Britain, 1966–1968,' in *Jewish Journal of Sociology*, Vol. XII, No. 1, London, June 1970.

Rayner, John D., 'Nonconformism in Anglo-Jewry,' The Jewish Quarterly, Vol. 46, No. 4 (176), winter 1999–2000.

Recorded Minutes of the First Meeting of Elected Members of the Vestry of the United Synagogue, London, 11 January, 1871; and Deed of Foundation and Trust, signed, sealed and delivered by Sir Anthony de Rothschild, Baronet; Lionel Louis Cohen; Sampson Lucas; Solomon Schloss; and Assur Henry Moses, in the presence of Algernon E. Sydney, Solicitor, 46 Finsbury Circus, London, EC, 13 January, 1871.

Reif, Stefan, 'Dilemma of Dr Jonathan and Rabbi Sacks,' in Jewish Chronicle, 30 April, 1993.

Report of the Royal Commission on the Laws of Marriage, in Reports from Commissioners, Vol. XXXII, Session 19 November, 1867–31 July, 1868, London: George E. Eyre and William Spottiswoode, 1868.

Rigal, Lawrence, and Rosenberg, Rosita, Liberal Judaism: The First Hundred Years, London: Liberal Judaism–Union of Liberal and Progressive Synagogues, 2004.

Romain, Jonathan A., 'The Establishment of the Reform Beth Din in 1948: A Barometer of Religious Trends in Anglo-Jewry,' in Jewish Historical Studies, Volume XXXIII, 1992–1994, London: Jewish Historical Society of England, 1995.

Romain, Jonathan A., Faith & Practice: A Guide to Reform Judaism Today, London: Reform Synagogues of Great Britain, 1991.

Romain, Jonathan A., The Reform Beth Din: The Formation and Development of the Rabbinical Court of the Reform Synagogues of Great Britain, 1935–1965, unpublished PhD thesis, University of Leicester, 1990.

Roth, Cecil, 'The Collapse of English Jewry,' in The Jewish Monthly, No. 4, London: Anglo-Jewish Association, 1947.

Roth, Cecil, A History of the Jews in England, London: Oxford University Press, 1941; reprinted, London: John Trotter, 1989.

Roth, Cecil, Archives of the United Synagogue: Report and Catalogue, London: United Synagogue, 1930.

Roth, Cecil, The Federation of Synagogues, 1912–1937, London, 5698-1937.

Rubinstein, W. D., A History of the Jews in the English-Speaking World: Great Britain, Basingstoke: Macmillan, 1996.

Sacks, Jonathan (ed.), Orthodoxy Confronts Modernity, New Jersey: Ktav, in association with Jews' College, London, 1991.

Sacks, Jonathan (ed.), Tradition and Transition: Essays Presented to Chief Rabbi Sir Immanuel Jakobovits to Celebrate Twenty Years in Office, London: Jews' College Publications, 1986.

Sacks, Jonathan, 'Prologue,' in Meir Persoff, Immanuel Jakobovits: a Prophet in Israel, London and Portland, OR: Vallentine Mitchell, 2002.

Sacks, Jonathan, 'The Origin of Torah,' Jewish Chronicle, 2 November, 1984.

Sacks, Jonathan, *A Decade of Jewish Renewal: Installation Address as Chief Rabbi of the United Hebrew Congregations of the Commonwealth*, 1 September, 1991, London: Office of the Chief Rabbi, 1991.

Sacks, Jonathan, *A Time For Renewal: A Rabbinic Response to the Kalms Report, 'A Time For Change,'* London: Office of the Chief Rabbi, 1992.

Sacks, Jonathan, *Community of Faith*, London: Peter Halban, 1995.

Sacks, Jonathan, *From Renewal to Responsibility*, London: Office of the Chief Rabbi, 2001.

Sacks, Jonathan, *One People? Tradition, Modernity, and Jewish Unity*, London: Littman Library of Jewish Civilization, 1993.

Sacks, Jonathan, *Studies in Renewal: 1. From Integration to Survival to Continuity; 2. The Crisis of Continuity; 3. The Secret of Jewish Continuity; 4. Rethinking Priorities; 5. From Jewish Continuity to Jewish Continuity*, London: Office of the Chief Rabbi, June–October 1993.

Sacks, Jonathan, *The Dignity of Difference: How to Avoid the Clash of Civilizations*, first edition, London and New York: Continuum, 2002; revised edition with new preface, 2003.

Sacks, Jonathan, *Tradition in an Untraditional Age: Essays on Modern Jewish Thought*, London: Vallentine Mitchell, 1990.

Sacks, Jonathan, *Traditional Alternatives: Orthodoxy and the Future of the Jewish People*, London: Jews' College Publications, 1989; published in the USA as *Arguments for the Sake of Heaven*, New Jersey: Jason Aronson, 1995.

Sacks, Jonathan, *Will We Have Jewish Grandchildren? Jewish Continuity and How to Achieve It*, London: Vallentine Mitchell, 1994.

Schmool, Marlena, and Cohen, Frances, *British Synagogue Membership in 1990*, London: Community Research Unit, Board of Deputies, 1991.

Schmool, Marlena, and Cohen, Frances, *British Synagogue Membership in 1996*, London: Community Research Unit, Board of Deputies, 1997.

Shaftesley, John M., 'Israel Brodie, Chief Rabbi: A Biographical Sketch,' in *Essays Presented to Chief Rabbi Israel Brodie on the Occasion of his Seventieth Birthday*, eds., H. J. Zimmels, J. Rabbinowitz, I. Finestein, Jews' College Publications, New Series, No. 3, London: Soncino Press, 1967.

Shaftesley, John M., 'Religious Controversies,' in *A Century of Anglo-Jewish Life, 1870–1970*, ed., Salmond S. Levin, London: United Synagogue, 1971.

Sharot, Stephen, 'Reform and Liberal Judaism in London, 1840–1940,' in *Jewish Social Studies*, Vol. XLI, Conference on Jewish Social Studies, New York, 1979.

Sharot, Stephen, *Judaism: A Sociology*, New York: Holmes & Meier, 1976.

Shashar, Michael, *Lord Jakobovits in Conversation*, London and Portland, OR: Vallentine Mitchell, 2000.

Simmons, Vivian G., *The Path of Life: A Study of the Background, Faith and Practice of Liberal Judaism*, London: Vallentine Mitchell, 1961.

Simon, Maurice, *Jewish Religious Conflicts*, London: Hutchinson, 1950.

Sorasky, Aaron, 'The Life and Times of Rabbenu Yechezkel Abramsky,' in *Emunah: Pathways in Contemporary Jewish Thought*, No. 2, January 1990, Tel Ganim: Kollel Tal Torah.

Sorasky, Aaron, *Melech Beyofyo* [*A King In His Glory*], Vols. I and II, Jerusalem: published privately, 2004.

Swift, Morris, *Jewish Marriage and Divorce*, London: Beth Din, 1962–5722.

Taylor, Derek, *British Chief Rabbis, 1664–2006*, London and Portland, OR: Vallentine Mitchell, 2006.

Taylor, Derek, *Chief Rabbi Hertz: The Wars of the Lord*, London and Portland, OR: Vallentine Mitchell, 2014.

Temkin, Sefton, 'A Crisis in Anglo-Jewry,' in *Conservative Judaism*, Vol. XVIII, No. 1, ed., Samuel H. Dresner, New York: Rabbinical Assembly, 1963.

Tessler, Gloria, *Amélie: The Story of Lady Jakobovits*, London and Portland, OR: Vallentine Mitchell, 1999.

Vallely, Paul, 'Jonathan Sacks: Defender of the Faith,' in *The Independent*, London, 8 September, 2001.

Wagner, Leslie (chairman), *Change in Continuity: Report of the Review into Jewish Continuity*, London: Jewish Continuity, 1996.

Waterman, Stanley, and Kosmin, Barry, *British Jewry in the Eighties*, London: Board of Deputies of British Jews, 1986.

Webber, Jonathan (ed.), *Jewish Identities in the New Europe*, London: Littman Library of Jewish Civilization, 1994.

Wittenberg, Jonathan, 'The Significance of Motivation in the Halachah of Conversion,' in *Judaism Today*, No. 3, London: Assembly of Masorti Synagogues, winter 1995–96.

Wolfson, Isaac, *Statement by the President of the United Synagogue*, London: United Synagogue, 1964.

Wolkind, Jack, *London and its Jewish Community*, London: West Central Counselling and Community Research, 1985.

Zolti, Bezalel, 'The "Man Of Freedom" Of Our Generation,' in *Sefer Zikaron* [*Memorial Volume to Rabbi Yechezkel Abramsky*], eds., Joseph Buchsbaum, Abraham Halevy Sher, Jerusalem: Moriah, 5738-1978.

Index

A
Abortion, 154
Abramsky, Yechezkel, 2, 204
Adath, 50
Adler, Hermann, 183
Adler, Nathan Marcus, 1, 183
Adultery, 99
Agunah ('tied woman'), 5, 27, 205
Ahavat Yisrael, 105
Aids, 147, 154
Akiva School (London), 116, 117
Amsterdam, 3
Anglo-Jewish Association, 83, 204
Anglo-Jewry, xi, xii, xiv, 4, 11, 17, 21, 36, 44, 45, 79, 85, 102, 104, 116, 119, 123, 126, 127, 138, 139, 157, 170, 178, 182, 187, 196, 217
Antisemitism, 195
Archbishop of Canterbury, 125, 157, 172, 178
Aschkenazi, M., 213
Assembly of United Synagogue Ministers, 76, 78
A Time for Change (Kalms), xviii, 203
Australia, 8

B
Baal teshuvah movement, 110
Baeck, Leo, 80, 197, 200, 209
Balfour Declaration, 183
Bar-Ilan University, 219
Barnet (London), 203
Baumgarten, J.H., 213
Bayfield, Tony, xv, 93, 100, 110, 118, 119, 121–124, 127–131, 133–135, 145, 146, 151, 152, 156–158, 185, 186, 188, 190, 216, 220
BBC, 121

Ben-Gurion, David, 207
Ben Zoma, 113
Berkovits, Eliezer, 60, 61
Bermant, Chaim, 180, 220
Bible (Higher) Criticism, 11
Birmingham, 145, 146
Board of Deputies, xvii, 1, 2, 13, 15, 32, 47–55, 83, 106, 115, 119, 120, 129, 130, 135, 136, 158, 167, 170, 191, 194, 202, 204, 210, 217
Bower, Marcus, 172
Boyd, Jonathan, xvii, 202
Brichto, Chanan, 197, 199
Brichto, Sidney, 5, 13, 14, 18, 27–29, 47, 56–60, 62–64, 75–77, 89–92, 96, 131, 140–145, 147, 150, 163–165, 168, 171–174, 176, 178, 179, 196, 197, 200, 201, 208, 216, 221
'Bridges of Understanding', 17, 22, 23, 26, 27, 110, 172
Brighton and Hove, 14
British Council of Synagogues, 15, 89
Brodie, Fanny, 12
Brodie, Israel, xii, 4–10, 24, 56, 183, 185

C
Cambridge, 82
Canada, 7, 207
Cardiff, 24
'Causeless hatred', 104, 189
Central/Modern Orthodox, 180, 203, 204
Chain, Benjamin, 82
Chalitzah ceremony, 5, 27, 205
Chanucah, 75
Chaplaincy Commission, 35
Chasidism, xix

Chief Rabbinate Conference, 16, 202
Chief Rabbinate Council, 54, 57, 59, 107, 177, 202
Chief Rabbinate, xi–xiv, xvi, xvii, 2, 12, 13, 84, 119, 128, 129, 166, 167, 170, 178, 186–188
Chief Rabbinate-in-Commission, 14, 16
Church of England, 1
Christianity, 36, 38, 40, 41
Clause 6 (Board of Deputies), 210
Clause 43 (Board of Deputies), 48, 50, 51, 54, 129, 210
Clause 50 (Board of Deputies), 47, 48
Clause 74 (Board of Deputies), 129, 131, 135
Cohen (McKenzie Wilson), Paula, 158, 161–164
Cohen of Walmer, Lord (Lionel), 27, 28, 56, 57, 192, 208
Cohen, Jeffrey, 108, 216
Cohen, Shimon, 216
Conference of Anglo-Jewish Preachers, 77, 84, 87, 88
Conference of European Rabbis, 3
Consultative Committee, 58, 59, 73, 86, 93, 107, 108, 111, 114, 120, 122, 124, 132, 136, 145–147, 151, 152, 157, 159, 177, 181, 185, 188–195
Conversion, 4, 5, 28, 46, 59–61, 63, 64, 69–72, 97, 101, 148, 161–163, 165, 217
Council of Christians and Jews, 55–58, 83, 115, 120, 185, 191
Council of Reform and Liberal Rabbis, 34, 47, 55, 58, 110, 113, 119–122, 127, 132, 134, 135, 158, 171, 190
Cousinhood, xi

D

Davis, Moshe, 55, 63, 69, 73, 76, 78, 114, 210
Decade of Jewish Renewal, 194
Diaspora, 10, 140
Divorce (*get, gittin*), 4, 5, 28–30, 59, 60, 63–66, 70–72, 97, 98, 101, 140, 141, 148, 213, 217
Dunner, J. H., 213
Dunner, H. D., 213

E

Economist, The, 125
Edgar, Leslie, 192
Edgware (Middlesex), 102, 201
Edinburgh, 180
Ehrentreu, Chanoch, 112, 169
Eimer, Colin, 188
Emeth Organisation, 212
England, 203
Epstein, Isidore, 195
Evening Standard, 221

F

Fackenheim, Emile, 68
Family purity, 139
Federation of Synagogues, xii, 15, 16, 24, 64, 168, 203
Feldman, H. I., 213
Fidler, Michael, 48, 50
Fifth Avenue Synagogue (New York), 8
Fisher, Michael, 63
Fisher, Samuel, 55
Free Churches, 172
Freehof, Solomon, 68
Friedlander, Albert, 216
Friedman, S., 213
Friedman, Theodore, 61
Frosh, Sidney, 176
Fundamentalism, 7

G

Gaon, Solomon (Haham), 14, 15, 23, 24, 29, 47–53, 56, 58–60, 62, 63, 90, 106
Gateshead, 79, 84
Gates of Heaven, 139
Germany, 24, 70, 80, 144, 197
Glasgow, xi
Gluckstein, Louis, 208
Goldberg, David, 62
Goldberg, P. Selvin, 31, 208
Golders Green (London), 112
Goldman, Raymond, 55, 58, 59, 101, 146, 160, 161, 216, 220
Goldstein, David, 28, 62
Gollop, Mark, 2
Goodman, Lord (Arnold), 171
Goren, Shlomo, 165, 217

Greater London, 203
Gurwitz, I., 213
Gryn, Hugo, 55, 58, 103, 108, 111, 114, 122, 132, 134, 143, 156, 157, 160, 186, 190, 194, 216, 220

H
Halachah with Humility (Brichto), 147–151, 176, 200
Halpern, E., 213
Hamilton Terrace (London), xx, 125, 158, 185, 193, 202
Hardman, Leslie, 62
Harris, Cyril, 75–78, 103, 119, 216
Haskalah movement, 11
Hertsmere (Hertfordshire), 203
Hertz (Freed), Rose, 204
Hertz, Joseph Herman, vi, viii, xi, xiii, 1–3, 56, 104, 183, 185, 195, 204
Herzog, Isaac Halevi, 12
Herzog, Yaacov, 12, 16, 207
Hildesheimer, Ezriel, 195
Hirsch, Samson Raphael, 195
Hoffman, David, 195
Holocaust, 64, 143, 144, 153
Homa, Bernard, 50, 51, 54, 210
Homosexuality, 104, 153, 192
House of Lords, 153

I
Independence Day (Israel), 30–33, 37, 76, 84, 212
Independent, The, 146
Institute of Jewish Policy Research, xvii, xix, 202
Intermarriage, 5, 196
Islam, 128

J
Jacobs, Louis, 6, 7, 15, 62, 89, 126, 177, 178
'Jacobs Affairs', xvi, 7, 183, 195
Jakobovits, Amélie, 115, 116, 158
Jakobovits, Immanuel, xi, xii, xv, xvi, xxi, 3, 4, 8–10, 12, 16–20, 22, 25–43, 49–51, 56, 61, 63, 72, 76, 79, 92, 107, 108, 110, 112, 113, 117, 126, 128, 134, 135, 142, 144, 147, 148, 150, 154, 157, 162, 166, 172–175, 179, 181, 183, 185, 192, 194, 196, 199, 201, 202, 208, 216, 218

Jakobovits, Julius, 197
Jewish Agency (London), 75
Jewish Chronicle, xi, xiii, xv, xvii, 4, 21, 55, 58, 76, 79, 85, 86, 104, 108, 112, 119, 126, 131, 136–138, 143, 159, 161, 163, 168, 170, 172, 174, 194, 202
Jewish defence, 84
Jewish Gay and Lesbian Helpline, 190
Jewish National Fund (London), 77, 78
Jewish Tribune, 220
Jewish Values (Jacobs), 7
Jewish Welfare Board, 113
Jews' College (London), 6, 35–37, 112, 115, 118, 177, 180, 195, 205
Jerusalem, xiii
Jerusalem Talmud, 209
Joint Standing Committee, 15
Jung, Leo, 8, 10, 206

K
Kagan, Israel Meir (Chafetz Chaim), 83
Kalms, Stanley, xviii, 203
Karaites, 74, 97
Karminski, Seymour, 91, 208
Kashrut, 70, 98, 99, 139, 168
Kenton (Middlesex), 108
Khomeini, Ayatollah, 165
King David School (Birmingham), 145
King-Hamilton, Alan [Committee], 14, 15, 20, 21, 106, 111, 208
Kirzner, Eliezer, 24
Klal Yisrael, 69, 105, 148, 154, 190, 193
Kokotek, Jakob, 14, 208
Königsberg (Germany), 197
Kopelowitz, Lionel, 167, 168, 170, 171, 217

L
Langdon, Harold, 54, 55, 216
Laski, Neville, 1, 204
Law and Parliamentary Committee (Board of Deputies), 49
League of Nations, xiii
Leeds, 212
Leigh, Michael, 102, 208
Leo Baeck College (London), 35–37, 45, 111, 116, 117
Lerner, Isaac, 97–100
Levirate marriage, 205
Lew, Jonathan, xv, 156, 160, 161, 220

Lew, Myer, 14
Liaison Committee, xv, 160, 181, 185, 187–189
Liberal Jewish Synagogue (London), 21, 204
Liberal Judaism, 203
Lieberman, Saul, 9, 206
Lipman, David, 160
Liverpool, 205
Living Judaism (Reform journal), 22, 85
London Beth Din, xii, xvi, 1–3, 7, 8, 12, 13, 15, 29, 141, 159, 162–165, 168, 169, 181, 186, 194
Longley, Clifford, 166, 168, 176
Lubavitch, 193
Lucas, Victor, 216

M

Machzike Hadath, 50, 79, 183
Mackay of Clashfern, Lord, 164
Magonet, Jonathan, 146
Maimonides, Moses, 10, 74
Mamzer (adulterous/incestuous child), 65, 98, 148
Manchester, 13, 31, 39, 79, 101, 102, 104, 106, 112, 203
Manna (Reform magazine), 180
Manor House (Sternberg) Centre, 114–117, 119, 122, 123, 191
Marble Arch Synagogue (London), xv, 30, 33, 124, 159, 177
Marmur, Dow, 22, 60, 61, 63, 64, 66, 73, 85, 86, 88, 100, 101, 105
Marriage, 1, 3–5, 13, 27, 28, 39, 46, 59, 60, 63, 70–72, 97, 98, 101, 141, 148, 210, 217
Mashiah, Donatella Casale, 202
Masorti (Conservative Judaism), xv, xvi, xviii, 7, 47, 102, 168, 180, 190, 193, 194, 203, 220
Mattuck, Israel, 209
Maybaum, Ignaz, 12
Michaels, Maurice, 216
Middleburgh, Charles, 220
Milah (circumcision), 102, 103
'Mission Statement' (Sacks), 187
Mizrachi, 78
Montagu, Ewen, xi
Moratorium (Unterman), 133, 155, 217
Moses (biblical), 7
Mount of Olives, 201
Munk, Ezra, 80, 197

Museum of the Jewish East End, 116
Muslims, 159

N

National Rabbinical Council, 15, 89
Ner Yisrael Synagogue (London), 169
New London Synagogue, 7, 13, 45
New Synagogue (London), 113
New West End Synagogue (London), 6–8, 12
Newcastle, 161, 164
New York, 10, 12
Northern Ireland, 203
North-Western Reform Synagogue (London), 116

O

Oral Law, 103
Ordman, N., 213

P

Padwa, Hanoch, 79, 213
Palestine Liberation Organisation, 217
Palestinians, 142, 217
Paul, Geoffrey, 168, 219
Pearl, Chaim, 7, 13
Peres, Shimon, 138
Philadelphia, 197
Pinner, Hyam, 216
Pluralism, 106, 108, 111, 112, 191, 219
Pointer (Liberal magazine), 17–20
Polarisation, 110
Prelude to Service (Jakobovits), 207
Prince of Wales (Charles), 113
Princess of Wales (Diana), 113
Purim, 75

R

Rabbinic Advisory Council, 76–78
Rackman, Emanuel, 10, 206
Rakow, B.Z, 213
Rayner, John, 20, 21, 24, 30–43, 83, 106, 110, 114, 115, 122, 123, 132, 134–136, 158, 159, 162, 163, 172, 191, 193, 208, 216
Redbridge (Essex), 203
Reform (USA), xii
Reform Association of Ministers/Rabbis, 3, 5, 65, 100, 171
Reform Beth Din, xii, 3, 204

Reform Judaism, xii, xv, xvi, xviii, 1, 10, 24, 25, 47, 80, 109, 181, 203
Registrar-General, 1, 3
Reinhart, Harold, xiii
Rich, Danny, xvii
Riverdale (New York), 13
Roberts, P., 213
Rocker, Simon, 202
Rogosnitzky, Mordechai Dov (Ber), 24, 25, 27, 213
Roman Catholicism, 128
Ronson, Gail, 113
Rose, Maurice, 27–29, 59, 210
Rosenberg, Rosita, 166, 170, 216
Rosenblum, Erwin, 14
Rothschild, Lord, xiii
Royal Society of Medicine, 150
Rubin, S., 213
Rushdie, Salman, 165
Ruth (biblical), 161, 162

S

Saadya, 74
Sabbath, 73, 98, 99, 139, 182
Sacks, Jonathan, xi–xiii, 96, 170, 176–180, 185–187, 189, 190, 193, 194
Sadducees, 97
Samaritans, 97
Sanderson, Harold, 166, 170
Sassover Rebbe, 79
Schauss, H., 209
Schlesinger, E., 213
Schneebalg, M. M., 79, 213
Schwab, S. G., 208
Scotland, 203
Second World War, xi, 1, 2
Segal, Y., 213
Sephardim, xix, 203
Shechitah, 51, 70
Silverman, Alfred, 206
Silverman, Bobby, 112
Simmons, Vivian, 2
Six-Day War, 23, 30, 44
Slovakia, 204
Slowe, Malcolm, 14, 15, 208, 216
Solidarity with Israel, 75–77, 79
Solomon, Norman, 216
Soloveitchik, Joseph, 8–10, 206

South Africa, 204
South Hertfordshire, 203
South-West Essex, 203
Soviet Jewry, 74, 84, 139, 195
Spanish and Portuguese Synagogue, 16, 204
Spiro Institute (London), 116
St John's Wood Synagogue (London), 22, 75, 103
Stamford Hill (London), 84, 203
Stanislower Rebbe, 79
Stanton, Linda, 160
Sternberg, Sigmund [Centre], 94, 115, 116, 173–175, 192, 215, 216
Sternbuch, A., 213
Strictly Orthodox, 203
Swift, Harris, 15
Swift, Lionel, 160, 218, 220
Swift, Morris, 4–6, 62, 103, 105, 112

T

Teff, Solomon [Committee], 13–16, 22, 28, 35, 43, 47
Temple, William (Archbishop of York), 56
Tevilah (ritual ablution, *mikveh*), 5, 62, 66, 102, 103
Thirteen Principles of Faith (Maimonides), 10
Times, The, 119–121, 125, 143, 159, 162, 164, 166–168, 171–174, 221
Torah im derech eretz, 184
Torah min Hashamayim, 7, 10, 99
'Traditional Alternatives' conference, 169

U

ULPS News (Liberal), 62
Union of Liberal and Progressive Synagogues, xv, xviii, 2, 92, 95, 116, 158, 166–168, 170, 171, 174, 199
Union of Orthodox Hebrew Congregations, 79, 80, 82–84
United Hebrew Congregations, 15, 16, 21, 95
United States, 7, 8, 60, 204
United Synagogue of America, 7
United Synagogue (London), xii, xv, xviii, 1, 9, 22, 41, 43, 84, 108, 118, 128, 156, 158, 160, 166, 168–170, 186, 194, 202, 204, 206
University Chaplaincy Board, 45
Unterman Committee, 94, 124, 135, 136, 156
Unterman, Issar Yehudah, 9

Unterman, Maurice, xv, 124, 133, 145, 146, 151, 152, 154–156, 159–161, 188, 215, 220

V
Van der Zyl, Werner, 5, 14, 32, 111, 208
Victory in Europe, 1

W
Wales, 203
Waley Cohen, Robert, 2, 204
Warnock Report, 123, 215
We Have Reason to Believe (Jacobs), 6
Westcliff-on-Sea, 7
Western Synagogue (London), 12
West London Synagogue, 1, 2, 31, 58, 91 111
Westminster (London), 203
Winston, Clive, 216
Wolfson, Isaac, xi, 7, 12, 16, 23, 202
Wolkind, Jack, 136, 137
World Zionist Organisation, 83
Written Law, 103

Y
Yakar Centre (London), 109, 169
Yeshiva University (New York), 206

Z
Zahn, S., 213